POLICE RESEARCH: SOME FUTURE PROSPECTS

Police Research:
Some Future Prospects

Edited by
MOLLIE WEATHERITT

Published in association with The Police Foundation

Avebury
Aldershot · Brookfield USA · Hong Kong · Singapore · Sydney

Published by

Avebury

Gower Publishing Company Limited
Gower House
Croft Road
Aldershot
Hants GU11 3HR
England

Gower Publishing Company
Old Post Road
Brookfield
Vermont 05036
USA

ISBN 0 566 07030 8

Contents

Acknowledgements

The conference on which this book is based was made possible by grants from the Home Office and the Economic and Social Research Council. Chapters 2 and 4 are covered by Crown copyright and I am grateful to the Controller of Her Majesty's Stationery Office for permission to reproduce them.

I am also grateful to Jill Knight for her considerable help in preparing the typescript for publication.

Mollie Weatheritt
Police Foundation

Contributors

Robert Baldwin is a Lecturer in Law at Brunel University and a member of the Regulation Group at the Centre for Socio-Legal Studies, Oxford. His publications include Police powers and politics (1982) (with Richard Kinsey), Regulating the airlines (1985) and various articles on policing, regulation and public law.

John Burrows is Group Security Adviser at Dixons Group plc. At the time of writing he was a Principal Research Officer at the Home Office Research and Planning Unit, where his work included studies of police investigation of and victims' reactions to burglary.

Michael R. Chatterton is Senior Lecturer in the Department of Social Policy and Social Work, University of Manchester. He has done extensive research on the police and his publications include 'Police work and assault charges' in M. Punch (ed.) Control in the police organisation (1983), 'Assessing police effectiveness: future prospects, British Journal of Criminology, Winter 1987, and 'Front-line supervision in the British police service' in G. Gaskell and R. Benewick (eds) The crowd in contemporary Britain (1987).

Nigel Fielding is Lecturer in Sociology at the University of Surrey. He has published on the ethics of observation research, legal training and extensively on the police. His current research interests arise from a fieldwork-based study of community policing and include the definition of practical competence and the implications of community policing skills and techniques for the deployment and management of constables. He is editor of the Howard Journal of Criminal Justice.

Keith Hawkins is a member of the Centre for Socio-Legal Studies at the University of Oxford. He has published a variety of papers on the sociology of legal and regulatory processes and is the author of Environment and enforcement (1984). He is currently researching prosecution practices in a number of regulatory agencies and is writing a book on legal decision-making with Peter K. Manning.

Simon Holdaway is Lecturer in Sociology in the University of Sheffield. He is a former police officer who has published widely on aspects of police work. His publications include The British police (1979) and Inside the British police: a force at work (1983).

Mike Hough is a Principal Research Officer in the Home Office Research and Planning Unit. He has worked on the British Crime Survey since its inception in 1981, and has also carried out research on policing - especially police effectiveness - crime prevention and attitudes to punishment.

Peter K. Manning is Professor of Sociology and Psychiatry at Michigan State University, a former fellow Balliol and Wolfson Colleges, Oxford, and at the time of writing was a member of the Centre for Socio-Legal Studies at Wolfson College, Oxford. He has published a number of works on British policing, including Police work (1977). He is currently writing a book on legal decision-making with Keith Hawkins.

Rod Morgan is Senior Lecturer in Criminology, University of Bath, and Visiting Fellow, Centre for Criminological Research, Oxford. He is the author of books and articles on criminal justice and penal policy, most recently (with M. Maguire and J. Vagg) Accountability and prisons: opening up a closed world (1985). He is engaged on research into police community consultation arrangements funded by the Economic and Social Research Council and the Police Foundationn.

Clive Norris is research fellow in community policing at the University of Surrey. In 1983-4 he was research consultant to the Police Foundation.

Robert Reiner is Reader in the Faculty of Law, University of Bristol. He is author of The politics of the police (1985) and The blue-coated worker (1978) and several other papers on criminal justice.

Mollie Weatheritt is Assistant Director of the Police Foundation and former research secretary to the Royal Commission on Criminal Procedure. She has published books and articles on various aspects of criminal justice and policing, including Innovations in policing (1986).

Preface

In his introduction to a book of readings on police research, published in 1979, Simon Holdaway wrote that 'the relative dearth of research into the British police has achieved the status of a cliche amongst sociologists'. He said that the police had not been helpful in getting research started nor in welcoming sociologists who wanted to do research in police forces. He spoke of the 'unhealthy gap' that existed between the academic and police worlds (Holdaway, 1979, p.1). Holdaway's words were penned less than 10 years ago yet it is clear that the situation they describe is in marked contrast to that of today. As several contributors to this volume testify, the 1980s have seen an enormous growth of research on the police and on policing: so much so, that this observation is itself in danger of becoming something of a cliche. Research access – once so difficult to gain and restricted to a very few – is now relatively easy to negotiate. The gap (unhealthy or not) between police and academia is still wide but the points of contact have increased as the empirical language of research has become an increasingly important part of the language of professional and managerial accountability in the police and as police officers themselves have undertaken, commissioned and cooperated in more and more research projects. Sources of official funding for police research have grown, reflecting the increasingly prominent place which policing occupies in social policy and in political debate. (See, for example, the Economic and Social Research Council's special intiative on the Police and Criminal Evidence Act 1984 and the Home Office Research and Planning Unit's current research programme.) And alongside this officially sanctioned and supported body of work has grown up a wide variety of smaller and less ambitious projects (Police Foundation, 1987) whose successful outcome nonetheless depends on good working relationships being established between the researched – the police – and those doing the research.

The chapters in this book stand as evidence both of the growth of police research in recent years and its variety. Each began life as a paper prepared for a two-day conference on the future of police research which was organised by the Police Foundation and which took place in Harrogate at the end of 1985. The participants were academics with an interest in or direct experience of research on the police, others doing research on the police, and police officers. While the main purpose of the conference was to take a forward look at both the likely and desirable future directions of police research, the conference also served as a retrospective. Contributors were asked to take stock of research in their respective fields and to assess where policing research had got to and how it had arrived there. The resulting contributions ranged from broad conceptual reviews (see the chapters by Reiner, Holdaway and by Manning and Hawkins) to concentration on specific pieces of empirical work, some of which was being reported for the first time (see the chapters by Norris and Chatterton). Other papers were concerned with the relationship - actual and potential - between research and policy (those by Burrows, Weatheritt and Hough); yet others on charting and accounting for developments in policing policy and speculating about their likely effects (Morgan and Baldwin's respective chapters).

For the purposes of this book, the papers to the conference have been arranged in three parts. Those in Part One each address, in different ways, the current political and policy context in which police research is carried out and the kind of research that emerges from this context. Robert Reiner's key paper sets out a provisional framework for examining the development of police research over the past 30 years. He argues that at any one time the nature and scope of police research is but one aspect of a wider political debate about policing. Thus, academic writing on the police in the 1950s, which Reiner characterises as largely celebratory, reflected the then high degree of political consensus about and public acceptance of the police. By the 1970s a number of causes celebres centred on alleged corruption and maltreatment of suspects had begun to undermine this consensus. Reiner characterises this period as one of substantial growth for academic police research, with an emphasis on civil liberties issues. By the end of the decade, wider political questions of who controls the police had begun to be raised, with police research itself becoming more overtly politicised. Reiner represents the current period as a contradictory one. There is greater scepticism about what can be achieved by mechanisms of control, stemming in part from a greater appreciation of their complexity. There is concern with looking at how policies and procedures actually work in practice; and with identifying, and thus helping to spread, good practice rather than, as in the 1970s, with identifying the bad. As to the future of police research, Reiner is sceptical about its likely practical and political impact. Given that developments in policing tend to be attended by political conflict, police policy, he argues, is unlikely to be greatly influenced by research.

Each of the following three papers takes up this challenge. Writing from within what Reiner describes as the 'official' perspective, Mike Hough and John Burrows each provide a view of how things appear from within central government. As one of the main architects of the British Crime Survey, Mike Hough is concerned with the kind of questions that can be asked in public surveys that will produce information which is relevant both to policy planning and to the development of theory. His Home Office colleague, John Burrows, provides something of an antidote to Reiner's pessimism in arguing that research sponsored by and carried out within central government has indeed contributed towards the development of policing policy in the form of principles of good management which the government has sought to foster through its Financial Management Initiative and through the work of Her Majesty's Inspectors of Constabulary. Burrows cites patrol activity studies and studies of CID work as examples of how research can help improve management decisions and police effectiveness.

In Burrows' words, 'research has tended to dictate the language used and the assumptions made in the current debate' about improving management and effectiveness. Mollie Weatheritt takes a sceptical line in asking whether, from the perspective of the police service rather than that of central government, research has, or indeed can, do more than this. She questions whether the rational empirical models of management that are being promoted by central government are workable ones, or whether they will not be subverted in practice. Like Robert Reiner, she raises questions about the hidden purposes and unintended consequences of research when it is used for organisational ends.

Part Two of this book takes the reader away from the political and policy context in which research is done to the actual practice of policing, on the streets and in the police station. Simon Holdaway's introductory chapter sets the scene by reviewing the literature on the occupational culture of policing and charting its intellectual bases in social theory. Holdaway reminds us that the early work on policing was not policy led but was instead directed at addressing problems and issues with sociology, in particular the idea that the police were merely the puppets of social control by the powerful. Key early studies of policing using humanistic, participatory methods and informed by a keen concern for the development of theory, sought to study the mundane, everyday aspects of police work. Holdaway sees this tradition of research as in danger of being subverted and submerged by a new generation of police research which is largely policy led. 'Theoretical questions and the longer term work of consolidating research findings' will, he says, 'take second place to the primary task of analysis of contemporary policies, with a view towards the pragmatic relevance of research results'. Holdaway sees this change of emphasis not just as a loss to learning, but also, ultimately, to the development of sound policy and practice.

That the tradition which Holdaway wishes to resuscitate is not entirely lost is evidenced, in different ways, by the three subsequent chapters. Nigel Fielding's paper about appropriate ways of understanding how police officers handle encounters with members of the public makes the case for a complex analytic framework which is sensitive to the interplay of formal organisational rules, local variants of the occupational culture and officers' own experience. Like Holdaway, he argues that the occupational culture is not unitary and fixed but is complex and shifting, with its members actively participating in creating and recreating its content and meaning.

Fielding's paper argues that it is important to take notice of the ways in which officers themselves define and negotiate good policing practice. This theme is developed in Clive Norris' paper which documents, from the stance of a participant observer, how officers manage (that is, handle and subsequently account for) troublesome encounters with members of the public. Norris is particularly concerned with the language and tactics that officers use to defuse trouble and to account for it in ways which will make it organisationally acceptable. He warns against defining competent practice solely in terms of how smoothly officers manage to defuse - and subsequently explain - difficult situations.

Michael Chatterton's paper reports on a study of first-line supervisors (sergeants) and in particular how they use paperwork to monitor, oversee and control the work of subordinates. Chatterton starts from the familiar complaint that officers have too much paperwork and that this prevents them from spending time out on patrol. But, argues Chatterton, not all paperwork is wasted work: on the contrary, it is a vital form of quality control. In a detailed comparison of how paperwork routines are used in two contrasting sub-divisions, Chatterton shows how such routines can be more or less effective in achieving quality control, depending on the managerial structure and ethos in which they are embedded. Paper checking systems can be used either to encourage or to undermine officers' scope for discretion and their sense of autonomy.

Part Three moves to wider considerations about regulating the police and in particular to how police decisions, police action and police regulation reflect and exemplify wider issues of law and policy. Peter Manning and Keith Hawkins' opening chapter treats police decisions not necessarily as unique but as just one species of more general legal decisions. Manning and Hawkins set out an analytic framework, derived from natural decision making, in which, they argue, police decisions need to be viewed in terms of their consequences, their generality, their visibility and their complexity. They go on to argue that an important key to understanding police decisions is the use the police make of information and they develop a framework in which different sorts of information, its use and its relationship to police policy and police action can be understood.

Manning and Hawkins demonstrate that because most research on the police has been confined to describing decisions taken by patrol officers on the street, our knowledge of the full range of police decision-making remains slight. They make a plea for a future research agenda, to be derived analytically, and to be informed by a fuller appreciation of the range of decisions that fall to be made, by whom, and on the basis of what information.

Like Manning and Hawkins, Robert Baldwin is at pains to characterise policing as a system (for his purpose, a regulatory system) which has much in common with other systems. Baldwin takes as his starting point developments in administrative law which have been aimed at deregulating services, freeing them from legal and administrative controls of various kinds and in encouraging self-regulation in place of oversight from outside. Baldwin sees much the same processes at work in relation to the police in the form of the Police and Criminal Evidence Act 1984 and its associated codes of practice. The Act and codes, says Baldwin, constitute a shift of policing away from an activity regulated by legal powers and duties under the law towards a largely self-regulated activity. While it is clear that he has qualms about these developments, Baldwin nonetheless concludes by seeing them as presenting new opportunities. First are the research questions they raise, such as the relationship between the new mechanisms of self-regulation and the potential for more effective supervision. But there are also potential practical gains to be made from viewing policing as a self-regulatory system having characteristics in common with other such systems. Comparative study of the ways in which self-regulation is applied to and in other institutional contexts can suggest new and potentially radical ways in which improved regulation of the police might be secured.

Rod Morgan's final chapter puts us back firmly in the world of practical politics. Morgan charts existing policy on police accountability, sketches the relevant debates and speculates about the likely effects of the former on the development of the latter. Morgan reviews government policy on police accountability in terms of what he discerns as a number of major themes: that the police should give value for money, amongst other things through better priority setting; the encouragement of self help; the wish to identify and respond to consumers' wishes; and the requirement for the police to account more fully for their activities. Morgan reviews the possible practical and political consequences which could flow from attempts to apply these concepts in relation to two initiatives - lay visiting and consultative groups. He concludes that these are difficult to predict.

What then of the future for police research? In an attempt to rough out an agenda, this question was addressed in four discussion groups on, respectively, public attitudes, perceptions and opinions and methods of performance measurement; police organisation, culture, role structure and function; police decision-making, discretion and its control; and law and accountability.

In the field of public attitudes and performance measures it was felt that one of the most useful things to have come out of crime and victimisation surveys was information about sub-groups. It was felt that future work should concentrate on attitudes towards and experiences of crime of women, householders and organisations as well as the kinds of policing services that different groups in the population actually received. It was suggested that the police themselves might collect information on how satisfied members of the public were with the way they had been dealt with and use this as a performance measure.

Participants addressing the subjects of police culture and organisation stressed the importance of at least being open to the possibility that there were many cultures of policing and the need to delineate and differentiate between them on the basis of rank, specialism and geographical area. Here a major concern was the ways in which police occupational culture(s) could undermine or facilitate good policing practice.

Some not dissimilar prescriptions emerged from the discussion on police decision-making. Taking their lead from Manning and Hawkins' paper, participants argued for a shift in research emphasis away from the kinds of decisions made by generalist patrol officers towards those made further up the chain of command and by specialist units. The important questions identified were: what kinds of decisions fall to be made; who makes them; and what information contributes to those decisions, both in terms of its source and its content. Ironically these are not new concerns. It seems appropriate and instructive to quote here from Maurice Punch's preface to a collection of papers prepared for a conference which took place in 1980. '[T]here can be little doubt that we remain fundamentally backward in exploring the police organization ... generally, we have not access and inside information on levels of political control, negotiations with power groups, debates related to the allocation of resources and to criteria of accountability, and on how the police organization copes in relation to its political-economic power base.' (Punch, 1983, p.xiii.) Unsurprisingly, parallel research prescriptions also emerged from the discussion group on law and accountability. These included the influence of non-statutory bodies on policing policies; more detailed study of the translation of policing policy into police operations; the role and influence of Her Majesty's Inspectors of Constabulary; the relationship between the Metropoitan Police and the Home Office as police authority; and police complaints. There was a plea for British researchers to be less narrow and parochial. Comparative studies of police in other countries were needed, as was a wider definition of what constitutes policing.

This kind of shopping list approach to agenda setting inevitably conceals a diversity and divergence of theoretical and practical concerns, the implications of which surfaced - and from time to time were heatedly debated - throughout the conference. As one might expect from a conference which looked back as well as forward, many of these debates involved familiar tensions between ethnographers, interactionists and structuralists and between those whose interests lay in improving policing and those whose prime concern was to seek to understand it.

It is clear from many of the papers in this book that the policy context in which British police research is carried out and with which it has to engage is creating new opportunities for - but also obstacles to - its future development. On balance, the emphasis in the papers is on the opportunities. Policy makers have become more interested in the kinds of messages that research conveys and certain kinds of research language look set to become part of the common currency in which debates about policing are carried on. Yet, as many of the papers suggest, the potential benefits of these developments are by no means certain. Nor are they without cost. The price of greater policy relevance must be that research comes to reflect the concerns of administrators and managers, who are interested in solutions rather than knowledge, in small rather than large questions. There are many who feel uneasy about these developments, for reasons which hardly need labouring here: it is not difficult to guess which items on the research agenda outlined above are least likely to attract funds.

The results of the changes which are taking place in the opportunity structure of research seem to me to be more ambiguous and less predictable than its detractors would allow. This is partly because there is an important sense in which the results of research - even that which is policy led - are by no means predictable in advance and are apt to produce a picture of the world which emphasises its ambiguity and complexity. Nor it such research necessarily intellectually or theoretically irrelevant. Whatever the concern of the researcher, the results produced by investigation can be used by others of widely differing theoretical and political persuasions.

In the context of contradictory arguments about the future of policing such considerations suggest that it would be unwise to try and predict with certainty the future course of British police research. To adapt the words with which Rod Morgan's chapter ends, it is clear that there is still a great deal to play for.

References

Holdaway, S. (ed.), (1979) Inside the British police, Blackwell, Oxford
Punch, M. (ed.), (1983) Control in the police organization, MIT Press, Cambridge, Mass

PART I
THE CONTEXT AND
POLITICS OF
POLICE RESEARCH

1 The politics of police research in Britain

ROBERT REINER

Introduction

This paper will attempt to provide a framework for examining the development of police research in Britain over the last thirty years, and the prospects for the future. It is, of course, a personal view, a preliminary attempt to gain an overall perspective. My purpose at present is primarily to stimulate discussion, not to give a definitive statement. The theme I want to stress above all is that the development of police research, like policing itself, is inherently and integrally bound up with political conflict and debate, whether or not this is overt. But this connection is not necessarily evident in any <u>one</u> piece of research. The patterns emerge clearly only when an overall view is taken.

Definitional preamble

In an influential review of the sociological literature on the police, Maureen Cain criticised most earlier studies for not attempting 'a definition of the object of their analysis . . . it has been taken for granted that we "know" what the police, as an institution, really is' (Cain, 1979, p.143). This point has been repeated by several critiques of the police literature (e.g. Tomasic, 1985, ch.4; and Mike Brogden in a review of my book, <u>The politics of the police</u>, in the January 1986 issue of <u>British Journal of Criminology</u>). The 'missing' definition is that 'Police, then <u>must be defined in terms of their key practice</u>. They are appointed with the task of maintaining the order which those who sustain them define as proper' (Cain, op.cit., p.158). In other words, what is suggested as appropriate is a <u>functional</u> definition of the police. However, so broad a conceptualisation fails to convey what is <u>specific</u> about the police within the array of institutions and processes charged with maintaining order. The specificity of the policing function is, I believe, best brought out in Egon Bittner's well-known work which

3

is strangely missing from both Cain's and Tomasic's review of the literature. (Bittner is in fact listed in the bibliography to Cain's review, but not discussed in this context.) Bittner gives a more specific delineation of the particular set of order problems which constitute the police task - those involving 'something that ought not to be happening and about which someone had better do something now!', i.e. emergency order-maintenance exigencies (Bittner, 1974, p.30). More importantly still, Bittner defines the police not primarily in functional terms, but by their unique capacity to use legitimate force: 'the capacity for decisive action . . . The policeman, and the policeman alone, is equipped, entitled and required to deal with every exigency in which force may have to be used' (Bittner, op.cit., p.35). Bittner's 1974 analysis well deserves its sub-title, 'A theory of the police' (Klockars, 1985, ch.1 is a useful elaboration of Bittner's argument). But it has been largely ignored in the critical literature, most strangely by Marenin in his systematic and penetrating radical analysis of the concept of policing (Marenin, 1982). However, Marenin does distil a definition of the police from earlier work (such as Manning, 1977; and Bayley, 1979) which is within the Bittner mould. This defines the police as 'the privately and publicly employed guardians of interest who are entitled to use force to do whatever needs doing' (Marenin, op.cit., p.252). In my work I start from a similar definition, drawing explicitly on both Skolnick and Bittner:

> 'The civil police is a social organisation created and sustained by political processes to enforce dominant conceptions of public order' (Skolnick, 1972, p.41) . . . 'Their specific role . . . is as specialists in coercion . . . ultimately the capacity to use legitimate force' (Bittner, 1970 and 1974). (Reiner, 1985, p.2)

This definition fits the basic criteria of a useful definition: reasonable unambiguity, fit with commonly held conceptions, and simplicity 'in the sense that it associates "police" with only a few activities' (Bayley, op.cit., p.113). It opens up rather than forecloses the analytic problems of what in particular social contexts the function, impact and legitimacy of the police might be.

I have embarked on this definitional excursus because it seems necessary to establish rather than take for granted the theoretical coherence of the object 'police' and a fortiori 'police research'. As indicated earlier, a number of influential statements have argued that because 'policing and social control need not necessarily be undertaken by those designated as "the police"' (Tomasic, 1985, p.86), a theoretically adequate conceptualisation must operate with the broader notion of 'policing' rather than the parochial colloquialism 'the police'.[1] Evidently, the work of 'the police' (men and women in blue uniforms) is only a part of wider social processes of 'policing' and control. Moreover, 'policing' is only part of the work undertaken by people in blue uniforms (and those working in plain clothes alongside them as part of 'police' organisations). We can distinguish between the following: a. 'Ordering' - the set of processes concerned with the reproduction of a social order. [2] These include the positive processes of socialisation, culture formation, and institution building, as well as negative constraints. b. 'Controlling' - regulating potential breaches of order by the application of sanctions, positive and negative. c. 'Policing' - monitoring potential breaches of order with the capacity to respond with legitimate force if necessary. 'The police' as an institution specially charged with 'policing' is evidently a relatively recent historical phenomenon. 'Policing' is not confined to 'the police' even when there exist specialised police organisations, nor are 'the police' confined to 'policing': they engage in 'ordering', 'controlling', and ad hoc other tasks not immediately related to reproducing social order. But in contemporary societies where specialised police organisations have developed, their activities are adequately coherent, and distinct from other institutions, to constitute a clear and recognisable area for research and study.

The centre of concern in this paper will be to chart the development in Britain over the last thirty years of such a tradition of research on the police, conceiving of this explicitly as work on the police organisation per se, rather than control processes or 'policing' of a more diffuse kind.

'Research' here will be defined in a broad sense as any sustained and organised writing on the police, not just empirical studies. [3] It encompasses historical or theoretical analyses of the police, as well as substantial works of polemic or journalistic comment.

The development of police research will be related to wider political conflicts and controversies surrounding the police. Each stage in the emergence of various kinds of police research is dependent on certain conditions of existence in terms of the political context of policing itself. Before looking at the development of police research, however, I will briefly recount the periodisation of the recent history of policing which informed my book on The politics of the police, as the backdrop to the periodisation of police research which I will elaborate subsequently.

The politicisation of the police [4]

The development of the police in the last thirty years can be divided into four stages, demarcated in terms of the nature of political debate about policing. The early and mid-1950s were the high point of political consensus about, and public acceptance of, the police institution in Britain. Since the inception of the Metropolitan Police in 1829 (and the spread of the 'New Police' idea nationally by 1856), a rough U-shape trajectory can be traced for the rise and fall of police legitimacy. As has been thoroughly documented, the British police were established against widespread opposition, stemming from a range of political interests and philosophies (and going back through nearly a century of debate preceding the 1829 Metropolitan Police Act). The landed gentry saw them as superfluous irritants in a paternalistic social order; many of the middle class disliked the burden on the rates; and the working class resented the coercive interference with their everyday lives. Middle and upper class opposition was speedily won over, but working class suspicion lingered on, bursting out sporadically in violence, and symbolised by the host of colourful slang epithets for the police: 'crushers', 'blue locusts', etc. (Storch, 1975; Cohen, 1979; Brogden, 1982; and others).

By the 1950s the police had come to be widely accepted, to the extent of being cornerstones of national pride. This can be shown by many contemporary accounts (e.g. Gorer, 1955) as well as by opinion poll data, notably the large scale survey mounted for the Royal Commission on the Police in 1960. The methodology of this survey - which found 'an overwhelming vote of confidence in the police' - has been criticised, both at the time and subsequently (Whitaker, 1964, pp.15-17; Brogden, 1982, p.205). There is no doubt that the interpretation of the survey in the Royal Commission's final report underplays the elements of discord to be found in its own data, and furthermore that the sample was biased against groups likely to be more hostile to the police (notably by excluding the under-18s, and under-representing the 18-21 age group). But these points do not demolish the overall implication of widespread public support, at least as much to be found among working class as middle or upper class respondents.

The picture given by the 1960 Royal Commission survey is a high point of consensus about policing, coming as the culmination of a century-long process of legitimation of the police institution. [5] Although polls continue to register high overall levels of acceptance of police legitimacy (e.g. the Times/MORI poll reported in Police Review, 15 November 1985, pp.2322-4), there are now clear dents in this. There is both widespread suspicion of particular kinds of wrong-doing, and general hostility to the police in some sections of the population, particularly young males, the unemployed, the economically marginal, and blacks (especially if they are also in the other three categories) (Policy Studies Institute, 1983, vol.I, pp.314-5 and vol.IV, pp.162-8; Jones and Levi, 1983; Southgate and Ekblom, 1984, pp.28-30). Numbers aside, the U-turn in legitmacy is sharply indicated by two recent events, with obvious parallels in the early years of police development: the attacks on police officers and stations during the miners' strike (recalling Storch's account of anti-police riots in the nine-teenth century) and the murder of PC Blakelock (the first Metropolitan police officer to be killed in a riot since PC Culley at Coldbath Fields in 1832).

The movement from the consensus of the 1950s to the present situation is divisible into three stages: the 'controversy' stage, the 'conflict' stage, and the 'contradictory' stage.

The 'controversy' stage

The first signs of wider questioning of the police came with the late 1950s causes celebres (minor with the benefit of hindsight) that led to the establishment of the Royal Commission on the Police in January 1960. The years immediately before and after the Commission's Final Report in 1962 were marked by controversy about the constitutional issues it was asked to consider, with continuing scandals about police abuses accentuating the debate. (These included the notorious cases of Challenor, the Sheffield 'rhino whip' inquiry, and the issue of rough police handling of anti-nuclear demonstrators.) The Royal Commission report, and the Police Act 1964 which derived from it, restated the respective roles of Home Secretary, local police authority and chief constable, with the latter firmly in the saddle as far as operational policy was concerned. This laid the seeds of future conflict, and indeed there was some sharp contemporary criticism (Hart, 1963; Marshall, 1965). But at first the 1964 Act constituted a settlement which was generally accepted. The reorganisation of policing in the mid-1960s into the unit beat system, now much reviled, was then widely welcomed as a 'police revolution' in the fight against more sophisticated forms of professional crime. However, by the late 1960s a series of related changes began to re-politicise the police, culminating by the early 1980s in a degree of conflict about police legitimacy which was unprecedented in the last century and a half.

The 'conflict' stage

During the 1970s the elements making for the legitimation of the police in Britain became unravelled and reversed. The series of revelations of police deviance, both in the sense of corruption and other violations of the rule of law, undermined the image of the police as professional symbols of legal authority. The strategy of minimal force appeared to be departed from increasingly, as police responded to spiralling problems of containing public disorder by stiffening their capacity in terms of rapid mobilisation, mutual support and defensive and offensive equipment. The service role of the friendly Dixonesque bobby was downplayed as an unintended consequence of the technology and specialisation associated with unit beat reorganisation. Police involvement in political controversy grew apace as the 'bobby lobby' developed following Robert Mark's Dimbleby Lecture in 1972 and the Police Federation's 1975 'law and order' campaign. The souring of police relations with blacks provided a self-conscious focus of questioning of the legitimacy of police tactics, which has now been expanded to the labour movement more generally, especially since the miners' strike. Police effectiveness has been called increasingly into question as crime rates have rocketted, and clear-up rates plummetted. Finally, the 1960s counter-culture and its legacy brought the police into regular conflict with sections of the articulate and politically aware 'chattering classes' as many forms of deviance came to be politicised. By the early 1980s, the tradition of 'law and order' being regarded as a non-party issue had clearly ended, and partisan controversy became increasingly marked, especially after the election in 1981 of several radical Labour local authorities (notably the Greater London Council) which provided a focal point for political criticism. In this already highly politicised context, the 1981 riots, the subsequent Scarman report and their fall-out have become the stimulus for a reorientation of police thinking and policy and a more confused current stage of debate.

The 'contradictory' stage

Since 1981 there have been two contradictory pressures at work shaping the development of policing. On the one hand, the riots underlined in the starkest way that the police institution had lost legitimacy, at any rate in the eyes of substantial sections of the population. The response was the Scarman report and a host of changes in the style of police policy intended to restore police legitimacy. The Newman strategy for policing London epitomised this, but the reorientation was encouraged on a wider scale by the Home Office and the Inspectorate (Reiner, 1985, pp.199-208). A key aspect of this has been the proliferation of police/community consultative committees around the country, initially following the Home Office guidelines issued in June 1982, and now the statutory encouragement of s.106 of the Police and Criminal Evidence Act 1984 (Morgan and Maggs, 1984 and 1985).

The contradictory pressures, making for continuing delegitimation, stem ultimately from the increasingly acute economic, social and political divisions of Britain. The main structural basis for the loss of police legitimacy since the 1960s continues. It is the de-incorporation of increasing sections of the working class population, 'who are being defined out of the edifice of citizenship' (Dahrendorf, 1985, p.98). This is not just a matter of high and growing levels of unemployment. It is, as Dahrendorf put it starkly in his recent Hamlyn lectures, that 'the majority class does not need the unemployed to maintain and even increase its standard of living . . . The main point about this category - for want of a better word we shall continue to call it "under-class" - is that its destiny is perceived as hopeless' (ibid., pp.101-7). To this structural source of division and conflict is added the cultural process of 'de-subordination' (as Miliband (1978) calls it from a Marxist perspective) or 'anomia' (as Dahrendorf's more conservative approach labels it): a weakening of the validity of traditional social 'subordinations' or normative controls. When in addition a substantial section of the 'de-incorporated' is ethnically distinct, a self-consciousness of exclusion from political citizenship is facilitated. As both the miners' strike and the recent riots underlined in various ways, for all the changes in the style and direction of police policy since 1981, the structural pressures for conflict have been exacerbated rather than reduced.

7

Moreover, the consequence of social conflict and political polarisation is the foregrounding within the array of police tactics of the 'harder' elements. Lord Scarman was right to argue that 'policing is . . . too complex a job to be viewed in terms of a simplistic dichotomy between 'hard' and 'soft' policing styles . . . There will . . . continue to be circumstances in which it is appropriate – even essential – for police commanders to . . . deploy special units' (Scarman, 1981, para.5.46). But he went on to warn:

> There should . . . be no change in the basic approach of the British police to policing public disorder. It would be tragic if attempts, central to the thrust of my report, to bring the police and the public closer together, were to be accompanied by changes in the manner of policing disorder which served only to distance the police further from the public. (ibid., para.5.74)

In fact it is now plain that the capacity of the police to respond toughly to public disorder has been considerably accentuated. [6] It is possible to debate how far this is an extension of the traditional approach, and how far it represents a qualitatively new departure (Northam, 1985). It is also possible to argue about whether the developments in riot control strategy are chosen policy or thrust upon the police by events; whether they are completely to be condemned or a regrettable necessity. But what is clear is that the tragic contradiction, warned about by Lord Scarman, between the legitimating reforms he advocated and 'changes in the manner of policing disorder', has come about and seems set to continue. It is set to continue not because it is inherent in any chosen directions for police policy, but because policing continues to operate in a context of widening conflict. There is a contradiction between the overt recognition of the need for legitimating reforms and the structural pressures vitiating these. The consequence of this contradiction for thinking about the police is that all viewpoints are in a condition of some confusion and self-questioning.

Politics and police research

The development of police research in Britain can be distinguished in terms of stages corresponding to the process of politicisation of policing itself. The focal concerns of each stage of police research embody those wider political conflicts about policing. In charting the stages of development of police research, I will distinguish four institutional bases from which police research emanates. (As already stated, I am defining research broadly, to include any systematic writing on the police, not just empirical data-gathering.) The four sources of police research are the academic world; 'official' research (i.e. government-funded or by serving police officers); 'critical' bodies (e.g. National Council for Civil Liberties, Institute of Race Relations, non-government political parties); and journalists. This distinction between the institutional bases from which research on the police flows is far from watertight, and individual works are often hard to classify. For example, academics may do 'official', 'critical' or 'journalistic' work, while journalists may write for 'critical' organisations. But the distinction does correspond to fairly clear inflexions of concern about the police in different periods. It is, however, rough and ready, and there are insuperable problems in pigeon-holing individuals.

The basic theme that will be developed is the across-the-board differences in focal concern at different stages. Because of the frequently long span of time between the conception of a work and its publication, and the fact that its tone and theme may be ahead or behind the predominant concerns of a period, there is some degree of arbitrariness in the placement of an author into a specific stage of development. Moreover, authors may change tack and appear in different guises, or alternatively plug away at similar themes, straddling more than one stage in any typology. The upshot of all these classification problems is that I wish to apologise in advance for the failure to do justice to individual works which is perhaps inevitable in constructing any general typology. With these caveats, a periodisation and typology of police research in Britain is offered in the table overleaf as a way of understanding its development.

Perhaps the most immediately striking aspect of the table is the explosive growth of work on the police in the 'conflict' stage, emanating from all four institutional sources. (I am reasonably confident that this is not a mere artefact of amnesia about earlier work.) Academic and journalistic interest had already begun to grow in the 'controversy' phase, which saw the development of the core interactionist perspective in sociological research on policing. But there is nonetheless a marked acceleration of academic and journalistic writing on the police in the 'conflict' stage. The growth of academic and 'official' research on the police is associated in part with the overall expansion of social scientific research in this period. (A useful account of the development of social science research in government - 'official' research - is Clarke and Cornish, 1983, Part 1.) But 'official' social science interest in the police, as distinct from other aspects of crime and criminal justice, is very much a feature of the 'conflict' phase. The first Home Office Research Study specifically on the police (Ditchfield, 1976) appears towards the end of the 'controversy' stage, as no.37 in the monograph series (which started in 1969, and was preceded by fifteen years of publication of 'Studies in the Causes of Delinquency and the Treatment of Offenders'). Sustained attention to the police by the Home Office Research Unit is evident only at the end of the 1970s (e.g. Clarke and Hough, 1980). But it is now a central concern, as shown by the 'Research Unit Papers' series which began in 1980 (called 'Research and Planning Unit Papers' since 1982 and the reorganisation of the Research Unit as the Research and Planning Unit). Of thirty-one Research and Planning Unit Papers published between 1980 and 1985, ten (i.e. one third) are specifically focused on the police. (There are too many to consider individually, but a useful selection is collected in Heal et al., 1985.)

The growth of work on the police during the 1970s, from all institutional sources, is an evident reflection of the politicisation of policing as an increasingly partisan issue, more and more central to political conflict. But the changing pattern of conflict within which the issue of policing is embedded is matched more particularly by the varying focal concerns in each period. [7] This will now be examined more closely for each stage, through a consideration of some characteristic works.

The 'consensus' stage

The key theme which marks the 'consensus' stage is celebration: the writing of a national success story. The problematic for most of these works is to explain the development and/or functioning of what is clearly taken to be a police institution which has solved a perennial political puzzle: how can order be maintained without unduly sacrificing liberty? Gorer, writing in the heart of the 'consensus' period, is the most explicit in claiming that 'the police represent an ideal model of behaviour and character' (Gorer, 1955, p.213). He suggests that 'started as an expedient to control the very great criminality and violence of large sections of the English urban population . . . the policeman has been for his peers not only an object of respect, but also a model of the ideal male character' (ibid., pp.310-11). Later 'consensus' period works are, of course, aware of the signs of tension preceding and following the establishment of the Royal Commission on the Police in 1960. But they are nevertheless still writing within the success story

9

	Academic	Official	Critical	Journalistic	Focal concerns
Consensus	Radzinowicz, 1948-69 Gorer, 1955 Banton, 1964 Martin & Wilson, 1969	Royal Commission on the Police, 1962 Critchley, 1967	Bowes, 1966	Rolph, 1962 Whitaker, 1964 Grigg, 1965	Order and legitimacy
Controversy	Lambert, 1970 Rock, 1973 Cain, 1973 Punch & Naylor, 1973 Chatterton, 1976, 1979, 1983 Holdaway, 1977, 1979, 1983 Manning, 1977, 1979 Reiner, 1978a Punch, 1979, 1983, 1985	Judge, 1972 Belson, 1975 Ditchfield, 1976	Pritt, 1972	Laurie, 1970 Humphry, 1972 Evans, 1974 Lewis, 1976 Cox et al., 1977	Civil rights and police deviance
Conflict	Rosenberg, 1971 Storch, 1975 Russell, 1975 Brogden, 1977, 1982 Cain, 1977, 1979 Miller, 1977 Bowden, 1978 Hall et al., 1978 McBarnet, 1978, 1979, 1981 Reiner, 1978b Cohen, 1979 Hall, 1979 Mawby, 1979 Bottomley & Coleman, 1981 Jefferson & Grimshaw, 1982, 1984 Steedman, 1984 Baxter & Koffman, 1985	Mark, 1977, 1978 Alderson, 1979, 1984 Ascoli, 1979 Jones, 1980 Royal Commission on Criminal Procedure, 1981 Policing London, 1982– McNee, 1983	Institute of Race Relations, 1979 Ackroyd et al., 1980 Blake, 1980 Gordon, 1980, 1983 Hewitt, 1982a, 1982b Christian, 1983 BSSRS, 1985 Coulter et al., 1985 Fine & Millar, 1985 Spencer, 1985	Bunyan, 1976 State Research, 1977–82 Hain, 1979, 1980 Whitaker, 1979 McClure, 1980 Kettle & Hodges, 1982 Manwaring-White, 1983	Who controls the police? The police in the social/political structure
Contradiction	Bailey, 1981 Fielding, 1931, 1984 Taylor, 1981 Politics and Power, 1981 Baldwin & Kinsey, 1982 Waddington, 1983, 1984, 1985 Jones & Levi, 1983 Lea & Young, 1984 Reiner, 1984, 1985 Geary, 1985	Home Office Research & Planning Unit, 1979– Clarke & Hough, 1980 Pope & Weiner, 1981 Policy Studies Institute, 1983 Weatheritt, 1983, 1985 Kinsey, 1984, 1985 Morgan & Maggs, 1984, 1985 Heal et al., 1985 Loveday, 1985 Thackrah, 1985	Scraton, 1985	Kettle, 1984, 1985	Realism: how is good policing to be done?

framework. Michael Banton's pioneering sociological study starts with 'the idea that it can be instructive to analyse institutions that are working well in order to see if anything can be learned from their success' (Banton, 1964, p.vii). Critchley's history (which I have classified as 'official' because the author was a senior member of the police department at the Home Office when the book was originally published) makes the national success story problematic explicit in his introduction: 'It is a priceless national heritage that the police system whose growth is described in this book combines the two virtues of all good policing. It sustains our civilisation; and, at the same time, it promotes the freedom under the rule of law without which civilisation is worthless (Critchley, 1967, pp.xvii-xviii). It is hard to conceive of studies being written nowadays which fall so unabashedly with a celebratory mode. [8]

The pervasiveness of the consensus assumptions in this period is brought out most sharply by examining the critical and journalistic literature. Bowes' 1966 book (and the police chapter in Pritt's 1972 study of legal institutions) both emanate from a well-known Marxist publishing house. Yet they are written from a straightforward civil libertarian perspective, as indeed the very title of Bowes' book makes plain. The blurb on the dust jacket explicitly states that the revelations of police misbehaviour which aroused concern (e.g. the 'rhino whip' and Challenor cases) were 'exceptional'. For evidence of more systematic abuse, the book has to delve back into the past. The clear difference between the traditional civil libertarian perspective of Bowes' book and later Marxist analyses in the 'conflict' phase is brought out by the absence of any discussion of the key issue of accountability, other than in the context of the complaints system and the question of individual police discipline (ch.11). The reform proposals are within an individualistic framework (recruits' educational standards and the like), aimed at 'improved police behaviour' (p.234). The history chapters apart, the book is squarely within the framework of liberal debate at the time. Pritt starts his chapter on the police with the assertion that they 'stand plainly in the middle of the class struggle', but this has the air of an a priori deduction from the general Marxist theory of the state, rather than growing out of his subsequent discussion of the civil liberties issues raised by individual police abuses.

Whitaker's influential 1964 Penguin Special was explicitly sold by the publishers as 'the first radical analysis of the police in our society'. It is indeed much more systematically questioning of the police role and organisation, as well as individual abuses, than most books in this period. But it is inconceivable that any later work could conclude with recommendations which advocate increasing police numbers, equipment and legal powers! (Whitaker, 1964, pp.168-9).

Altogether, then, the focal concern of works in the 'consensus' period is with analysis of the successful way that the police were seen as combining the maintenance of order and legitimacy. Even the avowedly radical works limit criticism primarily to individual abuses of civil liberties, and do not see any problem of excessive police power. Completely missing is any discussion of accountability, the rallying concern of later criticism. [9]

The 'controversy' stage

During the early 1970s, concern and controversy about policing increased over a variety of issues, notably police powers and the treatment of suspects, the handling of disorder, as well as the flurry of corruption revelations signalling the 'fall of Scotland Yard' (Cox et al., 1977). All these issues were, of course, present even in the 'consensus' period. But now the critical theme (among journalists and academics) became the systematic sources of police deviance and threats to civil liberties, as a function of police organisation and the nature of policing, transcending the individualistic 'one bad apple' approach. Those who were essentially defensive of the police in the face of this criticism had to support positively the 'one bad apple' approach, or indeed to concede the widespread prevalence of abuses but suggest these were remediable by reforms already in hand (Judge, 1972, pp.185-6; Lewis, 1976, pp.290-2). But the essential correctness of police organisation and procedures could no longer be taken for granted by any writers in the face of the evidently increasing controversy over the police role and practices.

The truly significant departure of the 'controversy' period was, however, the growth of a substantial body of academic research on the police. None of this research is overtly directed at politically contentious issues surrounding policing (with the possible exceptions of Lambert, 1970 and Reiner, 1978a). For the most part it is developed within the theoretical framework of symbolic interactionism, adopts the methodology of participant observation, and is concerned with laying bare the social relations and perspectives of the rank-and-file police culture. Unlike some of the pioneering American work in this tradition (notably Skolnick, 1966), it is not explicity constructed within a civil libertarian problematic, and does not address head-on the questions of the extent, sources and control of police deviation from the rule of law. (For an analysis of how the early American research reflected this civil rights perspective, see Cain, 1979, pp.144-5.) However, it remains true that the English academic research, at least implicitly, also 'regarded police deviancy as the central issue' (Cain, op.cit., p.146).

Key examples of this stage of academic police research are collected in Holdaway's important 1979 volume of essays. Holdaway's perceptive introductory comments make the civil rights/police deviancy problematic, which tacitly informs this research, quite explicit. As he sums up: 'one of the basic themes running through this book . . . is that the lower ranks of the service control their own work situation and such control may well shield highly questionable practices' (Holdaway, 1979, p.12). Holdaway foreshadows the central concern of the next phases of research when he concludes 'If, in a British society itself pervaded by social inequality, we desire a more accountable police, then we will check police power and we cannot expect the police to do this themselves' (Holdaway, op.cit., p.13). But for the most part accountability was still conceived of as a matter of internal organisational control. As Cain argues, these studies were limited in their explanatory scope by the boundaries of the police organisation, partly as an unintended by-product of the participant observation technique (Cain, op.cit., p.145-8). The 1962 Royal Commission's well-known aphorism that 'the problem of controlling the police can . . . be restated as the problem of controlling chief constables' (para.102) was implicitly inverted. The problem of controlling the police was re-conceptualised as the problem of control by, not of, chief constables.

The 'conflict' stage

The issue of accountability, in the more evidently political sense of who controls police organisational policy, moved to the forefront in the 'conflict' stage, marking a climax in the politicisation of police research. A much more explicit Marxist perspective, clearly raising the 'macro' issues of where the police stand in the social and political structure, informed much academic, critical and journalistic work in this period (foreshadowed by Rosenberg's pioneering 1971 paper). Much blunter evidence of the highly politicised debate is that some examples of what (on any objective criterion) must be counted as 'official' research now reflected a radical perspective, sponsored by the left wing Labour local authorities elected in 1981, notably the Greater London Council. This structurally critical analysis of the political role of the police thus appeared across the board in all forums of debate, and had to be confronted (if only as a menace!) by police establishment opinion. The world of difference which separates the autobiographical volumes of Sir Robert Mark and Sir David McNee, suffused by political apologetics, from the traditional genre of celebratory police autobiography bears this out. (Contrast Mark, 1978 or McNee, 1983 with the police memoirs tradition from Fabian, 1950 to Slipper, 1981 or Wicksteed, 1985.)

The relationship between the approach to police deviance embodied in the interactionist studies of the 'controversy' stage, and the structural Marxist work of the 'conflict' phase, is brought out most explicitly in the very influential writings of Doreen McBarnet (one of whose articles is contained in Holdaway's 1979 collection). McBarnet argues that the civil libertarian and interactionist approaches wrongly assimilated generalised ideological rhetoric about the values underpinning the rule of law and concrete legal rules. She shows rather that there is 'a distinct gap between the substance and the ideology of law' (McBarnet, 1981, p.155). The laws governing police practice are sufficiently permissive in formulation (especially as enforced by the courts) to give officers a wide range of discretion. The civil libertarian and interactionist emphasis on police deviation from the rule of law makes the rank and file 'the "fall guys" of the legal system taking the blame for any injustices' (ibid., p.156). Responsibility ought to be placed on 'the judicial and political elites' who make rules of sufficient elasticity to assimilate departures from the ideals of the rule of law. This raising of analysis to a structural rather than interactional level was enthusiastically endorsed by the expansion of more explicitly Marxist work (notably Cain, 1979; Brogden, 1982; and Jefferson and Grimshaw, 1984). All these works centre on the issue of accountability in the strong sense of 'who controls the police?' This also was the core concern of the proliferation of historical studies of the origins and development of the police written from a 'revisionist', radical perspective (Storch, 1975; Miller, 1977; Cohen, 1979; Brogden, 1982; and Steedman, 1984).

Congruent with this flourishing tradition of academic work on the issue of accountability and control was the influential study of the 'moral panic' about 'mugging' by Stuart Hall and his associates at the Centre of Contemporary Cultural Studies. This advanced the argument that the police and other elements of the social control apparatus had constructed the issue of 'mugging' in a way that resonated with a wider set of concerns about social disorder and decline, legitimating the development of a strong state and a 'law and order' society (Hall et al., 1978; Hall, 1979). These academic studies about the drift towards a police force which was increasingly authoritarian and 'beyond the limits of the law' (Bowden, 1978), were echoed by a proliferation of journalistic and critical writing in the same vein (Bunyan, 1976; Hain, 1979 and 1980; Institute of Race Relations, 1979; Ackroyd et al., 1980; Blake, 1980; Hewitt, 1982a and 1982b; Gordon, 1983; Christian, 1983; Manwaring-White, 1983; British Society for Social Responsibility in Science, 1985; Spencer, 1985; Fine and Millar, 1985; and Coulter et al., 1985).

By the mid-1980s it had become a new left orthodoxy, cemented by the reactions to policing developments during the 1984 miners' strike (Kettle, 1984 and 1985). Even more traditional studies of the public demand for police service, the construction of crime statistics, and the internal organisation of police forces (e.g. Mawby, 1979; Jones, 1980; Bottomley and Coleman, 1981) reflected the pervasive political concern with the issue: who controls the police? The

Royal Commission on Criminal Procedure, which mounted an extensive research programme, itself emphasised the theme of 'safeguards' over police power (however inadequately it may have accomplished this object in the eyes of its many critics, e.g. Baxter and Koffman, 1985).

The 'contradictory' stage

There are peculiar difficulties in assessing the current state of play in any field, and it is perhaps this that makes me see the present stage as 'contradictory'. But it may be that even with the benefit of hindsight the police research of the mid-1980s will be seen as reflecting the contradictory trends and pressures which have beset policing since 1981.

The key theme of the period is 'realism', a lowering of sights away from Utopian idealism, whether aspiring to a crime-free, orderly society, or a democratically accountable policing system animated by values of socialist justice. 'Realism' is espoused across the political spectrum, although of course with different inflexions. But it is evident in the 'left realism' of Taylor (1981), Politics and Power (1981), Baldwin and Kinsey (1982), Lea and Young (1984), and Kinsey (1984 and 1985); the 'administrative criminology' which informs the policing research of the Home Office Research Unit (the label is taken from Young, 1985); and the 'new right' realism, associated with James Q.Wilson in the USA. (There is no clear counterpart in England. But the work of Waddington (1983, 1984 and 1985) comes closest, with its explicit defence of the police against radical criticism, not by simple assertion of a 'law and order' model but a review of the research evidence on what the police actually do.)

There are two themes in the 'new realism'. One is a recognition of complexity, producing a crossing of previously maintained ideological boundaries, a borrowing of ideas and cross-fertilisation of themes, even if this is not acknowledged, indeed fervently denied. [10] An example is the 'left realist' emphasis that crime really is a problem, as indicated by judicious appraisal of crime statistics, and a consequent berating of police ineffectiveness on the basis of low clear-up rates. Meanwhile, the police and Home Office have adopted the erstwhile 'new criminology' arguments about the limited role of the police as a crime-control agency, and the pitfalls in interpreting official statistics.

The more important theme of the 'new realism' is a tendency to concern itself not so much with the documentation of bad policing as a quest for the good. The improvement of policing is also seen as raising deeper issues than the formal structure of police powers and accountability alone. There is an enthusiasm for monitoring new police initiatives, not in a spirit of seeking to discredit them, but aiming at constructive critical feedback intended to realise their aspirations. [11] (This attitude animates the Police Foundation's work; the 1983 Policy Studies Institute study of policing in London; much of the Home Office research; and the Economic and Social Research Council initiative on the Police and Criminal Evidence Act 1984.) Above all, there is a new concern to ground conceptions of 'good' policing not in a priori ideals, but a distillation and projection from best current practice. (The first example of this approach is Muir's originally neglected but increasingly influential 1977 American study. In England, this concern with analysing 'good' practice is evident in recent interactionist studies, e.g. Chatterton, 1983 and Fielding, 1984, as well as Geary's 1985 historical study of the policing of industrial conflict.) Similarly, there has been an interest in looking at how accountability actually works (even if critical and pointing at reform possibilities) rather than just lamenting its absence (Morgan and Maggs, 1984, 1985; Loveday, 1985). How the new 'realism' will develop is still very much open. In principle there is the possibility of a limited new consensus around shared ideas, but in practice at present this is still suppressed by ideological boundary-maintenance. As with policing itself, the current stage of debate and research on policing is beset by contradictions.

Conclusions

What can the role of policing research be in the future? As is evident from the table, there is much more police research than ever before, and much more of it is officially sponsored. But what will its practical and political impact be? Will it be to legitimate policing trends; to look on without influence; or to act in a leadership role? The worst case scenario is that the greater readiness of police organisations to be associated with research will merely serve to cloak their activities in an aura of legitimacy derived from presenting policy as rational and research-based. Alternatively, research may be irrelevant to practice. As in the past, policy fashions may flourish enthusiastically, impervious to evidence of ineffectiveness (Weatheritt, 1983 and 1985). Alternatively, a concern with the effectiveness and long-term legitimacy of policing could make police policy actually led by research; to spread identified 'good' practices; and to modify innovations which monitoring shows to be ineffective. On past experience, this is the least likely outcome - apart from anything else because of the political conflict which attends all policing developments. Perhaps empirical research can only have a negative monitoring function: assessing whether initiatives which have their roots in the practical exigencies and political direction of police organisations have their intended consequences. It is arguable that deepening the understanding of policing now requires theoretical synthesis rather than more empirical data (although this too is bedevilled by the inherently political character of policing). Perhaps we need further research to monitor the progress and impact of policing research!

Notes

[1] In addition to the previously cited critique of police studies by Cain, this point is developed from another theoretical viewpoint by Sykes: 'only a conceptualisation of policing that transcends local definitions and is related to a broader theoretical orientation is adequate for . . . scientific understanding' (Sykes, 1977, p.239).

[2] Within specific societies two 'orders' can be conceptually distinguished: what Marenin calls 'general order, the interests of all in regularity . . . public tranquillity and safety' and 'specific order . . . the use of state power to promote particular interests' (Marenin, 1982, pp.258-9). As I have put it elsewhere, 'the most fundamental difficulty in analysing and dealing with policing in a capitalist society is that the police have the inextricably dual function of handling troubles derived both from the problems of any industrial society and from its specifically capitalist form' (Reiner, 1985, p.34).

[3] But this excludes brief journalistic reports (and certainly 'news'), and the well-established 'true crime' genre of celebration of individual detectives and their casebooks. I am also not concerned here with non-social research on forensic and management techniques for the police (e.g. the work of the Home Office Scientific Research and Development Branch), or with black-letter expositions of the law on police powers (e.g. Leigh, 1985, or the clutch of recent texts on the Police and Criminal Evidence Act, e.g. Zander, 1985; Freeman, 1985; Bevan and Lidstone, 1985).

15

[4]   The points in the next section are developed more fully in Reiner, 1985, ch.1 and ch.2.

[5]   For all the bumps and wobbles in this, e.g. the clashes between police and the organised unemployed of 'Outcast London' in the 1880s, or the conflicts in the 1930s with the unemployed movement or anti-Fascist demonstrators, the overall trajectory towards a pacification of social relations seems unmistakable (Gatrell, 1980; Gurr, 1976; Geary, 1985).

[6]   The degree of this is ironically underlined by the growing scale of police injuries during riot control training, indicating its intensity. Already at the 1978 Police Federation annual conference demands were made for the 'realism' to be toned down because of the extent of injuries inflicted on police officers during training. In March 1982 during a riot control training exercise in Kent, ten officers were hurt, one suffering a serious head injury for which he eventually received £99,500 damages in the High Court (the Guardian, 16 November 1985).

[7]   By 'focal concerns', I mean those issues that constitute the axes of debate. Evidently in periods of controversy and conflict the concrete way in which these concerns are addressed will vary between different theoretical and political approaches.

[8]   Stead's recent (1985) book is, however, very reminiscent of this period in its tone.

[9]   Accountability was of course the key issue in the terms of reference for the Royal Commission on the Police in 1960. This was, however, seen very much as a problem of the potential abuse of the powers of watch committees, and certainly the Police Act 1964 did not increase the accountability of chief constables over operational policies. The tame (and ambiguous) approach of the Royal Commission was severely criticised by Marshall (1965) in the only book of the period to focus on the accountability issue (albeit from a perspective of constitutional and legal principle, which is why it does not feature in the table).

[10]   This is evident in the counter-revisionist histories of the early 1980s, e.g. Bailey, 1981. (See Reiner, 1985, ch.1).

[11]   This is reflected even in the avowedly adversarial 1985 book by Scraton. After a spirited resume of the worst aspects of the police, the book concludes not with a call for democratic accountability as similar works in the 'critical' period would have done, but advocacy of the potential of 'monitoring', an indication of the lowering of sights I identify as the hallmark of the 'realism' of the present phase.

References

Ackroyd, C., Margolis, K., Rosenhead, J. and Shallice, T., (1980) The technology of political control, Pluto Press, London
Alderson, J., (1979) Policing freedom, Macdonald and Evans, Plymouth
Alderson, J., (1984) Law and disorder, Hamish Hamilton, London
Ascoli, D., (1979) The Queen's Peace, Hamish Hamilton, London
Bailey, V., (ed.) (1981) Policing and punishment in the nineteenth century, Croom Helm, London
Baldwin, R. and Kinsey, R., (1982) Police powers and politics, Quartet Books, London
Banton, M., (1964) The policeman in the community, Tavistock, London
Baxter, J. and Koffman, L., (1985) Police: the constitution and the community, Professional Books, Abingdon

Bayley, D., (1979) 'Police function, structure and control in Western Europe and North America: comparative and historical studies', in Norris, N. and Tonry, M.(eds), Crime and Justice, I, University of Chicago Press, Chicago

Belson, W., (1975) The public and the police, Harper and Row, London

Bevan, V. and Lidstone, K., (1985) A guide to the Police and Criminal Evidence Act 1984, Butterworths, London

Bittner, E., (1970) The functions of the police in modern society, National Institute of Mental Health, Chevy Chase, Maryland

Bittner, E., (1974) 'Florence Nightingale in pursuit of Willie Sutton: a theory of the police', in Jacob, H. (ed.), The potential for reform of criminal justice, Sage, Beverly Hills

Blake, N., (1980) The police, the law and the people, Haldane Society, London

Bottomley, A.K. and Coleman, C., (1981) Understanding crime rates, Gower, Farnborough

Bowden, T., (1978) Beyond the limits of the law, Penguin, Harmondsworth

Bowes, S., (1966) The police and civil liberties, Lawrence and Wishart, London

British Society for Social Responsibility in Science Technology of Political Control Group (1985) TechnoCop, Free Association Books, London

Brogden, M., (1977) 'A police authority: the denial of conflict', Sociological Review, 25, 2

Brogden, M., (1982) The police: autonomy and consent, Academic Press, London

Brown, J. and Howes, G. (eds), (1975) The police and the community, Saxon House, Farnborough

Bunyan, T., (1976) The political police in Britain, Quartet Books, London

Cain, M., (1973) Society and the policeman's role, Routledge and Kegan Paul, London

Cain, M., (1977) 'An ironical departure: the dilemma of contemporary policing', in Jones, K. (ed.), Yearbook of social policy in Britain, Routledge and Kegan Paul, London

Cain, M., (1979) 'Trends in the sociology of police work', International Journal of Sociology of Law, 7, 2

Chatterton, M., (1976) 'Police in social control', in King, J. (ed.), Control without custody, Cropwood Conference Series No.7, Institute of Criminology, Cambridge

Chatterton, M., (1979) 'The supervision of patrol work under the fixed point system', in Holdaway, S. (ed.), The British police, Edward Arnold, London

Chatterton, M., (1983) 'Police work and assault charges', in Punch, M. (ed.), Control in the police organisation, MIT Press, Cambridge, Mass

Christian, L., (1983) Policing by coercion, GLC/Pluto Press, London

Clarke, R. and Hough, M., (1980) The effectiveness of policing, Gower, Farnborough

Clarke, R. and Cornish, D., (1983) Crime control in Britain: a review of policy research, State University of New York Press, Albany

Cohen, P., (1979) 'Policing the working class city', in Fine, B., Kinsey, R., Lea, J., Picciotto, S. and Young, J., (eds), Capitalism and the rule of law, Hutchinson, London

Coulter, J., Millar, S. and Walker, M., (1984) State of seige: miners' strike 1984, Canary Press, London

Cox, B., Shirley, J. and Short, M., (1977) The fall of Scotland Yard, Penguin, Harmondsworth

Critchley, T.A., (1967) A history of police in England and Wales, Constable, London

Dahrendorf, R., (1985) Law and order, Sweet and Maxwell, London

Ditchfield, J.A., (1976) Police cautioning in England and Wales, Home Office Research Study 37, HMSO, London

Evans, P., (1974) The police revolution, Allen and Unwin, London

Fabian, R., (1950) Fabian of the Yard, Naldrett, London
Fielding, N., (1981) 'The credibility of accountability', Poly Law Review, 6, 2
Fielding, N., (1984) 'Police socialisation and police competence', British Journal of Sociology, 35, 4
Fine, B. and Millar, R., (1985) Policing the miners' strike, Lawrence and Wishart, London
Freeman, M.F.D., (1985) The Police and Criminal Evidence Act 1984, Sweet and Maxwell, London
Gatrell, V., (1980) 'The decline of theft and violence in Victorian and Edwardian England', in Gatrell, V., Lenman, B. and Parker, G. (eds), Crime and law, Europa, London
Geary, R., (1985) Policing industrial disputes 1893-1985, Cambridge University Press, Cambridge
Gordon, P., (1980) Policing Scotland, SCCL, Glasgow
Gordon, P., (1983) White law, Pluto, London
Gorer, G., (1955) Exploring English character, Cresset, London
Grigg, M., (1965) The Challenor case, Penguin, Harmondsworth
Gurr, T.R., (1976) Rogues, rebels and reformers, Sage, Beverly Hills
Hain, P. (ed.) (1979) Policing the police 1, Calder, London
Hain, P. (ed.) (1980) Policing the police 2, Calder, London
Hall, S., (1979) Drifting into a law and order society, Cobden Trust, London
Hall, S., Critcher, C., Jefferson, T., Clarke, J. and Roberts, B., (1978) Policing the crisis, Macmillan, London
Hart, J., (1963) 'Some reflections on the Report of the Royal Commission on the Police', Public Law, 283
Heal, K., Tarling, R. and Burrows, J. (eds), (1985) Policing today, HMSO, London
Hewitt, P., (1982a) A fair cop: reforming the police complaints procedure, NCCL, London
Hewitt, P., (1982b) The abuse of power, Martin Robertson, Oxford
Holdaway, S., (1977) 'Changes in urban policing', British Journal of Sociology, 28, 2
Holdaway, S. (ed.), (1979) The British police, Edward Arnold, London
Holdaway, S., (1983) Inside the British police, Basil Blackwell, Oxford
Humphry, D., (1972) Police power and black people, Granada, London
Institute of Race Relations (1979) Police against black people, Institute of Race Relations, London
Jefferson, T. and Grimshaw, R., (1982) 'Law, democracy and justice', in Cowell, D., Jones, T. and Young, J. (eds), Policing the riots, Junction Books, London
Jefferson, T. and Grimshaw, R., (1984) Controlling the constable: police accountability in England and Wales, Muller, London
Jones, M., (1980) Organisational aspects of police behaviour, Gower, Farnborough
Jones, S. and Levi, M., (1983) 'The police and the majority: the neglect of the obvious', Police Journal, LVI, 4
Judge, A., (1972) A man apart, Barker, London
Kettle, M., (1984) 'The police and the left', New Society, 6 December
Kettle, M., (1985) 'The left and the police', Policing, 1, 3
Kettle, M. and Hodges, L., (1982) Uprising! The police, the people and the riots in Britain's cities, Pan, London
Kinsey, R., (1984) Merseyside Crime Survey, Merseyside County Council, Liverpool
Kinsey, R., (1985) Survey of Merseyside police officers, Merseyside County Council, Liverpool
Klockars, C., (1985) The idea of police, Sage, Beverly Hills

18

Lambert, J., (1970) Crime, police and race relations, Oxford University Press, Oxford

Laurie, P., (1970) Scotland Yard, Penguin Books, London

Lea, J. and Young, J., (1984) What is to be done about law and order? Penguin Books, Harmondsworth

Leigh, L., (1985) Police powers in England and Wales, Butterworths, London

Lewis, R., (1976) A force for the future? Temple Smith, London

Loveday, B., (1985) The role and effectiveness of the Merseyside Police Committee, Merseyside County Council, Liverpool

McBarnet, D., (1978) 'The police and the state', in Littlejohn, G. et al. (eds), Power and the state, Croom Helm, London

McBarnet, D., (1979) 'Arrest: the legal context of policing', in Holdaway, S. (ed.), The British police, Edward Arnold, London

McBarnet, D., (1981) Conviction, Macmillan, London

McClure, J., (1980) Spike Island: portrait of a police division, Macmillan, London

McNee, D., (1983) McNee's law, Collins, London

Manning, P., (1977) Police work, MIT Press, Cambridge, Mass

Manning, P., (1979) 'The social control of police work', in Holdaway, S. (ed.), The British police, Edward Arnold, London

Manwaring-White, S., (1983) The policing revolution, Harvester, Brighton

Marenin, O., (1982) 'Parking tickets and class repression: the concept of policing in critical theories of criminal justice', Contemporary Crises, 6

Mark, R., (1977) Policing a perplexed society, Allen and Unwin, London

Mark, R., (1978) In the office of constable, Collins, London

Marshall, G., (1965) Police and government, Methuen, London

Martin, J.P. and Wilson, G., (1969) The police: a study in manpower, Heinemann, London

Mawby, R., (1979) Policing the city, Gower, Farnborough

Miliband, R., (1978) 'A state of de-subordination', British Journal of Sociology, 29, 4

Miller, W., (1977) Cops and bobbies, University of Chicago Press, Chicago

Morgan, R. and Maggs, C., (1984) Following Scarman? Bath Social Policy Papers, University of Bath

Morgan, R. and Maggs, C., (1985) Setting the PACE, Bath Social Policy Papers, University of Bath

Muir, Jr, K.W., (1977) Police: streetcorner politicians, University of Chicago Press, Chicago

Northam, G., (1985) 'A fair degree of force?', The Listener, 31 October

Policy Studies Institute (1983) Police and people in London (Vols I-IV) by Smith, D.J., Gray, J. and Small, S., Policy Studies Institute, London

Politics and Power (1981) Politics and Power 4: Law, politics and justice, Routledge and Kegan Paul, London

Pope, D. and Weiner, N. (eds), (1981) Modern policing, Croom Helm, London

Pritt, D. (1972) Law, class and society, Book 4: The substance of the law, Laurence and Wishart, London

Punch, M., (1979) 'The secret social service', in Holdaway, S. (ed.), The British police, Edward Arnold, London

Punch, M. (ed.), (1983) Control in the police organisation, MIT Press, Cambridge, Mass

Punch, M., (1985) Conduct unbecoming: the social construction of police deviance and control, Tavistock, London

Punch, M. and Naylor, T., (1973) 'The police: a social service', New Society, 17 May

Radzinowicz, L., (1948-1969) A history of English criminal law, Vols I-IV, Stevens, London

Reiner, R., (1978a) The blue-coated worker, Cambridge University Press, Cambridge

Reiner, R., (1978b) 'The police, class and politics', Marxism Today, March

Reiner, R., (1984) 'Is Britain turning into a police state?', New Society, 2 August

Reiner, R., (1985) The politics of the police, Wheatsheaf Books, Brighton

Rock, P., (1973) Deviant behaviour, Hutchinson, London

Rolph, C.H. (ed.), (1962) The police and the public, Heinemann, London

Rosenberg, D., (1971) 'The sociology of the police and institutional liberalism', unpublished paper, Sociology Department, University of Bristol

Royal Commission on the Police (1962) Final report, Cmnd 1728, HMSO, London

Royal Commission on Criminal Procedure (1981) Report, Cmnd 8092, HMSO, London

Russell, K., (1976) Complaints against the police, Milltak, Leicester

Scarman, Lord (1981) The Brixton disorders, Cmnd 8427, HMSO, London (reprinted by Penguin Books, 1982)

Scraton, P., (1985) The state of the police, Pluto, London

Skolnick, J., (1966) Justice without trial, Wiley, New York

Skolnick, J., (1972) 'Changing conceptions of the police', Great Ideas Today, Encyclopaedia Britannica, Chicago

Slipper, J., (1981) Slipper of the Yard, Sidgwick and Jackson, London

Southgate, P. and Ekblom, P. (1984) Contacts between police and public: findings from the British Crime Survey, Home Office Research Study 77, HMSO, London

Spencer, S., (1985) Called to account: the case for police accountability in England and Wales, NCCL, London

Stead, P.J., (1985) The police of Britain, Macmillan, New York

Steedman, C., (1984) Policing the Victorian community, Routledge and Kegan Paul, London

Storch, R., (1975) 'The plague of blue locusts: police reform and popular resistance in Northern England, 1840-57', International Review of Social History, 20

Sykes, R., (1977) 'A regulatory theory of policing', in Bayley, D. (ed.), Police and society, Sage, Beverly Hills

Taylor, I., (1981) Law and order: arguments for socialism, Macmillan, London

Thackrah, J. (ed.), (1985) Contemporary policing, Sphere, London

Tomasic, R., (1985) The sociology of law, Sage, Beverly Hills

Waddington, P.A.J., (1983) Are the police fair? Research Paper 2, Social Affairs Unit, London

Waddington, P.A.J., (1984) 'Community policing: a sceptical appraisal', in Norton, P. (ed.), Law and order and British politics, Gower, Farnborough

Waddington, P.A.J. and Leopold, P., (1985) Protest, policing and the law, Conflict Studies 175, Institute for the Study of Conflict, London

Weatheritt, M., (1983) 'Community policing: does it work and how do we know? A review of research', in Bennett, T. (ed.), The future of policing, Cropwood Conference Series No.15, Institute of Criminology, Cambridge

Weatheritt, M., (1985) 'Policing research and policing policy', Policing, 1, 2

Whitaker, B., (1964) The police, Penguin Books, London

Whitaker, B., (1979) The police in society, Eyre Methuen, London

Wicksteed, B., (1985) Gang buster, Futura, London

Wilson, J.Q., (1975) Thinking about crime, Vintage, New York

Young, J., (1985) 'The failure of criminology: the need for a radical realism', unpublished mimeo, Sociology Department, Middlesex Polytechnic

Zander, M., (1985) The Police and Criminal Evidence Act 1984, Sweet and Maxwell, London

2 Achieving 'value for money' from police expenditure: the contribution of research

JOHN BURROWS

Introduction

Several contributions to the recent debate about ways and means of achieving 'value for money' from the police start with the opening gambit that 'efficiency' is not a new concept in policing. It is a point worth making, but it is also worth stressing – as Collins has done – that the interpretation of what constitutes 'an efficient force'· has changed over the years: in current usage, she notes, it is concerned specifically with the relationship between inputs and outputs (Collins, 1985). In this sense, the recent drive towards monitoring the efficiency of the police service is more ambitious in its scope than the programme which many see as its natural predecessor – the Planning Programming Budgeting (PPB) experiment which was carried out between 1969 and 1974; although this initially intended to embrace measurement of output, it commenced with the more limited aim of costing different police 'inputs', and floundered (see Southgate, 1985, for a summary of this initiative and Christian, 1982, for a fuller account).

There have been two main pressures behind this renewed interest: the rapid increase in the costs of policing at a time when government has sought to restrain public expenditure generally, and the fact that crime has continued to rise despite this increased expenditure. Research on the wider issue of police effectiveness has, however, been another factor prompting this resurgence of interest. Expenditure on the police was, for quite a substantial period in the 1970s, insulated from the restraint experienced in other parts of the public sector, and undoubtedly one reason for this was that increased police strength was viewed as the means of meeting governmental commitments on law and order. However, in the late 1970s and early 1980s a stream of research findings on police effectiveness, whether about aspects of patrol or investigative work, served to undermine the faith that increased resources would provide the expected returns (Clarke and Hough, 1984, provide a review of these). [1]

21

The most positive indication of the government's commitment to police efficiency is Home Office Circular 114, issued in November 1983. The debate that this has engendered, which is clearly reflected in several of the chapters in this book, suggests that it must constitute the most widely scrutinised Home Office circular in recent years. What the circular does – in the context of an introduction that outlines the general need for restraint in public expenditure, notes the recent increases in police expenditure and indicates that the 'golden days' are over [2] – is outline the criteria that will be employed when considering applications for increases in police establishments. Four specific criteria are given [3]: that increases will only be given to forces whose resources are directed in accordance with 'properly determined objectives and priorities' (in the view of HM Inspectors (HMIs)); that bids will have to be for specific posts; that the police authority will fund them; and that they will take effect in the current or following financial year. The bulk of the circular is then devoted to expanding on this first principle – that is, specifically what is expected from forces when setting objectives (to ensure, for example, that these are based on sound management information, that they reflect the needs and wishes of the community and the views of junior ranks of the police), and implementing them (for example, the need for objectives to be clearly understood by those pursuing them and the need to monitor how far objectives are met).

The intention of this paper is to review some of the ways in which research has contributed to the development of these 'good management' principles which the government has sought to foster. It is thus concerned almost exclusively with what Robert Reiner's chapter calls the 'new realism' theme in police research. It has been argued that the research on police effectiveness has a crucial role in prompting Circular 114, but it is important to ensure that those funding police research do not construe this as its only – and perhaps negative – contribution (particularly so, when research 'contractors' are as closely bound to the wishes of their 'customers' as they are so often in the field of police research). The circular and the other components of the present government's initiatives of course provide a wide scope for research [4] on various issues, although many would question how far the key principles have been adopted by the police service. Moreover the fact that these clearly make certain presuppositions about 'proper' policing functions may certainly be unwelcome to some. [5]

Given that 'good management' can be said to touch on almost every aspect of policing, there will be clear limitations to the scope of the issues that can be discussed in the context of a short paper. The focus of this paper is thus primarily on the input/output aspect of the efficiency initiative, which is one particularly close to the spirit of Circular 114 and to several other aspects of the government's 'value for money' initiative. To develop precisely what this means, the paper first focuses on some of the key elements of the current initiative. It thus gives disproportionate weight to the role of the Home Office, at the expense of the police authority's 'statutory duty of securing an adequate and efficient force' (para.8 of Circular 114). [6] It then moves on to discuss, in a more practical vein, some of the ways in which research has affected good management in two particularly important areas of policing – patrol work and investigation – and how it can continue to do so.

Existing policy

Circular 114, while certainly the most 'visible' element of the present government's thrust at ensuring efficiency within the police service, is not of course its only component. The other features of this initiative have been outlined elsewhere (see Collins, 1985; Southgate, 1985) but these features, and the thinking underlying them, deserve some elaboration here. This is important in order to develop more precisely what the Home Office has demanded from the police, but also in order to pinpoint some of the limitations on the control exercised by central government and to give a concrete idea of the Inspectorate's functions and role.

It is traditional to distinguish two ways in which the Home Secretary exercises power over the police service: directly, for example in the payment of police grant and the provision of support services (training, forensic science, etc.) and indirectly, for example by approval of changes in police establishment or through the work of HM Inspectorate of Constabulary. While current moves to ensure efficiency of course emanate from a direct source - specifically restrictions on police grant (the Government's intentions are summarised in the White Paper on the Financial Management Initiative (FMI) of 1982: they include the intention to ensure 'critical scrutiny of output and value for money' in all departments), the Home Office has clearly opted to achieve this end primarily through indirect means. Control is largely focused through the work of the HMIs. This approach is seen as reflecting the principles underlying the Police Act 1964 - in particular, that policing is a local service and that more direct intervention would impinge on the operational independence of chief constables and the powers of police authorities.

The revised inspection guidelines now employed by HMIs constitute the backbone of this approach [7] and HMIs' visits the 'sharp end' of the intiative. To assess an individual force's performance, HMIs now require considerably more thorough information about manpower deployment and financial expenditure within a force. [8] This information is requested prior to the HMI's annual visit and requires expenditure to be grouped under three main headings: 'activities', 'management' and 'manpower'. It is designed to provide a basis by which HMIs can discuss with local chief constables their policing priorities for their force, and whether their resources are deployed in line with these priorities.

Development of a financial information system

What is of particular interest is the way in which the financial information system currently employed by HMIs was developed and the thinking that underlay this approach. The system was developed by a team called the Financial Information System (FIS) Project Group, which was established in 1983 as part of the programme of work carried out in response to FMI. Inevitably, it lent heavily on experience of programme budgeting of the early 1970s. On the resource allocation side, members of the project group sought to obtain a comprehensive categorisation of all police expenditure under a range of different functional headings which could be employed either to look at a police force's priorities in the very broadest sense - for example its distribution between 'operational' and 'non-operational' activities - or in comparative detail, by looking at principal headings and specific sub-headings within each (thus the main 'operational' activities could be broken down to such activities as 'community relations', 'crime', 'traffic', etc; these were then further sub-divided amongst appropriate sub-categories). In addition to this, the group sought to delineate the way in which money was spent on each of these functional activities (the 'types of spend') breaking each down into three principal headings ('operational manpower time', 'training' and 'support') and then again into sub-headings (thus 'support' was sub-divided into 'transport', 'buildings', 'computers', etc.)

These broad functional categories designated the areas for measurement when the FIS project group moved on to address the issue of performance indicators, and possible measures HMIs might ask chief constables to provide. Inevitably, they tended to the view that the best that could be hoped for was that police forces could assemble a wider range of 'intermediate' measures of their performance rather than any 'final' outputs (as the latter more often than not required the views of the ultimate 'consumers' of most police services – the public – in one form or another).

Professional regulation

The developmental work of the FIS project group was thus in line with the Home Office's overall response to FMI: broadly, this has been to employ circulars (like 114/1983 and its successor 8/1984 on crime prevention) to outline the sort of approach expected from the police, to ask chief constables to provide a great deal of more detailed information about how they organise their resources and to provide some general performance indicators, primarily as a means of prompting HMIs to ask more searching questions. Some have argued that this emphasis on statistics has inevitably increased pressure to produce results 'comparable' with other forces and is thus a major step towards centralisation, and a step backwards from the belief that policing needs to be geared to local conditions. On the other hand, the Home Office has implemented this policy within the constraints of the tripartite structure (which effectively precludes, for example, any thought of setting quantifiable targets for the police). It has also chosen not to publish either policy guidelines or forces' returns to HMIC. There has been criticism from some quarters about the secrecy of an arrangement which effectively involves police officers reviewing their peers (see New Society, 19 July 1985), but the overall strategy of 'professional regulation' was one that tended to be endorsed by a review by Ian Sinclair and Clive Miller (1984) of the National Institute of Social Work. Sinclair and Miller were asked by the Home Office to explore questions about measures of effectiveness and efficiency for the police through interviews with senior police officers, civil servants and academics: they took the view that qualitative assessment provided by fellow professionals was the only feasible policy to adopt when it was not possible to obtain 'unambiguous routine measures of the relationship between inputs to the police and desired final outputs'.

Consultation

The emphasis on proper 'consultation' as an integral part of good management – consultation both with the community policed and junior ranks within the service itself – emerges as a recurring theme of the current efficiency initiative. It is worth noting here – without wishing to stray too deeply into the debate on 'consumerism' raised in Rod Morgan's chapter (and especially the question of whether the public are suitable judges of policing priorities) – that this could be construed as exerting pressure on senior officers to enlist professional research assistance to ensure this sort of consultation is properly carried out. However, with one or two notable exceptions (such as the, now regular, work by National Opinion Polls for the Metropolitan Police in London, or Kinsey's survey of police officers in Merseyside), it is clear that the service has generally not chosen to follow this path. There are undoubtedly several reasons for this, and it may be that behind the various ostensible explanations lies a gut resistance to assuming either the public or junior officers have a legitimate right to offer comment. One more respectable objection, however, is that of the cost incurred: primarily in order to ensure a degree of objectivity in survey work, the police have been advised not to utilise their own officers to carry out surveys themselves (Home

Office, 1984) and this tends to leave them with the option of having to employ a survey research organisation to carry out the task. Another explanation is that although HMIs require to know who was consulted when force strategies were formulated, they do not attempt to set standards about how systematically this should be done. Although there has been a long tradition of survey work examining public perceptions of the police (Southgate and Ekblom, 1984 provide a recent example), systematic research aimed at assembling community views about local policing policies and their priorities remains in its infancy. It is however an important area where the contribution of research may come to be more in demand, particularly in inner city areas where many increasingly perceive that existing community representatives present views which may be essentially at odds with those of the community they serve (especially the young and disadvantaged).

There are, in summary, a great many strands to the current 'value for money' initiative directed by the Home Office. It goes without saying that, while the overall policy is welcomed by some within the police service (see, for example, Butler, 1984), almost each and every strand has drawn fire from critics. It is not possible to catalogue all these here – especially those lacking any more substance than a resentment that police expenditure should be held in check – but it is clearly important to outline some recurrent themes.

One common criticism, emanating from junior ranks in the police service, is that senior ranks seldom consult them in setting objectives. The views of constables and sergeants, the great majority of those in the service, are obviously central to the way management will develop. Unfortunately, if the columns of force newspapers are taken to be representative, many voice the view that current 'management' initiatives lack anything but lip service to the idea of consultation with junior ranks and that planning serves as yet another police function that withdraws officers from the streets; moreover many fiercely resist the idea of management encroaching into areas of policing – such as patrol work – where hitherto the individual constable seemed assured of a degree of autonomy in his work. The Police Federation, for its part, is certainly well aware that the 'policing by objectives' policy implicit in Circular 114 may manage to involve the individual constable more closely in decision-making and so undermine the collective strength of the Federation (see Rowlands, 1984).

Another theme is that police officers of all ranks have warned against the tendency to look for 'tangible' results from 'purposeful' policing and the likely development of 'league tables' (of prosecutions, process cases and arrests) as the measure of the individual officers' achievement (see Templeton, 1984). This is an argument echoed in the views expressed by academic researchers who – to summarise their views so briefly as to do injustice to them – tend to focus on the difficulties of defining concise objectives for much of police activity, and the resultant difficulty of deriving any final outputs. In this opening section, the intention has been to make it clear that, by focusing on the professional judgement of HMIs, current Home Office policy has not intended to foster a purely quantitative approach. The department has not, for example, followed the line pursued by the Department of Health and Social Security, which was to develop performance indicators like those collected in CIPFA's police statistics. It is not easy however to say with any conviction that the pressure to provide measurement of performance within forces has not resulted in this sort of development, in other words that this is not the unintended result of the present FIS initiative.

Monitoring patrol and investigative activity

Much of the existing literature on the efficiency of the police service tends to deal with the subject en bloc. This necessarily gives rise to some unwarranted generalisation about the scope and desirability of extending the 'efficiency' concept. An obvious point, though perhaps a little ridiculous, is that some components of the police budget – like police buildings, vehicles or equipment – are, or could be, managed as efficiently as in any profit-making organisation. In an attempt to avoid this pitfall, the discussion in the remainder of this paper is focused on two distinct but clearly central areas of police activity: patrol and investigation. The discussion deals specifically with the current preoccupation with the relationship between the 'inputs' of policing and their 'outputs' in these two areas; it is largely directed at the impact of recent research conducted in this country.

Patrol

The problems of monitoring patrol activity are substantial: in fact it is more than a little ironic that such a central plank of police activity should constitute probably the most complex activity to manage efficiently. The root of the problem is of course that 'ground cover' policing, in whatever form it is conducted, can be claimed to achieve a range of diffuse objectives, or even several objectives at one and the same time: thus the constable on the street corner can be said to be preventing reckless driving, deterring the thief or fostering that elusive concept of 'public tranquillity'. In a real sense, therefore, patrol work confounds the central premise of any planning system: that all resources should be directed towards a clearly understood and specific purpose. The FIS Project Group were well aware of the difficulties here, not least because of their familiarity with the same problems confronted by the PPB initiative in this area, but were unable to make any significant headway in coming to terms with it, primarily because the police officers they spoke to could provide no consensus view of why patrol activity was necessary. [9] Thus while the group were broadly content to live with a range of general assumptions in their attempt to define broadly the 'functions' of the different elements of police activity – that, for example, the CID is are predominantly concerned with crime investigation – they reported that patrol work could not be said to achieve any specific function: they were thus reluctantly forced to admit 'patrol activity' into their financial information system as a functional category in its own right, alongside specifically orientated objectives of police work.

The long-term solution to this problem, at least to the FIS Project Group, lay in the Home Office policy of fostering the 'directed patrol' philosophy within the police service: that is patrol work informed by detailed crime analysis and carried out with clear objectives in mind. To central government, and local police management, this has both working and analytical advantages: it provides evidence of closer management supervision and would allow any financial information system to categorise all patrol activity under the objective that was being pursued at the time – whether this be crime prevention, road traffic control, or any other activity. Few however are oblivious to the practical difficulties of implementing such policy. Quite apart from differences in view about what directed patrol should consist of [10], there are, for example, doubts about whether existing management information is sufficient for the task, whether middle management (particularly sergeants and inspectors) are appropriately trained and about the responses from constables actually on patrol. It is for these reasons that in its 1985/86 programme, the Research and Planning Unit of the Home Office has elected to devote a substantial proportion of its police research budget to the various components of patrol. Three studies are relevant. One of these has explored in two divisions of the Metropolitan Police District (MPD) the extent to which current patrol activities are directed by senior officers, and the way in which constables themselves choose their priorities when on patrol. The work by Mike Chatterton in Derbyshire, described in Chapter 8, looked specifically at the role of the uniformed sergeant but will go on to look at the implementation of directed patrol in both that force and Greater Manchester. Finally, the implementation of directed patrol is an essential ingredient of the management initiative conducted by Hampshire Police with the research assistance of David Smith.

Directed patrol, however, is viewed as a long-term objective for the police service and one critically dependent on the development of more sophisticated crime analysis within the police service, in order that managers can identify precisely how, when and where problems requiring police attention arise. Researchers are taking a lead in developing this work (see, for example, Ramsay, 1982, and the research publications of the Home Office Crime Prevention Unit). The more immediate problem for the police manager, however, has been to explore what can be done about monitoring current patrol activities. Some of the issues are discussed here by resorting, once again, to the guiding principle of the current initiative: the measurement of 'inputs' and their relationship to 'outputs'.

A major pitfall that confounds informed management judgement in the police service – particularly about patrol work, but also about many other aspects of police activity – is that few can actually claim to have reliable information about how resources are presently deployed. Of course senior management are aware of how officers are allocated between departments, between headquarters and division, between permanent station duties and relief; they also have recourse to the 'duty state', or its equivalent, at each police station as a means of obtaining information about the allocation of duties on a daily basis. In a few areas command and control computers provide both an immediate 'snapshot' of manpower deployment, and trends over time. Nonetheless, these sources seldom provide an accurate breakdown of how patrol officers spend their time [11], and this naturally is an essential prerequisite if this time is to be managed more efficiently. It is, for example, axiomatic that patrol time can only be more precisely directed when officers are not responding to calls from the public or other necessary duties. This begs the question of whether this 'uncommitted' time constitutes a major, or insignificant, portion of existing patrol time.

These sorts of, essentially very basic, management questions have prompted renewed interest in activity surveys as a means of looking at the 'input' to patrol. It is no coincidence, of course, that these activities came to attract particular interest around the time of the PPB experiment (see, for example, Martin and Wilson, 1969; Comrie and Kings, 1975; Home Office, 1974); the subject attracted little interest in the late 1970s and early 1980s. Several of the recent studies by academic researchers can now boast considerably larger samples than their predecessors: these have either employed the strategy of asking police officers to complete a retrospective questionnaire of how time was spent on their 'last tour of duty' (by this means, the Policy Studies Institute (PSI) looked at the activities of 1,770 officers in the MPD, and Kinsey of 1,190 in Merseyside) or resorting to the more traditional method of requiring officers to complete a log of their activities over a given review period. The current Research and Planning Unit survey, while covering only two divisions of the MPD, concentrated on all ground-cover activities over a four-week period, and yielded information about some 2,500 'duty tours' by officers. These studies, however, lack the breadth of earlier work (where typically similar methodologies were employed in different forces) and therefore do not allow differences between forces to be pinpointed: the only recent study of this nature was Brown and Iles' (1985) work in five police forces, and this was restricted to the work of community constables. Nonetheless, this study, like those of the PSI and Kinsey, did serve to underline the fact that the demands on the police, and consequent manpower deployment, do vary significantly from one area to another; they suggest the comparative element needs to be tackled, not least better to inform decisions about the deployment of resources between police forces.

There can be little doubt that these published studies represent the 'tip of an iceberg'; the recent experience of the Home Office Research and Planning Unit is that a sizeable number of police forces has conducted activity surveys, but without the assistance of the outside research community. This is probably indicative both of the encouragement of HMIs (responding specifically for the need to match 'resources' with 'priorities' outlined in para.7 of Circular 114) and the increasing research independence within the police generally (there are - particularly within planning and management service departments - an increasing number of those with research experience to call on). Whoever conducts such surveys, it is clear that police officers should take key roles in interpreting their results. While there is no difficulty for the researcher in producing a broad brush picture of what activities are carried out, by whom or in what circumstances (and indeed in drawing attention to apparent anomalies), it is primarily for management to decide whether this resource deployment is in line with what they expect, whether 'paperwork' is necessary or superfluous, and so on.

Set against the major inroads now being made into exploring the 'inputs' of patrol work, the work on defining 'output' measures for patrol has been more restricted. The reasons largely lie in the multiplicity of objectives for patrol work (which were discussed earlier) but also derive from the longstanding difficulty of assessing preventive action by police officers. Once again, the problem was put in very plain language by the FMI Project Group: 'where there is effective prevention there is nothing to count'. [12]

This is not to say that existing research has had no impact, for the general research on police effectiveness - and indeed the fruits of recent work on victimisation - has tended to dictate the language used and assumptions made in the current debate. On the one hand, the generally negative findings that have emerged about the preventive capabilities of the officer on patrol have tended to prompt questions about the extent to which his presence reassures the public. Thus reduction of the fear of crime has tended to take the limelight as a primary objective of patrol activity. On the other hand, the findings of recent victim surveys have persuaded more and more police officers (as well as civil servants) to accept that careful evaluation of policing strategies generally requires 'before' and 'after' observation by means of victim surveys, as well as reference to recorded crime. Victim surveys have thus come to be viewed as the desirable 'tools' for the job. This does not mean, of course, that evaluation by means of recorded crime statistics has come to be seen as a thing of the past - these of course still predominate the debate on policing - but that research on victimisation has created a climate where most accept the deficiencies of evaluations which have not employed these methods. Victim surveys - such as those employed in Trevor Bennett's evaluation of neighbourhood watch in London - enjoy two distinct advantages: the ability to detect changes in unrecorded crime but also the ability to incorporate questions about the fear of crime and its consequences.

One major contribution to this development was David Farrington and Lizanne Dowds' work in Nottinghamshire. This study directly highlighted the <u>differences across areas</u> in the relationship between recorded crime and victimisation data in a way the British Crime Survey (BCS) had not done. The BCS sample is not large enough to produce an 'alternative' crime rate for each force in the country and, although its second sweep has done much to inform us about how trends in recorded crime and victimisation data may change in relation to one another, it was never intended as an instrument for looking at recording anomalies across force or divisional boundaries. It thus left open the danger that many, in the absence of contradictory evidence, could assume that the statistics on recorded crime are generally an accurate - <u>pro rata</u> - reflection of victimisation in an area, and can be interpreted as such. Farrington and Dowds' useful study, designed to account for the extremely high crime rate of Nottinghamshire and drawing heavily on the BCS questionnaire, confounded this view quite dramatically. It showed that while Nottinghamshire had a higher 'true' crime (victimisation) rate than the areas with which it was compared (Staffordshire and Leicestershire), the <u>main reasons</u> why its crime rate was so disproportionately high was because of police recording practices (specifically, Nottinghamshire recorded a greater number of crimes originating from admissions, and a greater number of crimes involving stolen property of little value). This research has perhaps not changed things to the extent that <u>only</u> victimisation data will do to evaluate policing strategies - their cost alone remains the prohibitive factor -but its message has not been lost.

On the patrol front generally, experience seems to suggest that most forces have been content to devise intermediate measures of output - such as the number of officers posted to patrol duties who actually went out on patrol - in preference to assessment by means of crime statistics or other more 'final' outputs. Not surprisingly, those that have proposed more ambitious criteria have fallen under fire from the critics of purely 'quantitative' measurement. There has been a range of arguments against such a development (see Sinclair and Miller, 1984; Southgate, 1985) primarily pointing to organisational evidence that the setting of quantitative goals will motivate respondents to achieve these in preference to - and indeed at the expense of - less finite goals. It is worth repeating that the Home Office have not taken the view that quantitative measures of assessment should take ascendancy over qualitative (indeed Kate Collins (1985), formerly of the Home Office police department, has indicated that forces which 'use performance indicators in a mechanistic way would be misunderstanding the style of management advocated in Circular 114'). But set against this, Jones and Silverman (1984) have coined the convincing argument that because 'figures have an authority of their own', senior officers are bound to favour them rather than simple 'value judgement'. The Jones/Silverman argument makes the important point that researchers are <u>not</u> necessarily tilting at imaginary windmills when referring to this danger: the Home Office emphasis on the need for 'professional' judgement can quite easily be lost when instructions are interpreted at the local level, and forces may quickly refer to figures in their keenness to impress on the Inspectorate that their resources are efficiently employed.

Investigation

On a theoretical level, the investigation of crime accords far more clearly with the paradigm of the classic planning model: that activity should be directed towards 'achievable' goals. Although the long-term goal of investigation may be to deter future criminal activity, its immediate goals are more concrete: to identify and arrest those responsible for crime (increasingly, many now add to this the provision of a 'satisfactory' service to victims). Moreover the 'input' to police crime investigation work is again finite – crimes recorded by the police. While there may be some fuzziness at the margins on this issue (where crimes may not be formally recorded precisely because they offer no prospect of being solved), clearly the police cannot be expected to solve unreported offences. Given this relatively straightforward relationship, it is no surprise that advances have been made on the measurement of the output of investigation. In this area, it is the measurement of input that lags behind.

On the face of things, detectives and their work seem to have frequently escaped the careful scrutiny that their uniform colleagues have been subjected to. Research has of course provided useful analysis of how they achieve results – studies like those by Keith Bottomley and Clive Coleman (1981) or David Steer (1980) have illustrated the means by which crimes are cleared up. What remains largely unexplored is the quantitative assessment of inputs – that is, detailed breakdown of how detectives spend their time (the fruits of activity surveys) – and, at a more sophisticated level, any analysis of which aspects of investigative work are the most productive (Eck, 1983, provides a perspective from the USA). A recent summary of CID activity surveys carried out in some four forces has started to throw some light on this area (see Tarling and Burrows, 1985) but this essentially remains a first step.

While this lack of 'background' has not inhibited several forces from exploring ways and means by which their investigative capabilities could be more product- ively organised, it has almost certainly proved a stumbling block which confounds rigorous evaluation of the impact of such initiatives. The adoption of 'case screening' – the procedure employed to separate 'solvable' cases that warrant CID attention from those that do not – is a case in point. The primary aim of the various systems being employed (particularly in the larger metropolitan forces where the CID have traditionally been responsible for all investigation; in rural forces 'uniform' investigation is nothing new) is to channel scarce detective resources to where they can be put to best effect. This being the case, evaluation seems invariably to incorporate simply an account of how clear-up rates have changed. This overlooks the basic proposition that informal case screening may well have achieved approximately the same effect (that is, the shuffling process by which the 'hopeful' cases in the CID officer's in-tray have traditionally been sorted from the 'no-goers') or even that the attention given by uniform branch to the more hopeless cases may be more than that previously given by CID. In this instance there is a need for research effort to be directed at the impact of case screening – ideally incorporating measurement against some finite control (either analysis in the same area before, or by comparison with one not practising case screening); the same need exists to look at the other organisational fad of the police service – the squad system. Squads go in and out of fashion, but do they provide a more, or less, efficient means of investigation?

Recent research evidence has done much to inform the debate on clear-up rates and indeed has led to some refinements being made to the actual statistics required from the police. This evidence, particularly that derived from a programme of work by the Home Office Research and Planning Unit aimed at looking at why clear-up rates vary so widely, has prompted the search for ways and means of investigating cases efficiently, notably by undermining the contention that most crimes could be solved provided there were sufficient resources to devote to the task. It has also suggested more concise means of measurement (see Burrows and Tarling, 1982). One central, perhaps in retro- spect obvious, finding of this research is that the crime 'mix' of an area is a critical determinant of its clear-up rate; a point taken on board by the FMI Project Group in their search for performance indicators.

The other important finding in the quest for suitable measures of investigative output is that clear-up rates - particularly for important crimes like burglary - do not reliably indicate a force's success in arresting offenders (Burrows, 1986a). One reason for this of course is the reliance on offences taken into consideration. But recent evidence suggests that - although the development is not uniform across the country - 'prison write-offs' have also grown rapidly in importance as a means of obtaining 'secondary' clear-ups to crime (see Burrows, 1986b). Indeed force statistical officers have recently been asked to provide the Home Office with information about such clearances on a regular basis. Although space does not permit full discussion of the issues this prompts, it seems that the current differences in practice across police forces signal the fact that the service remains divided about the ultimate objectives of investigation. Obviously the identification and arrest of offenders warrants top priority everywhere, but while some see this as their only objective (with little effort given to exploring previous offending by those arrested), others direct considerable energy to extracting admissions from those they detain. In the same way it also seems that there are differences of view about whether victim satisfaction should be seen as a legitimate objective of investigation.

Postscript

This paper has attempted to sketch how existing research on the police has made a substantial contribution to the present 'efficiency' initiative, and indeed to argue that it was itself a major catalyst in prompting that initiative. It has attempted to show the various ways research has contributed: both indirectly - by experimental evaluation of standard policing practices - and more directly by analysis of the inputs of various policing activities, their outputs and by action research focused on the means of implementing new ideas. It would be foolish to maintain that this contribution has been successful on every count (or that the current 'efficiency' initiative itself has been entirely successful), but many difficulties that have arisen are a natural consequence of the complex and varied nature of policing as an activity: here the intractable problem of identifying the objectives of patrol serves to illustrate the grand scale of the task. It has been suggested that the fact that police forces have not produced a limited number of generic quantitative output measures does not signify, ipso facto, that current initiatives have failed: quantitative indicators cannot be the sole criteria to be applied.

For the future, it seems that there will continue to be a substantial interest in efficiency-related issues, and that this will continue to demand research [13] that adopts the range of different designs and methodologies that characterises present efforts. It seems appropriate, however, to add that one, comparatively unused, research approach (not covered here) is likely to grow in importance: namely, 'aggregate' studies (see Morris and Heal, 1981) that analyse relationships between the input and outputs of policing. In this country, the work by Carr-Hill and Stern (1979) remains the prime example of this approach, although similar studies - also employing econometric methods - have been carried out by Burrows and Tarling (1982) and Joyce (1985). The reason for anticipating major developments in this area is that as data about inuts and output grow in sophistication (allowing, for example, police 'presence' to be measured in actual hours on the street rather than by some substitute like 'police per capita'), so this methodology becomes increasingly credible. Statistical models of policing offer the police manager a predictive capability and ability to identify divisions or areas unusual in their performance; to the researcher they offer a valuable chance to explore, from a different angle, the web of inter-relationships between social and demographic factors, policing and crime.

Notes

[1]   Much of this drew on from the results of research carried out in the United States, but - in some notable instances - it was also supported by in-house Home Office studies of the 1960s and early 1970s which had not previously received wide coverage.

[2]   'The restraints in public expenditure at both central and local government level make it impossible to continue with the sort of expansion which has occurred in recent years' (para.2).

[3]   The need for civilianisation - if this is practicable and more economic - is not specifically included as one of these four criteria; it is, however, given due prominence elsewhere.

[4]   It is important that Circular 114/1983 and subsequently 8/1984 (on crime prevention) specifically mention the need for research both to decide objectives and to evaluate initiatives.

[5]   A simple example may be the emphasis on 'opportunity reduction' (or the 'situational' approach) as the principal means of crime prevention which receives prominence rather than any consideration of ways and means of altering the initial disposition to offend.

[6]   This issue is addressed in Chapter 11.

[7]   These are reviewed each year: they are not publicly available.

[8]   Set against this increased demand for statistics from HM Inspectorate, it is worthy of note that the statistical demands on the police made by the Home Office statistical department have reduced substantially, rather than increased. This is not to say that new information is not being requested, but that requests for new information have been accompanied by reduction in other areas (this derives from a commitment to keep the statistical requirements of all policy divisions under regular review).

[9]   The report of the group is succinct in its identification of the major difficulty: 'in essence, if those in charge of police officers on the ground cannot tell us what objectives they are seeking, we cannot tell them. That remains the essential problem'.

[10]   The 'textbook' accounts of directed patrol in the USA, for example, clearly indicate that direction, although requiring the official endorsement of middle management, should primarily emanate from junior ranks (see Crowe, 1985), not that direction should derive solely from middle and senior management (as many in this country seem to interpret the concept).

[11]   Computers seldom provide a comprehensive record; for several reasons police controllers do not always 'log out' relief officers engaged on non-urgent duties (because they frequently wish to keep them logged as 'available' in the event that their assistance is required urgently elsewhere) and equally PCs do not bother to record tasks they take up on request from people in the street. Another obstacle is that few controllers log the patrol activities of officers who are not part of the relief strength, like home beats.

[12]   The problem applies particularly to prevention where the agency concerned is only one of a range of 'inputs' contributing to a diffuse

'output' such as law and order: a useful analogy is to equate the police impact on crime with that of the National Health Service on the nation's health (see Southgate, 1985).

[13]   Largely because the police service cannot defend its budget without being seen to have taken the quest for efficiency seriously, but also because research findings invariably prompt new questions or initiatives that themselves require assessment.

References

Bottomley, K., and Coleman, C., (1981) Understanding crime rates, Gower, Farnborough

Brown, D. and Iles, S., (1985) Community constables: a study of a policing initiative, Research and Planning Unit Paper 30, Home Office, London

Burrows, J., (1986a) Investigating burglary: the measurement of police performance, Home Office Research Study 88, HMSO, London

Burrows, J., (1986b) 'Prosecution decisions in respect of the repeat offender', Home Office Research Bulletin 20

Burrows, J. and Tarling, R., (1982) Clearing up crime, Home Office Research Study 73, HMSO, London

Butler, A., (1984) 'Yesterday's people', Police, XVII, 4

Carr-Hill, R.A. and Stern, N.H., (1979) Crime, the police and criminal statistics, Academic Press, London

Christian, J.D., (1982) A planning programming budgeting system in the police service in England and Wales between 1969-74, MA dissertation, University of Manchester

Clarke, R.V.G. and Hough, M., (1984) Crime and police effectiveness, Home Office Research Study 79, HMSO, London

Collins, K. (1985) 'Some issues in police effectiveness and efficiency', Policing, 1, 3

Comrie, M.D. and Kings, E.J., (1975) 'Urban workloads', Police Research Bulletin 23, HMSO, London

Crowe, T.D., (1985) Directed patrol manual: juvenile problems, Office of Juvenile Justice and Delinquency Prevention, US Department of Justice, Washington DC

Eck, J., (1983) Solving crimes: the investigation of burglary and robbery, Police Executive Research Forum, Washington DC

Farrington, D.P. and Dowds, E.A., (1985) 'Disentangling criminal behaviour and police reaction', in Farrington, D.P. and Gunn, J. (eds), Reactions to crime: the public, the police, courts and prisons, Wiley, London

Home Office (1974) Police activity analysis in a territorial division, Economic Planning Unit, Home Office and Avon and Somerset Constabulary

Home Office (1984) Guidelines on local surveys, HM Chief Inspector of Constabulary

Jones, S. and Silverman, E., (1984) 'What price efficiency? Circular arguments. Financial constraints on the police in Britain', Policing, 1, 1

Joyce, M.A.S. (1985) Spending on law and order: the police service in England and Wales, National Institute of Economic and Social Research, London

Kinsey, R., (1985) Survey of Merseyside police officers, Merseyside County Council, Liverpool

Martin, J.P. and Wilson, G., (1969) The police: a study in manpower, Heinemann, London

Morris, P. and Heal, K., (1981) Crime control and the police, Home Office Research Study 67, HMSO, London

Policy Studies Institute (1983) Police and people in London, Vol.III A survey of police officers, by Smith, D.J., Policy Studies Institute, London

Ramsay, M., (1982) City centre crime: a situational approach to prevention, Research and Planning Unit Paper 10, Home Office, London

Rowlands, D., (1985) 'PBO: the Tokyo connection', Police, XVI, 8

Sinclair, I. and Miller, C., (1984) Measures of police effectiveness and efficiency, Research and Planning Unit Paper 25, Home Office, London

Southgate, P., (1985) 'Police output measures: past work and future possibilities', in Heal, K., Tarling, R. and Burrows, J. (eds) Policing today, HMSO, London

Southgate, P. and Ekblom, P., (1984) Contacts between police and public: findings from the British Crime Survey, Home Office Research Study 77, HMSO, London

Steer, D., (1980) Uncovering crime: the police role, Royal Commission on Criminal Procedure, Research Study No.7, HMSO, London

Tarling, R. and Burrows, J., (1985) 'The work of detectives', Policing, 1, 1

Templeton, H., (1984) 'PBO. Something is wrong: do we need medicine or the surgeon's knife?' Police, XVI, 9

3 Why should the police use police research?

MOLLIE WEATHERITT

The background to this paper is a review that the Police Foundation asked me to carry out to document and assess innovatory and experimental policing projects and schemes and new methods of working. The Foundation's concerns were political and pragmatic. It felt that much public discussion of policing proceeded from and emphasised a negative image of the police and that this needed to be counterbalanced by a more positive picture of what the police were about and what they were doing to respond to changing demands and pressures on them. The Foundation was concerned that much of the constructive work being done by police forces was hidden from view and so played a less important part in informing public debate than it should do. On a practical note, the Foundation was concerned that a lot of the good work being done in separate forces was never communicated to other forces; or, to use the words of Home Office Circular 114/83, that forces were failing to 'contribute their own experience to the common stock'. Some way was therefore needed of bringing together individual experience and reviewing it, so that news about good practice could be spread and others' mistakes avoided. With any luck, consolidating and assessing all this information would not only provide useful source material, it would also give a boost to processes of innovation and change that were already underway.

Like many research ideas, this one raised as many questions as it was designed to answer. Institutions already existed for doing the job I had been commissioned to do. For example, distilling the basis of good practice and spreading the word about it has formed a major part of the remit of Her Majesty's Inspectors since the early 1960s. The Home Office Crime Prevention Centre keeps an index of force crime prevention projects; and it is the job of Police Research Services Unit (also part of the Home Office) to see that forces are made aware of one another's experiments and initiatives. Yet many people, including many police officers, either did not know about these channels, or felt they were inadequate or were somehow not working properly. This obviously raised the questions why existing institutions seemed unable to do the job and whether a short-term, one-off piece of research, which would only provide a snap-shot of what was going on, could be expected to do any better.

Other questions were raised by what should count as innovatory and experimental. In compiling my review, I had decided to concentrate on what might broadly be termed 'community policing' initiatives: attempts to reorganise patrol in ways which are thought to be more acceptable to the public and to encourage behaviour more in line with public expectations; and approaches to crime prevention which involve the police working with other people and institutions to reduce opportunities for crime, or the motivation to commit it. Yet I soon discovered that a great deal of policing activity which is carried out under a community policing banner, and much that is specifically marketed and packaged as innovation, is either not new at all, or represents less of a break with the past than is often assumed. Some of the current (and sometimes avowedly experimental [1] approaches to patrol for example, bear a surprisingly close resemblance to unit beat policing in terms of their supporting philosophy, their aims, their organisation and their claimed effects. (The resemblance is surprising because new forms of patrolling are usually designed to counter the adverse effects of 'firebrigading' for which unit beat policing is held responsible.) Similarly, approaches stressing community participation in crime prevention, far from involving a recent 'redefinition' [2] of crime prevention, form a recurrent theme of official policy statements of the last 20 years or so. [3]

The discovery that innovation is not always what it masquerades as, raised a new set of questions about why organisational memories seemed to be so short; why past attempts to achieve the same objectives by similar means appeared to have failed; and what purposes were served by ignoring the lessons of the past. I thus became interested not only in documenting innovations, but also in why certain activities came to be packaged and marketed as 'new' and 'better' and how these effects were achieved.

Putting aside these definitional problems, a final set of questions was raised in relation to what specific innovations achieve and how we come to know what they achieve. Although the broad themes which run through changes in police policy are fairly well documented – in other words, we often know what it is the police are trying to do – what actually happens when the policy tries to engage with everyday life is not. The gap between intention and achievement is potentially enormous, but accurate, unvarnished accounts of what happens in the process of trying to implement change are hard to find. Not only is basic description lacking, honest assessments of the effects of new initiatives are also rare. For the most part, such assessments have tended to come from outside the police service rather than being generated within it. As Robert Reiner argues in his paper, there is a growing number of people who are either actively willing or are prepared to be cast in the role of critical friend, and to provide the police with research-based evidence about their performance which might help them improve it. Yet however influential this body of work conducted by outsiders might become, it is likely to remain numerically small in comparison with the amount of research the police generate themselves, mainly for their own consumption but occasionally (and perhaps now increasingly) for a wider audience.

Police accounts are often the only source of information on innovatory initiatives and I read quite a lot of them in preparing my review. The way these accounts are constructed, the assumptions they embody, the questions they address, the data they appeal to, the conclusions they draw and the ways in which ambiguous, inadequate and inconsistent information is handled in them go to the heart of the question posed in the title of the paper. As research, the quality of these accounts is patchy – a few are excellent, some passable, others indifferent and some unambiguously unsatisfactory. But virtually all of them share a significant feature. This is that the kind of research that the police do on and for themselves is used to legitimate the activity to which it is addressed rather than to critically evaluate it. It lacks critical distance from what it aims to study and is often aimed instead at presenting police activity in the best possible light. At worst, mere nominalism is involved: the language of empirical evaluation is used to convey the sense that something important has been going on, or that important effects have been achieved when really nothing very much has happened. At best, problems are reassessed and solutions revised or discarded as a result of empirical enquiry. More usually, and hardly surprisingly, research becomes subverted to other organisational goals: the need to create a sense of pride in the job and a sense of the organisation's positive achievements; and the need to be seen to be actively establishing and reaffirming the basis of consensus. This last is often of particular importance in relation to community policing activities because an emphasis on consensus lies at the heart of what community policing itself is about.

These observations are general and generalised and do not universally apply. Nonetheless I think it is fair to characterise a great deal of research that the police do on and for themselves as forming an important part of the consensual package and as being inseparable from the demands for a certain kind of organisational performance – or the appearance of it. I have chosen three, not atypical examples to illustrate this. The first comes from a 'prevention of fear' project, which involved improving home security on a local authority housing estate with the aims of making residents feel safer and reducing domestic burglary (Northumbria Police, undated). The second comes from a description of the work of two local beat officers who were given the job of doing something about vandalism in their area and set about it with considerable verve and enthusiasm (Hall, 1981). The third example is a description of the work of Devon and Cornwall Constabulary's Crime Prevention Support Unit and its offshoot, the Exeter Community Policing Consultative Group (Moore and Brown, 1981). All three assessments were undertaken by police officers, the first as a research exercise by the force, the other two as MSc projects. All three were aimed at describing and evaluating what was done.

In assessing each account, I shall refer to four sets of questions. First, how was the initial policing problem defined, using what sort of information? Second, how were solutions to the problem arrived at? Third, how were these solutions implemented and what difficulties were encountered along the way? Fourth, how were the effects of the solutions assessed and what information was considered to be relevant to doing this?

Prevention of fear through security

Here the problem was a housing estate with inadequate security and a rate of recorded burglary offences of around twice the national average. (About 10 of the estate's 200 dwellings were burgled each year.) How fearful the residents were is impossible to assess because the force appears not to have collected any systematic information about this. The solution to these (actual and implied) problems was seen as being more and better locks. These were duly fitted on ground floor windows and on doors and the doors were also reinforced.

The force assessment of this project is reasonably thorough. It compared recorded burglary rates on the estate before and after the new locks were fitted and it collected similar information for a likely displacement area and for a separate control area. In addition, a small number of residents (30) was asked what they thought about the security devices.

The small absolute number of burglary offences on the estate in effect made it impossible to test whether burglary had been reduced there. The force evaluation document admits this. It is also disarmingly honest about how ineffectual the locks were: many could not be used by residents because they had been ineptly fitted. The main difficulty with the evaluation is its treatment of 'fear' and how it assessed this elusive concept. On this it remains inscrutable, but concludes: 'Since the title of the project was 'The Prevention of Fear', there is every reason to suppose that fear was reduced and to that extent, the experiment can be deemed successful'.

Reducing vandalism

In this project, two beat officers were told to go out and 'do something' about vandalism in their town. They were given no guidance and were left entirely to their own devices in tackling the problem. They chose informal reparation. By asking around, and some judicious reading of graffiti, they identified likely culprits, who were asked to clear up the mess they had made or face the possibility of a prosecution.

Hall studied this scheme by accompanying the two beat officers on patrol and by talking to key local residents, children, offenders and victims. He did not collect any information on the incidence of vandalism either before or after the beat officers began their work; nor was he able to document how much damage was made good by offenders. He concentrated instead on the public relations and public contact aspects of the officers' work. He claims that there was widespread support for the officers' methods and that because of this people were prepared ·to come forward with more information. Hall says that this helped prevent and detect more crime. In addition, he claims that the officers' helpfulness and approachability and their willingness to get involved in community activities, helped to encourage those activities, promote community solidarity and improve police–community relations. So far as I can tell, no independent check was made of these claims. They emerged instead from talks and interviews Hall had with residents and offenders (he does not say how many, or how representative they were, nor what questions he asked them); and from the fact that he clearly approved of the officers' policing style and admired what they were doing.

Community crime prevention: the Crime Prevention Support Unit

My final example comes from the account offered of the Crime Prevention Support Unit (CPSU) by the superintendent who was in charge of it.

CPSU's job was to identify crime prevention problems by examining facts and statistics. Its terms of reference directed it to produce and experiment with new crime prevention ideas, particularly those which would harness public support. The Unit began by trying to define exactly what the problem was. It produced spot maps of juvenile crime, showing how it was distributed in relation to public transport routes, pubs and schools. It gave these maps wide publicity, in order to alert people to what their local problems were and thence stimulate their interest in doing something about them. CPSU also used the maps to propagate its guiding philosophy that crime arose from certain features of community life (most notably the breakdown of informal community controls) and could therefore best be tackled by, with and in the community.

Two strategies evolved from this approach. One involved the police working with local residents in various community involvement schemes – the most important being play and recreational schemes organised by the police for young people otherwise at a loose end in the school holidays. The other was the creation of a forum (the Exeter Community Policing Consultative Group) for improving cooperation and coordination between the police and local authority agencies. The Group created a joint agency training programme and also took on a more general advisory role, which included advising on local authority planning applications.

The historical account of CPSU and the Consultative Group is, I think, unique amongst police accounts in charting the mutual suspicions, compromises and lack of progress that dog attempts to get people and institutions with supposedly common interests to work together. It ought to be read by all policy-makers and practitioners who believe that multi-agency or coordinated crime prevention is the answer to preventing crime. But of equal interest is what Moore and Brown's account leaves out and, in particular, how it fudges the question of CPSU's effectiveness.

CPSU was established to prevent crime by engaging in and encouraging community action. But although CPSU began its journey in an analytical spirit and the crimes analysis it carried out formed the rationale for its subsequent activity, there is no evidence that CPSU used crime figures to evaluate its own work. Reading Moore and Brown's account, one is left with the strong impression that to judge CPSU in terms of its original objective – that of preventing crime would somehow be missing the point. Ultimately we are left to admire the means and spirit by and which CPSU pursued its goal and which, in effect, are presented as the real measures of its achievement.

Each of the three accounts I have described illustrates, in different ways, the tendency for empiricist intentions to falter in the face of what is presented as self-evidently good. In the prevention of fear project, this effect was achieved fairly crudely by assuming a positive answer to a question without any supporting evidence for the conclusion drawn. The other two accounts use more subtle means and are consequently more beguiling. Essentially what they offer is an appeal to a set of assumptions which are virtually self-validating. This is perhaps less obvious in Hall's account than in Moore and Brown's because in the process of providing a justification for it, Hall appeals to the effects and effectiveness of what the two officers were trying to do. Thus he claims that the information they received from the public which was elicited by the policing style they adopted, enabled the officers to prevent crime. However, these 'findings' are more often assumed that proved. Hall slides (effortlessly) from admiration for the officers' aspirations and activities to satisfaction with their achievements.

Moore and Brown, in contrast, make almost no appeal to evidence of effectiveness. Instead, what they are describing stands or falls by the philosophy it appeals to and the claims to makes to embody a consensual policing ideal. The light emanating from this ideal puts empirical evidence in the shade.

It is against a background of the kind of evaluations that the police make of their own activity that attempts of central government to tighten up on existing forms of internal and external organisational accounting and to devise some new ones are of particular interest. Other contributors to this book will set out the background to these attempts and describe some of their main features. Their relevance here lies in the premium they place on forms of rational accounting, and the attitudes to the collection, analysis and presentation of evidence that lie at the base of them.

Circular 114/1983 sets the tone. It talks of the importance of forces setting objectives and priorities and of reviewing and reallocating resources in line with them. The emphasis is both on external review (through the Inspectorate of Constabulary) and on internal review. Forces are encouraged to undertake major reviews of their own policies and to collect and analyse relevant information in testing for effectiveness. This emphasis appears again in Circular 8/1984 on crime prevention. Its recipients are urged to collect and to collate systematically 'detailed and specific' information about crime. Both circulars refer to the importance of formulating and disseminating good practice and the need to base it upon empirical assessment. Both advertise the availability of Home Office research expertise, and encourage forces to call upon it in planning and evaluating what they do.

This breath of empirical wind is also blowing from other directions. Circular 114 gives HMIs a key role in helping to achieve the aims set out in it. In particular, the requirement to account in the language of objectives and of demonstrable achievements has been made an explicit part of the inspection process. This has meant that the content and style of inspections has had to change. Previously unregulated, save by custom and practice, inspections are now to be conducted within a framework of explicit written guidance. This guidance has been formulated within the Home Office and is aimed at giving the department additional, better and more systematic information about what is happening in forces. As to the style of inspections, a more explicit (and hence probably greater) emphasis is being put on analysis and on the need to probe more closely force performance. This change in style is clear from HMIs' inspection notes, which aim to solicit from forces, prior to the HMI making his formal inspection, basic information on force organisation, deployment and activities. In relation to crime prevention, for example, forces are asked to give details of new initiatives, including those undertaken in conjunction with other agencies and to say how and whether new initiatives, and patterns of crime are monitored and with what results.

These new departures are aimed amongst other things at promoting a more questioning management style in forces and at stimulating organisational self-assessment. But they do little more than establish a climate in which self-assessment is seen as desirable and necessary. They do not of themselves specify what forms that self-assessment should take. In this context, two other models of rational, information-based planning are relevant. They are situational crime prevention and policing by objectives.

Situational crime prevention

Situational crime prevention has developed as a research-based policy response to the message of the crime prevention research which the Home Office Research Unit undertook during the 1970s (see in particular Clarke and Mayhew, 1980). The general conclusions of this work were that traditional approaches to crime prevention were ineffective and that this was because they involved generalised solutions aimed at unspecific or excessively broad targets. The way forward was considered to lie in greater specificity, both in terms of initial problem definition and in terms of the kind of preventive responses that should be entertained. The Home Office diagnosed the problem as follows: 'In the development of . . . crime prevention measures what has tended to be lacking has been the coherent and systematic marshalling of . . . information in respect of the circumstances surrounding particular types of offence'. What was needed therefore was 'an examination of the situation in which a particular type of offence takes place' so as to 'suggest preventive measures which relate directly to those conditions' (Home Office, 1976). The Home Office termed this approach 'situational prevention'. It is essentially a method of problem analysis, characterised by the analysis of empirical data; the setting of limited, attainable and measurable objectives; the tailoring of action very closely to those objectives; and the monitoring and evaluation of the results of action. The need to approach crime prevention problems in this way has been stated in other Home Office policy documents (eg, Home Office, 1982) including circular 8/1984.

Policing by objectives (pbo)

Unlike situational analysis, which is aimed solely at force crime prevention activities, pbo is a thorough-going attempt to apply a rational/empirical approach to any or all aspects of a force's activity. In its emphasis on objective setting and performance measurement, pbo has clear parallels in the interests of central government in promoting more efficient use of resources and in the language of Circular 114/1983. Pbo extends this philosophy further, through the idea of a planning cycle, and through the uncompromising emphasis it places on the importance of delivering results.

The planning cycle lies at the heart of pbo. It is a means by which a publicly available force policy statement - general guidelines about what the force intends to do - is successively honed to create a set of force goals, then objectives and action plans. These last are specifications of what needs to be done and in theory are to be aimed specifically at achieving a set of pre-determined and explicitly stated objectives. The planning cycle culminates in an 'impact assessment' (viz empirical evaluation) of the action plans. The results of this are then fed back into the planning cycle and in the force objectives, goals and policy revised in the light of it. [4]

Pbo is both dynamic and results-oriented. It assumes that the pursuit of greater policing effectiveness is a realistic and desirable goal and it aims to harness the energies of every officer in the force in pursuit of that goal. Under pbo, change, and the assessment of change, become almost an organisational way of life. Officers in forces operating pbo have to know (or at least be able to say) exactly where they are going, why they want to go there and when they have arrived. Pbo is uncompromising in the stress it places on the importance of results. 'The PBO philosophy is that police activities are only as good as the results they produce, and have no value in themselves' (Lubans and Edgar, 1979, p.17, emphasis added). This means that nothing is sacred; that all value judgements must be suspended until activities have proved their empirical worth. This model of police management is by no means in widespread use (only two forces, Northamptonshire and the Metropolitan Police, have adopted it). Nonetheless, considerable interest is being expressed in it.

Some thoughts on the future

I have argued that the kind of research that the police do on themselves should more often than not be viewed as a form of legitimation of the very activity it seeks to investigate. If this is right, then an important question for the future is whether the kind of rational, problem-solving models I have described can reasonably be expected to provoke a more honest, thorough and objective approach to police efforts to examine their own organisational performance. There are contrary pressures at work, and ironically these mirror the picture I have given of police research as an empirical activity subverted to other organisational ends.

An important pressure is that from central government for the police to innovate in ways which have already been decided upon. One example is the perceived desirability of multi-agency crime prevention. The government has said that this is successful (Circular 8/1984, para.36), even though the evidence for it is, at the very least, equivocal. [5] If at the same time as being expected to pursue certain policies, the police are also being asked to examine all that they do, it will not be surprising if they oblige by coming up with the 'right' answers.

This has implications for the way in which 'best practice' is likely to be defined and the kind of evidence on which such definitions will draw. Although HMIs have been furnished with a new set of investigatory tools, it would be unrealistic to think that this will somehow liberate them from reliance on what forces tell them to be the case. (The government has, in any case, left a large - and largely undefined - area in which Inspectors' professional judgement is to reign supreme.) The Inspectorate has set little store by developing an analytical capacity of its own which might help it critically to examine the claims made to it by forces. This means that definitions of best practice, rather than being illuminated or informed by a critical ethic, are likely to remain reflective of current fashion.

Other pressures come from the sheer necessity to get on with the job. Action cannot wait for research but - happily - research can validate its results. Often too, the goods that empirical enquiry provides only serve to complicate the world to which people with jobs to do are required to respond. The purpose of research may often be to uncover impediments to action and to demonstrate how shaky are the assumptions on which action is based. The more this happens, the less useful and relevant is research likely to be regarded.

A final pressure comes from the attitudes to reflective detachment that an action-based culture like policing necessarily engenders. The rewards of action are short-term and decisive while those of research are deferred and potentially problematical. Perhaps it is no accident that police management is accused of being overly concerned with the day-to-day at the expense of the longer term and is characterised as flying by the seat of its pants. There is a sense which such attitudes help to sustain a more exciting approach to the job.

These arguments suggest that the reasons why the police should use police research are not necessarily very powerful. That they are being pressed to do more of it perhaps speaks less to the value placed on achieving a genuine understanding of the difficulties of action in a complex setting than to a need to demonstrate managerial competence consistent with certain political expectations. Unlike Robert Reiner, I do not believe that this possibility forms 'the worst-case scenario'. On the contrary, I believe it would be unrealistic to expect anything else. If this seems to be an unduly pessimistic conclusion, it is at least consistent with the idealised picture of research that I have given, which is its willingness to face the facts.

Notes

[1]   For example, the Havant policing scheme, which aimed to cultivate closer contacts with the community; enhance the status and job satisfaction of beat officers; and achieve a better disciplined response to public demand. (Hampshire Constabulary, 1981 and Males (ed.) 1982, pp.103-26.) Also the Highfields community policing scheme, which aimed to improve police-public relations; improve officers' self-image; reduce delinquency; and improve information flow between police and public (Pollard, 1979). These are only two of many similar schemes throughout the country.

[2]   The word 'redefinition' appears in a historical discussion of the development of crime prevention policy which formed part of the the the GLC's response to draft Home Office Circular 8/1984 (Greater London Council, 1983). Similar views are widespread in the police service. For example, in a review of neighbourhood watch schemes, the head of the Metropolitan Police crime prevention department has written: 'only in the last two years have we seen any contructive moves to restore the primacy of crime prevention through policies to encourage police to work with 'the community to reduce crime' (Turner, 1984, p.1).

[3]   Virtually the opening words of the 1965 report of Cornish Committee on the prevention and detection of crime are that 'the prevention of crime needs the cooperation and work of many elements in society' (Home Office, 1965). Identical sentiments appear in Home Office circulars on crime prevention issued in 1968 ('Crime prevention is not the responsibility of the police alone. It is a cooperative effort in which every part of the community is involved); in 1970 and in 1978.

[4]   This description is taken from Policing by objectives, by V. Lubans and J. Edgar, which has become the bible for forces wanting to implement pbo. The influence of Luban's and Edgar's work is acknowledged in A.J.P. Butler's recent book, Police management, which aims to help police managers assess what they are doing and plan how they might do it more efficiently.

[5]   See, for example the Home Office Research Unit's assessment of a multi-agency crime prevention project in Manchester (Gladstone, 1980 and Hope and Murphy, 1983).

References

Butler, A.J.P., (1984) Police management, Gower, Farnborough
Clarke, R.V.G. and Mayhew, P., (1980) Designing out crime, HMSO, London
Gladstone, F.J., (1980) Co-ordinating crime prevention efforts, Home Office Research Study 62, HMSO, London
Greater London Council (1983) Home Office draft circular on crime prevention - a response
Hall, A.S., (1981) Strategies against vandalism, MSc thesis, Cranfield Institute of Technology, Department of Social Policy
Hampshire Constabulary (1981) The Havant policing scheme, Chief Constable's Office, Winchester
Home Office (1965) Report of the committee on the prevention and detection of crime, (Cornish Committee), London

Home Office (1976) Report of the working group on crime prevention, unpublished

Home Office (1983) Crime prevention: a coordinated approach. Proceedings of a seminar on crime prevention, Police Staff College, Bramshill House, 26-29 September 1982, London

Hope, T. and Murphy, D.J.I., (1983) 'Problems of implementing crime prevention: the experience of a demonstration project', The Howard Journal, 22, 38-50

Lubans, V.A. and Edgar, J.M., (1979) Policing by objectives, Social Development Corporation, Hartford

Males, S.J., (ed.) (1982) Initiatives in police management, Police Research Services Unit, Home Office, London

Moore, C. and Brown, J., (1981) Community versus crime, Bedford Square Press, London

Northumbria Police (undated) Prevention of fear, Part 1, Felling

Pollard, B., (1979) A study of the Leicestershire Constabulary's Highfields community policing scheme, MSc thesis, Cranfield Institute of Techonology, Department of Social Policy

Turner, B.W.M., (1984) Neighbourhood watch. Review of the London experience. Paper prepared for the 59th intermediate command course, Police Staff College, Bramshill

4 Demand for policing and police performance: progress and pitfalls in public surveys

MIKE HOUGH

This chapter is intended as a stocktaking of research on police performance and on policing demand which has made use of sample surveys of the general public. Surveys of this sort can, very broadly, do three things. They can tap general attitudes towards the police: 'Do the police do a good job or a bad job?' They can also measure people's preferences for policing – how it ought to be done and how priorities should be arranged. Finally, they can collect information about respondents' experience of the police, and their rating of the treatment they received from the police.

The paper assesses some of the main findings to emerge under these three headings in the last few years. The surveys it draws on are, primarily, the Policy Studies Institute's (PSI) London survey (Policy Studies Institute, 1983, vol.I); the British Crime Survey (BCS), the first sweep of which contained many items on the police (Hough and Mayhew, 1983, 1985; Southgate and Ekblom, 1984); the surveys carried out by NOP for the Metropolitan Police (NOP, 1984, 1985); and the Merseyside Crime Survey (MCS) (Kinsey, 1985). [1] It aims to be illustrative rather than comprehensive. It excludes consideration of small scale depth interviews, such as those which Shapland and Vagg (1986) carried out in their recent study of rural policing. To summarise the main arguments, general attitudes to the police may look like a promising seam to mine, but closer inspection shows it to be well worked, if not exhausted. Secondly, measuring what people want of the police is an attractive enterprise but there is also a risk here of digging out fool's gold. Where sample surveys can contribute most, I would argue, is in getting to grips with people's direct experience of policing.

In survey work it is important never to lose sight of the reductionism involved in asking people to force their attitudes and experience into crude conceptual frameworks which are not of their own choice. It is not that the man in the street has limited intellectual skills, but that the interviewer imposes artificial

45

rules on the encounter with respondents in their sitting room. The following are worth remembering:

Respondents will give an answer of some sort to any question; they will do their best to accommodate the interviewer;

they won't allow ignorance to stand in the way of a reply;

they are Utopian, favouring, for example, reduced taxation and increased public services simultaneously;

they will be fearless in their support of socially acceptable positions.

How well the police do: general attitudes

General questions about the police show a generally well satisfied public. Innumerable polls have shown that the police vie with the medical profession as the most trusted occupational group, leaving trades unionists at the other end of the scale with the status of used car dealers. Even a more focused question about the performance of the police 'in your area' consistently shows over 80 per cent nationally rating 'very good' or 'fairly good'. The demographic correlates of general attitudes to the police are well established: the old are more favourable than the young; women more than men; non-manual households more than manual. Ethnic minorities generally rate the police lower than others. People in cities are only slightly less favourably disposed than others.

These strong demographic relationships pose a technical problem for surveyors. Any variations in rating over area or time may simply reflect differences in population mix; for example, the proportion of young adults is set to decline very rapidly – almost 30 per cent by 1995 – so that, other things being equal, ratings of the police by the overall population will improve. Any analysis must control for demographic factors; and as a result only large samples will escape the problem of 'running out of numbers'.

A more intractable problem is to be found in the likelihood that general questions about police performance reflect people's orientation not simply to the police, but to authority in a wider sense – their attitudes to the established social order. Certainly, the more focused questions evoke lower and more variable ratings; for example, in the PSI London study, only a third of respondents thought that the police were successful in fighting muggings, street robberies and burglaries (though 80 per cent said they were successful in coping with marches and demonstrations).

Insofar as responses are shaped by police action at all, the effects may be very diffuse: ratings of local police performance may be influenced by extraneous factors – police handling of the miners' strike, for example, or a major detective success in another police force. The questionnaire itself can amplify such effects by drawing respondents' attention to different features of policing. An example from the BCS: the proportion of people saying that the police in their area did a 'very good job' fell between 1982 and 1984; in 1984, the item followed questions unconnected with the police, but in 1982 it concluded a long section of the questionnaire on police contact, the immediately preceding question asking respondents to rehearse the detail of incidents where the police had treated them well. To my mind, the (unintended) sensitising effect of this ordering vitiates any comparison. [2]

Finally - admittedly, a speculative point - quite broad sectors of the public feel strongly that the police need their support, and think it irresponsible or disloyal to express critical attitudes about them. If this is so, unfocused questions about police performance will elicit what one could call a 'sacred cow' response.

What do these problems amount to? Certainly, they make it extremely difficult to confer any meaning on the single statistic: 'Seventy-five per cent think the police do a very good or fairly good job'. Is the pot three-quarters full ('As many as 75 per cent were satisfied with police performance') or quarter empty ('A worryingly large minority of 25 per cent were unhappy with police performance')? Comparisons across area and time can only safely be made by controlling for demographic variations. And when differences do emerge, it is impossible to know whether these should be attributed to factors within police control or to totally extraneous factors. In short, if questions about police performance are pitched at a general level, and are not tied to respondents' immediate experience, they are unlikely to earn their keep. [3] By the same token, it would be a rash police manager who entrusted his career to performance measures derived from survey questions of this sort.

Preferences and priorities

The use of surveys to tap policing preferences and priorities seems set to increase, given that the principle of police/community consultation is now on the statute book. Section 106 of the Police and Criminal Evidence Act 1984 requires that 'arrangements shall be made in each police area for obtaining the views of people in that area about matters concerning the policing'. Both the Act's provisions for the London area and Home Office guidance on consultation (Circular 2/1985) offer a model of consultation involving consultative committees, but the terms of the Act could, on the face of it, equally cover sample surveys as a means of tapping public priorities for policing.

The BCS, the MCS and the NOP surveys for the Metropolitan Police have all tried in varying degrees to see to what extent police practice and public priorities are in step. One approach has been in terms of perceived solutions to problems, asking people what problems their area has and how they could be solved:

> What do you feel are the most important problems in this area that the police should be concentrating on . . . ? And what do you think the police should do about these problems?

Questions like this will elicit burglary and robbery as primary problems in cities, though robbery may be displaced by vandalism in more rural areas. In the MCS, which offered a 'shopping list' of problems, sexual assaults figured at the top of the list, together with robbery and burglary. The main solutions offered to these problems will be more police, more police patrols and more police patrols on foot.

Another format is: 'Should there be more, less or about the same level of X?' Thus the PSI London survey found between two-thirds and three-quarters of respondents felt that too many policemen were on wheels. When asked a more difficult question, for example 'Do you think the police should stop and question more people, less people, or is it about right?', one in eight (only) answered that they didn't know, but over half gave the cautious man's version of the same sentiment: 'It's about right'.

Some questions which have been asked are hard to interpret (indeed hard to answer). For example, the MCS asked how important various police tasks are, and the BCS asked victims what priority the police should give to crimes like theirs. The importance of tasks bears no relationship to the effort required to do them. Doing something properly may require minimal effort, even if failure to do so brings catastrophic consequences (turning the bath taps off, for example). However people understand such questions, emergency response, crime investigation and deterrent presence on the street head the list of important tasks. (It would be odd if emergency work did not head the list; unimportant emergencies are few and far between.)

One feature of all these questions is that people will answer them in partial or complete ignorance of current police practice; the extent of demands on the police; the competences of the police (the relationship between practice and problems); and the opportunity costs incurred in reallocating resources. [4] This comparative ignorance about policing raises the possibility that the questions simply evoke 'pseudo attitudes' - ones which respondents generate on the spur of the moment, which they would readily modify or withdraw if they were provided with more information. This may indeed be the case for items about detail of tactics - for example whether stop-and-search levels are at the right level - but people have ample opportunity to form views on visible issues such as foot versus car patrol. Crime and policing form part of the staple of everyday conversation; and behind the survey responses, and the support for foot patrol, lies a very widely shared vision of old-style policing, where Bobby and community proceeded in step and in an orderly fashion.

Deciding what weight to attach to survey indices of public priority raises two intertwined issues: the extent to which police policy should fall under political control, and the extent to which political machinery should represent people's interests in contrast to their views. For example, should the general desire for foot patrols be met, given that it is questionable both whether this would affect crime levels and whether people would actually notice any increase? [5] I will not develop these issues here, except to state that in practice, large scale sample surveys will tend to paint a picture of priorities which is extremely consistent across area and social group. The survey method imposes the constraint of generalisation, and in general terms, I suspect, people will want the same sorts of thing. It would be surprising, for example, if a replication of the MCS in some other metropolitan area threw up very different results. Only when people talk bout specific problems in specific places which they want the police to tackle will variations emerge, and this is a process to which sample surveys are ill-suited.

Experience of the police

Where sample surveys have contributed most, and where they can continue to do so, is in tapping people's experience of the police: in characterising both demand for police services and contact initiated by the police. This is partly because it is technically simpler to survey people about events they have been involved in than to measure their attitudes; but also the information which surveys can yield about contacts has more relevance to actual police practice.

By demand for police service, I mean demands which are in practice made on the police. (One cannot, of course, infer public priorities from these demands, because what people want and what people ask for are quite separate things.) Surveys have a unique contribution to make here because much police 'response' work is ephemeral, and not captured in police recording machinery. The same is true of police-initiated contacts: a large proportion will never appear in any formal record, and those records which are maintained will inevitably have a bare minimum of information about the incident and people involved.

Those components of crime surveys to do with criminal victimisation also bear on demand for policing, of course, insofar as crimes reported to the police are a sub-group of calls for service. Their particular value lies in documenting demands not made on the police, as the police maintain quite full records of crimes reported to them; but at the same time they can show what crimes are reported to the police (and what reported crimes go unrecorded), why crimes are reported and how the victim rates the police response. (Farrington and Dowds' (1984) crime survey in Nottinghamshire was a path breaker amongst local crime surveys.)

Collecting information on contact with the police has its own special problems, of course. When asked about their experience of the police, respondents may

simply forget a relevant incident, or aspects of it;

remember the incident, but think it happened before the reference period;

remember an earlier incident as happening within the reference period;

remember a relevant incident but be unprepared to mention it; or

fail to realise that an incident meets the terms of the question;

or even make up an incident.

It is difficult to say which is the most severe of these problems; many of the more trivial contacts will simply be forgotten; there will be some 'telescoping', as crime surveys have shown; but most of all surveys will probably underestimate adversarial contacts. People are bound to be reticent about incidents where they were cast as the villain of the piece.

To date, the PSI London survey, the BCS and the MCS have collected information on demands made of the police; in aggregate, they have yielded a great deal of valuable descriptive material. A list of key findings would include:

Over a year's period, around half the adult population will have some contact with the police; most contacts are initiated by the public.

Men make more demands on the police than women; young people more than old; white more than ethnic minorities. People from non-manual background use the police more than manual workers.

The pattern of use may vary considerably over area; for example, it seems that the Merseyside public make more demands on the police than elsewhere, and a greater proportion of these are concerned with crime.

'Adversarial' contacts initiated by the police nationally comprise a large group of motoring offences and a smaller group of other offences; but in Merseyside the balance is reversed.

The police tend to stop (and search) youths and young men much more than other age groups, and ethnic minorities more than others; from the MCS, roughly four per cent of stops result in arrest and charge.

People stopped by the police – most of whom are not found to have committed any crime – become much more hostile to the police as a result.

A large proportion of those approached by the police are also police 'users'; and the unemployed frequently come into contact both as user and suspect.

Surveys including questions on victimisation suggest that reporting to the police, and recording by the police vary over time (BCS and General Household Survey) and place (Nottingham).

The future

The last five years have seen the publication of quite a substantial body of survey work on public contact with the police and attitudes to the police. Where will this work lead in the next five years?

First, there is probably some scope for broadening the range of areas covered by large scale sample surveys; the surveys which have covered police contact most extensively have been restricted to London and Merseyside. The next BCS is currently planned for 1988, and one proposal is to cover police contact in some detail in this third sweep.

There is considerable scope for improving the way in which demands for police service are classified by sample surveys; for example, the term 'service work' is pervasive in analysis of demand, but fails totally to characterise what it is about these demands which makes them appropriate for police attention.

A promising prospect lies in the trend data which could be produced by repeating parts of the MCS and London surveys. This is especially true for information on stop-and-search and other police-initiated contacts, given the changes in the law introduced by the Police and Criminal Evidence Act 1984 and the Public Order Act 1986. (An effective way of ensuring that findings are firmly grounded is to conduct surveys of the public and the police in parallel.)

An idea which may produce some fruit is to combine survey findings with systems of area classification derived from the census, such as Acorn. What I have in mind is to construct estimates of, for example, unreported crime, or of demands made on the police, for any specified area. If a survey can provide estimates by Acorn group, and an area's Acorn composition is known, it is a simple matter to extrapolate from the survey and generate estimates for the area.

Finally, something should be said about the relationship between survey research on the police and other work. Large scale sample surveys of the public's experience of and attitudes towards the police have all been commissioned by bodies with administrative responsibility for policing; in fact, all three corners of the 'tripartite structure' have stood as clients; and given the cost of survey work, future studies will continue to need their sponsorship. Inevitably, therefore, the surveys must justify themselves in terms of policy relevance. The findings I have listed on police contact have paid their way mainly in providing a factual backdrop against which policy can be made and adjusted.

Partly as a consequence of this sponsorship, and partly as a function of survey methodology, surveys about policing have tended towards the atheoretical, deploying the 'commonsense' concepts embedded in existing thought and practice. Surveyors should, perhaps, look more to theoreticians (or wear their own theoretical hats more often) in both designing studies and presenting results.

If surveyors should make more use of theory, the reverse is also true. The results of these surveys should inform theoretical issues to a greater extent. Findings on the social stratification of police users and police suspects spring to mind as a case in point; the survey findings are essential to any adequate analysis of police function. Both sweeps of the BCS are now available from the Economic and Social Research Council Archive, and I believe this is the case for most of the other surveys I have mentioned. I can only recommend them as a source of data ripe for secondary analysis.

Notes

[1]   At the time of writing, the Islington Crime Survey had not been published (Jones et al., 1986).

[2]   Another oddity about this question is that the number of 'don't knows' fell from 20 per cent in 1982 to seven per cent in 1984. Perhaps the earlier survey, in asking whether people had had any contact with the police, implied the legitimacy of ignorance amongst those without contact.

[3]   With one qualification: they can be more useful as independent or analysis variables than focused, concrete questions.

[4]   To a limited degree one can get round this by questionnaire design. For example, the MCS used an imaginative card sort technique to force respondents to think in terms of priorities.

[5]   Many forces were moving from mobile to foot patrol between 1981 and 1983, but BCS respondents did not report seeing foot patrols more often in the second sweep.

References

Farrington, D.P. and Dowds, E.A., (1985) 'Disentangling criminal behaviour and police reaction', in Farrington, D.P. and Gunn, J. (eds), Reactions to crime: the public, the police, courts and prisons, Wiley, Chichester

Hough, M. and Mayhew, P., (1983) The British Crime Survey: first report, Home Office Research Study 76, HMSO, London

Hough, M. and Mayhew, P., (1985) Taking account of crime: key findings from the second British Crime Survey, Home Office Research Study 85, HMSO, London

Jones, T., Maclean, B. and Young, Y., (1986) The Islington Crime Survey: crime, victimisation and policing in inner-city London, Gower, Aldershot

Kinsey, R., (1985) Merseyside Crime Survey: final report, Merseyside County Council, Liverpool

NOP, (1984) Policing needs and priorities in the Metropolitan Police District, NOP Market Research, London

NOP, (1985) Policing needs and priorities in the Metropolitan Police District, NOP Market Research, London

Policy Studies Institute, (1983) Police and people in London, vol.I, A survey of Londoners, by Smith, D.J. and Gray, J., London

Shapland, J. and Vagg, J. (1985) Social control and policing in rural and urban areas: final report to the Home Office, Centre for Criminological Research, Oxford

Southgate, P. and Ekblom, P., (1984) Contacts between police and public: findings from the British Crime Survey, Home Office Research Study 77, HMSO, London

PART II
POLICE CULTURE AND
POLICE ORGANISATION

5 Discovering structure. Studies of the British police occupational culture

SIMON HOLDAWAY

In my editorial introduction to The British police, which was written in 1977, I argued that, 'despite a significant growth of interest during the 1960s into the sociology of deviance and social control, the relative dearth of research into the British police has achieved the status of a cliche amongst sociologists' (Holdaway, 1979, p.1). That view was not contested; indeed, as a historical statement it remains uncontentious but is now possibly all the more striking for its contemporary irrelevance. Within less than a decade, a great deal of interest in the police is evident among academics working in universities and in research institutes, and among the staff of the Home Office Research and Planning Unit. But there is an irony here: as research findings are published they are generally not related to a body of sociological knowledge about crime, deviance and social control. The theoretical foundations that underpin their analyses are rarely discussed. Exceptions can be identified, of course. Scholars working in the Marxist tradition come most readily to mind as people who are consistent in their quest for a theory of the police (for example, Jefferson and Grimshaw, 1984; and Brogden, 1982). Nevertheless, if I wrote another editorial introduction summarising changes in research about the police during the last decade, my argument might well be that, 'despite a significant growth of research into the British police during the 1970s and 1980s, the lack of interest in the relevance of this research to general sociological knowledge may in future years achieve the status of a cliche amongst sociologists'. As a subject called 'Police Studies' seems to be securing its ground and status, we may be witnessing an erosion of the sociology of the police.

In this paper I want to focus on one area of study about the police that has received a considerable amount of attention from academics and has remained at the centre of the sociology of the British police. The occupational culture of the police has found reference points in virtually every publication about policing. One straightforward purpose of my paper is therefore to review the literature on the subject and to chart the intellectual context within which it has been written. Broadly speaking, my argument will be that the early British work on the occupational culture sprang from problems and issues within sociology rather more than it did from problems posed by police policy. In many ways the police were an interesting testing ground for sociologists concerned with theoretical questions who were fortunate to have access to a constabulary, rather than as a distinct subject matter begging some researchable questions.

Having reviewed the major literature, I then want to muddy the academic waters that characterise work on the occupational culture as a homogeneous corpus of knowledge to be placed within the interactionist tradition. Finally, some criticisms and remaining problems that arise from the literature will be discussed, and possible directions for future research will be identified.

Excavating the sociological foundations

In iconoclastic mood, Paul Rock has described the development of the sociology of crime and delinquency as an erratic and fragmented enterprise. Any perception of an incremental development of sociological knowledge about crime and delinquency is, he argues, more likely to be the gloss of a reviewer constructing historical coherence and continuity from the fragments of a chronological sequence than an accurate presentation of the orderly accumulation of literature. Rock is unambiguous about this point: 'the sociology of crime and delinquency has developed fitfully. Indeed, it may be misleading to describe it an an example of clear development at all' (Rock, 1979, p.52).

Scholars interested in crime, deviance and social control lay claim to an intellectual heritage derived from a vast sociological terrain. For example, Merton's theory of anomie is but one aspect of a larger sociological project within the functionalist framework. Any gleaning of references to crime in Marx's writings should be placed within an appreciation of his broader theoretical concerns. Caution should therefore be exercised when the historical field is perceived as an ordered whole, regardless of whether that orderliness is cemented by consensus, conflict or confusion. On the other hand, although he dismisses grand architectural ambitions for sociological theory, Rock is apparently suggesting that creative thinking is stimulated within an intellectual setting that enhances appreciation of the sociological theories that underpin questions about particular issues.

Although I have some reservations about the fragmented portrait of research drawn by Paul Rock, his argument that the sociology of crime and social control is an outcrop from an expansive terrain of sociological work is a helpful pointer along a route leading to some understanding of how research about the police occupational culture has progressed. The immediate point is that study of the occupational culture has grown out of precisely the appreciation of sociological theory and of philosophical anthropology that Rock invokes as the fresh air of creativity.

Michael Banton's pioneering work, The policeman in the community, is surely the general starting point of a contemporary sociology of the British police and for research about the occupational culture in particular. In his introduction to that book, Banton is careful to point out that he is not seeking to answer questions of value such as, 'are relations between the police and the public better or worse than in the past?' It is clear, nevertheless, that the state of police/public relations leading to the establishment of the Royal Commission on the Police in 1960 was certainly in his mind when he drafted his manuscript. Policy issues are there, as is Banton's personal interest in teaching police officers. Far greater importance should be attached to the influence of Emile Durkheim's dissertation, The division of labour in society, on Banton's thesis. The underpinning that Durkheim secures for The policeman in the community allows Banton to mould his data around the notions of the police officer as a law enforcer and as a peace-keeper, as well as weaving the threads of the argument that a particular mode of social control is dependent upon a particular societal density.

William Westley's doctoral thesis and published papers added a comparative dimension to Banton's research. George Homan's work on the human group and his insistence that social research should in the first instance be concerned with, 'the systematic examination of the commonplace events of everyday behaviour', informed Banton's observational method of research, harmonising with the traditions of his subject, social anthropology.

From this study we therefore gain insight into the different modes of policing officers have adopted in a Scottish and in some American cities. The detailed descriptions that led to the analysis of law enforcement and peace-keeping roles begged further research to discover if they are the only roles played by officers and to question if they are discrete. Although there is no reference to a police occupational culture in The policeman in the community, Banton's research began to map out some of the directions in which subsequent students might pursue this research (pp.vii-xiv). I suspect that Michael Banton knew from his observations that a distinct culture of policing exists amongst rank-and-file officers but his commitment to the most careful use of evidence prevented him from stretching his data to claim that particular discovery. Nevertheless the importance of this research as a theme setter and an encouragement to work on the occupational culture should not be underestimated.

Finally, I want to mention a feature of Banton's book that has often been overlooked. This is his cautious use of American research findings within the British setting. Reservations about the relevance of Westley's research findings are continually expressed. For example, Banton points out that when compared with the Scottish police rather than with other occupational groups in American society, American officers seem rather less socially isolated than Westley suggests. Other reservations are expressed about the comparative regularity of the use of illegal techniques of work employed by American and Scottish officers. Subsequent evidence places question marks against a number of the comparative inferences drawn but at least Banton was acutely aware of the value of comparative data and the need to use it with the utmost caution, which is not always appreciated by many contemporary researchers.

As Banton was finishing his fieldwork, Maureen Cain began her questionnaire and observational study of rural and urban policing (Cain, 1968 and 1973). The basic questions that Cain set for her doctoral thesis arise from role theory, being concerned with the mediation of power that is available to role definers through their reciprocal ties of interdependency with and perceptions of other role players. Questions from sociological theory - role and reference group theory - therefore set the framework for Cain's study of the police and in many ways her description of the lower ranks' world is a by-product of a larger sociological project. Indeed, it is clear from her later papers that Cain was keen to work from the smaller scale of study found in Society and the policeman's role to the larger scale of sociological enquiry concerned with questions of class structure. Studies of the occupational culture have subsequently been described by her as 'the icing sugar on the cake' which, she argues, is no substitute for research which deals, 'with the fundamental issues, with the chemical processes which make the cake of policing possible at all' (Cain, 1979). I happen to disagree with this view - a point I will return to - but it is clear that throughout her research into the police role, Maureen Cain has remained close to questions of socio-logical theory, strengthening the analytical benefits of her studies.

Cain's documentation of the lower police ranks' world continues to serve as an invaluable source of data and a benchmark for research. In Society and the policeman's role the lower ranks' perception of their role is clearly documented as one of crime fighting; the arrest for a criminal offence is the central act of 'good policing' and the primary feature of what appears to be an insatiable need for action amongst the rank-and-file. The chase and capture, the fight and scuffle before the taking of an offender are all close to the centre of the lower ranks' view. Time between bursts of action, which the lower ranks regard as boring, led to Cain's notion of 'easing behaviour'. Because easing is contrary to force regulations, a thread of secrecy and interdependency is woven through the lower ranks' role. This web of security is tightened by the requirement amongst the lower ranks to defend themselves from possible hindrances to their particular use of legal powers. They therefore protect themselves from members of the public and from senior officers, though the nature of the relationship between the junior and the senior ranks in Cain's urban force is not clear. The work group of constables is secured as the primary reference for the definition of the police role.

Although Cain does not dismiss some of the more recent studies of the occupational culture out of hand - indeed, she has been kindly appreciative of them - she is clearly sceptical about their analytical and explanatory power. The small section of Society and the policeman's role that I have outlined is probably not regarded by its author as having particular significance. As far as my own and other people's work is concerned, Cain's findings have served as an invaluable body of data, forming a clear bearing from which research can proceed. Like Michael Banton, Cain did not extrapolate the notion of a police occupational culture from her data but they surely warrant the use of this concept. Her documentation of the range of beliefs and associated strategies of action, spanning expressive and instrumental dimensions of police work, laid the foundations for the study of the British police occupational culture. At last a baseline of data was published to assist the work of the few people researching the police during the mid-1970s. At last someone had managed to pierce the public gloss of policing and describe its underlying reality.

Further, I think that Cain's research sensitised scholars to the American studies, expecially those by Westley (1970) and Skolnick (1966). The norms and working rules employed by Westville's officers and the idea of a police 'working personality' did not seem too far from the shores of British policing. This view added a stimulus to new work. On the other hand, the fillip given to British research about the occupational culture by the American writings also seems to have led to an often unstated assumption that the American work is applicable to the British context, give or take some smoothing of rough cultural edges. Banton's warnings were to be neglected as a notion of Anglo-American policing took shape.

Finally, Cain's research began to shed some light upon what has become a stock-in-trade enquiry for students of the police. From her study it became clear that the objective reality of police work - for example, its sporadic, mundane and peace-keeping character - is at odds with the perceived reality of the rank-and-file. Maurice Punch's (1973) article on the police as a secret social service and Martin's and Wilson's (1969) work on manpower and workloads enhanced our knowledge of the gap between the subjective and objective realities of police work. Other American research has also been of relevance here; the Cummings' (1965) study of calls for police assistance, with its evocative title 'The policeman: philosopher, guide and friend', and Bittner's (1967) study of police peace-keeping on an American skid-row raised further questions about how the peace-keeping role is played in British constabularies, especially questions about the content of the rules that script it.

Mention should be made at this point of Robert Reiner's (1978) study of police unionism. Although the main focus of his doctoral thesis is concerned with the development of the Police Federation and officers' attitudes to that organisation, it also includes a typology of 'orientations to work' amongst a sample of the federated ranks. The relevance of this typology to research about the occupational culture is a matter for future study.

Exploring some new territory

Robert Reiner's work got its first public airing, I think, at one of the three bi-annual seminars on the sociology of the police organised at Bristol by Michael Banton (Banton, 1971, 1973 and 1975). Michael Chatterton's work was also first presented at the seminars, which brought together academics and police officers to discuss research findings, and to explore how future research might be operationalised. I recall attending the final seminar and being struck by what has become an agenda item for most academic and police exchanges about research. Chatterton's paper on supervision under the fixed points system of patrol was being discussed and a number of us were appreciating his use of the concept of 'accounts', of rule use, and so on (Chatterton, 1979). One of the senior police officers present cut through the discussion with his strongly held view that the paper was of little relevance because the fixed points system of supervision that Chatterton had studied was no longer in use. Everything had changed. My lack of quantitative research skills should have been redressed from that moment. I am certain that the senior officer's statement is an expression worthy of statistical significance - I have heard it hundreds of times - but utterly insignificant as far as the reality it seeks to describe is concerned. Its corollary, of course, is that academic researchers are out of touch and naive.

Banton's seminars brought home a dilemma to be faced by sociologists of the occupational culture. Research is not really possible without the cooperation of the police. On the other hand, police cooperation can constrain sociological enquiry, framing proposals and findings in terms of their relevance to immediate policy issues. The sociology of the occupational culture seemed to face grave difficulties.

Stanley Cohen makes a brief reference to the Bristol seminars in his review of the history of the development of the sociology of deviance in Britain. He writes that 'there have already been a few isolated projects in this field, (the sociology of the police), over the last few years and attempts are currently being made - although one has some misgivings about the direction some of these might go - by Banton and others to evaluate recent research and define future priorities' (Cohen, 1974, p.21). If Cohen's misgivings signal the dangers of the subject being over-determined by police interests, they probably reflect the views of the sociologists attending the seminars.

Cohen is also signalling to another, rather different apprehension. He wonders if the police are a proper subject for sociological research; an idea that might seem somewhat bizarre in this new age of 'realism' in criminology. In the late 1960s and 1970s there was a clear tendency of 'new criminologists' who said little or nothing about the police and whose influence over the scope of research enquiry was strangely pervasive (see Taylor et al., 1974 and 1975). This neglect of the police within a popular sociological perspective on crime and social control was a powerful influence upon the people who wanted to study the occupational culture.

When I say, 'people who wanted to study the occupational culture' I am still referring to a very small number of academics. There was little interest in the police during the 1970s. Those of us researching the occupational culture, Michael Chatterton, myself, Peter Manning and, in Dutch exile, Maurice Punch, certainly wanted to break away from the portrait of the police painted by the new criminologists, which seemed to amount to little more than one of puppets who 'translate fantasy into reality', orchestrating that feat without any apparent consciousness (Young, 1971). When, in a later paper, Jock Young asserted that 'The criminal statistics represent the end-results of the deployment of social-control agencies by the powerful' (Young, 1975, p.87), and offered no evidence to substantiate the claim, it was becoming clear that a sociological vacuum needed to be filled with ethnographic data. Yet it was these developments within sociology we wished to take issue with, not any new police policies.

Of greater importance, perhaps, was the developing critique of positivism and an empiricism which was bound by an allegiance to statistical rather than any other types of data. Max Atkinson's paper on police coroners' officers, which was published in the first selection of papers from The National Deviancy Conference, indicated what the insights of one type of ethnomethodological approach might accomplish (Atkinson, 1971). More importantly, Atkinson's paper demonstrated how empirical study could challenge a dominant sociological notion that 'social facts should be treated as things'. Michael Chatterton, who was working in the same university department as Atkinson and other sociologists who were in sympathy with what amounted to a vigorous critique of sociology's accepted wisdom, turned his attention to the analysis of crime and arrest statistics.

David Matza's advocacy of an appreciative stance in sociology was further encouragement for our research, in the sense that it potentially restored humanity to the cardboard puppets portrayed as police by the new criminologists, though in Matza's case this is more of an unintended than intended consequence of his work (Matza, 1969). The labelling perspective similarly engaged our understanding and offered a link with the methodological and analytical themes of the Chicago school of the sociology of work and occupations. The focus of research on the occupational culture was to be in the first instance concerned with the mundane, repetitious and common employment called police work; our concern was to understand how the mundane is transposed to a dramatic, highly symbolic and vividly exciting realm (Hughes, 1953). A pre-requisite of this discovery is, as Robert Park put it to his students, to 'get the seat of your pants dirty with real research', meaning for us the observation of and perhaps participation in police work (reported in Manning, 1972).

Although unevenly marked in studies of the occupational culture, Alfred Schutz's social phenomenology draws attention to the study of what he calls 'the life world' and 'the natural attitude of everyday life' as the subject matter of sociology (Schutz, 1974). Here, then, is a perspective that helps us to understand the tenuous and fragile nature of social relationships and to conceptualise social structure as an equally tenuous construction of human accomplishment. Schutz advocates an anthropology that can cope with the perplexity and uncertainty of being human, which is the view developed by Peter Berger and Thomas Luckman in The social construction of reality. In many other writings published in the late 1960s and 1970s, sociologists began to shake the foundations of theoretical certainty that characterise social structures as massive and monumental.

Our understanding of anthropology was therefore markedly different from the highly deterministic and all too certain sociologies of crime and social control that manage to reduce everything to the correlation of statistically measured variables or neglect detailed study of the police because some over-arching force that plays upon all institutions has been de-mystified by deductive argument. We were concerned to retain humanistic, participatory methods of research; to study mundane aspects of police work; to discover the 'commonsense knowledge' and the rules of work employed by officers on routine patrol; and, I think, to re-conceptualise the relationship between the police organisation and the wider social environment which, it should be admitted, has tended to be characterised by a conspicuous silence on key issues like the analysis of power, of class and of domination.

A rather different feature of the intellectual context within which we worked was an implicit disquiet and sometimes a fear about the consequences of publishing some of our research findings. Remember that Maureen Cain published her research about ten years after she collected her data. There was a similar time-lag in William Westley's work. For us in Britain it seemed possible that the publication of some of our research findings could lead to a self-administered amputation of our research arm, and we naturally wished to develop our academic studies as well as influence police policy where this seemed possible. More worrying still was the possibility of legal action; remember again, these potentially stormy waters had not been tested by publications which documented possible illegalites committed by police officers.

Many strands of academic thought were therefore woven into the research context that I have described, setting the scene for the more recent studies of the occupational culture. Michael Chatterton's PhD thesis is one piece of work fostered within this setting (Chatterton, 1975, 1976 and 1979). Now mostly published in the form of papers, Chatterton's thesis is primarily a testing of Egon Bittner's conceptualisation of an organisation and of the sociological research that suggests official statistics of crime are the end product of a process of human decision making (Bittner, 1965). Major chapters of the thesis tackle Bittner's notions of 'competence', 'gambit of compliance' and 'corroborative reference'. This conceptualisation of the police organisation is allied to what Chatterton calls the action perspective that: 'required us to examine the meanings and uses of this blueprint for the goals and rules of the Division as these were manifest in the action and interaction between Divisional personnel and their various publics' (Chatterton, 1975, p.1). Policing is understood as a highly contextualised activity. Rules in use (working rules), seem to differ from the rules of law and policy directives (formal rules), both differing from rules concerned with the retrospective reporting of police action (accounting rules). The occupational culture is therefore conceptualised by Chatterton as a lexicon of working, formal and accounting rules, employed by officers when they are found to be appropriate within a particular context of police work.

This all too brief coverage of Chatterton's initial research on the occupational culture is intended to emphasise his conceptualisation of the occupational culture as a lectionary of rules to be employed in appropriate contexts. When operationalised, this notion leads to a research strategy of tracking one social process as it flows through the police organisation - the construction of a section 47 assault is his best example - which has in my view been an important advance in research (Chatterton, 1983). As well as tracking the construction of appropriate courses of police work, Chatterton (in his study of the use of resource charges) has also documented a range of styles of policing, and, following Bittner, has linked the law enforcement and peace-keeping aspects of police work (Chatterton, 1981).

Peter Manning's intellectual debts are more widespread than Michael Chatterton's. Manning's writings on policing, not least on the occupational culture, are now numerous; they draw on many academic sources and display a diverse range of objectives. If Police work: the social organisation of policing is taken as our starting point, this diversity soon becomes apparent. How are we to read this book? Is it an ethnography of police officers at work? Is it a critique of systems theory? Is it a theory of the police in general and/or of the occupational culture in particular? Or is it an exploration of Goffman's dramaturgy? Indeed, it is all of these, and more - a history of British and American policing and an analysis of the concept of Anglo-American policing, and so on!

I suspect that many people find Police work a difficult and possibly an annoying read which leaves them with the feeling that they have not got to grips with the precise purpose of the text. This could be reasonable criticism but for me misses the mark by miles. The value of this rewarding and challenging text surely lies in its launching of a provocative avalanche of ideas which, time and again, stimulates new trains of thought and new ideas for research. Goffman's thesis, The presentation of self in everyday life, lies at the heart of much of Manning's work. He employs this theory at the organisational level of analysis, documenting the dramatic, public presentations of the police which shield its mundane and rather secret and private, 'backstage' reality. A tension between the public and private domains of policing creates a dominant characteristic of police work - uncertainty. I wonder if at one level Manning is stating an anthropological fact here, which is to be associated with the existential theme in Goffman's writings. I am not sure. At another level of analysis, uncertainty sharpens the private world of the police occupational culture that is constantly threatening to break into public view. Again, I am not sure if Manning is arguing that the team work of the lower ranks and the professional/bureaucratic perspective of the senior police ranks are a consequence or cause of organisational uncertainty. The secrecy, lack of trust, unwillingness to resort to written records of work and the general protection afforded by the retention of team loyalty amongst the rank-and-file are welded together by a perceived uncertainty about police work, and the so-called ritualistic displays of the lower ranks are an attempt to resolve it. But is the uncertainty that Manning writes about a metaphor or a measurable concept, a cause or an effect?

Rather than follow Chatterton's strategy of tracking a process to chart the relatonship between formal, working and accounting rules, Manning chooses a rather elusive stance to substantiate this analysis. In Police work and in other papers we find lists of rules and of social types that officers identify but their application to specific incidents is not really clear. It is argued, nevertheless, that there is a separation between the lower ranks' working rules and the occupational culture which they frame, and the administrative theory of policing which is said to order the work of the managerial ranks.

Two problems arise from this view. First, the relationship between principles and rules, or to put it another way, between normative and contextual rules is not clarified and this has a knock-on effect for the whole of the thesis presented in Police work. It also tends to falsely separate instrumental and symbolic aspects of policing and, therefore, ritualistic from mundane features. Secondly, because he frequently draws on American and on English data to make a single point, Manning's notion of Anglo-American policing is certainly attractive but misleading. It might be replied that I am focusing on relatively minor matters that should be submerged in favour of an appreciation of the challenge to systems theory made in the text. That challenge is certainly not weakened by the criticisms.

If Police work is a critique of systems theory, The narcs' game changes key slightly to deal with problems of conceptualising the relationship between an organisation and its social environment. In the former book we are told that policing is both a public presentation and a private practice but the more precise relationship between these two domains is not spelt out. This is the primary issue taken up in The narcs' game, where Manning draws on Weick's notion of the 'enacted environment': 'A basic metaphor for articulating organisation-environment relations . . . Instead of discussing the "external environment" we will discuss the "enacted environment". The phrase the enacted environment preserves the crucial distinctions that we wish to make, the most important being that the human creates the environment to which the system then adapts. The human act does not react to any environment he enacts to it. It is this enacted environment and nothing else, that is worked upon by the process of organising' (Manning, 1982).

Although The narcs' game is concerned with a drugs squad and therefore a specialist unit, within its text Manning asks the more general question of how the occupational culture is constructed and sustained. Chatterton tracks some rules spanning law enforcement and peace-keeping work; Manning suggests that the meaning of various features of an interpreted social environment creates and mandates a certain application of rules within particular contexts of police action. Here, the occupational culture is a myriad of meanings and associated rules, 'what is taken for granted about the organisation and the world by any competent member', and therefore concerned with 'a cool emotional tone, properly executed tactics, properly applied skills and a fair and open-minded view of encounters with the public' (Manning, 1979, p.49).

Peter Manning has drawn attention to the expressive, dramatic and, though I disagree with his use of this notion, the ritualistic characteristics of police work. Hedonism, toughness and adventure pervade the occupational culture, as does the centrality of crime work. How far some of these features are importations from working class culture is another important question that he has raised. From Weick's perspective any importation, indeed, any perception of the wider social structure is to be analysed as a reflective discernment rather than a reactive response. Here lies the foundation of Manning's contribution to our under-standing of the occupational culture. He conceptualises this culture as a social construction and thereby advocates an anthropology that is humanistic and, I think, mindful of the precarious nature of human existence. In shoring up a public presentation of police work that can hold public confidence and attention, but working in a private context of rather different cultural dimensions, the lower ranks hold uncertainty at bay. The occupational culture retains its symbolic importance at both the personal and societal levels.

Rules and typifications of phenomena form a police 'commonsense'; this is a broader notion than that found in Chatterton's work. Policy, law and requests for some police service enter the police organisation from the external environment and are coded, 'under the umbrella of a commonsense theory. The facts are not taken as a means to disconfirm the police theory of human nature' (Manning, 1977, p.237). Manning leaves us with the question of how this body of knowledge is structured and how it is sustained in the course of routine police work. How are facts turned into 'police commonsense'? Other fascinating questions about the occupational culture overflow from Peter Manning's work and they should have led to a great deal of further research. The fact that this has not been the case is surely more indicative of the instrumental research climate we now work in, than a comment about their importance.

Police work was published after I completed my covert field work. When I returned to the police service after graduation, my research interests lay not so much in the aspects of police work that I have written about as they did in questions arising from sociological theory and methodology. Most of all, my attention was captured by the writings of George Herbert Mead, Alfred Schutz and Peter Berger and Thomas Luckman. All of these writers direct attention to the manner in which social structure is constructed and sustained. Peter Berger and Thomas Luckman attempt, in The social construction of reality, to weave together classical traditions of sociological theory, advancing an anthropology which stresses human creativity. The question that these and other writers working within similar theoretical frameworks do not address is that of how the social world is constructed and from what materials it is hewn.

Alfred Schutz argues that the starting point for sociological enquiry is 'commonsense knowledge' and he has formulated a theory of the relevancies of knowledge. Peter Berger and Thomas Luckman theorise about the dialectic of externalisation, objectification and internalisation, suggesting it to be normative, but they do not tell us how that dialectic creates a commonsensical world; how the dialectic of social structure creates its patternings from a particular content. These questions beg empirical study and when I returned to my force I found myself in a research setting that allowed me to begin to tackle them and with the opportunity to use the research method of participant observation, which flows naturally from a Schutzian and Bergerian anthropology.

From the initial data I gathered it appeared that many of Maureen Cain's findings extended across the decade that separated our research, forming a strand of continuity woven into the lower ranks' occupational culture. Chatterton's adherence to Bittner's formulations constrained an understanding of the police work I was observing. David Silverman's definition of an organisation as, 'a multitude of rationalities each of which generates the "in-order-to" motives of the participants and allows them to make their own sense of the actions and intentions of others', offered a more adequate touchstone of analysis (Silverman, 1970). Drawing on Schutz's work, this definition allowed me to describe and analyse clusterings of motive, strategy, tactic, intent and account (Holdaway, 1980). The definition also allowed me to exploit Schutz's work through an analysis mindful of the central and peripheral relevancies of the occupational culture. This excluded giving attention to styles of policing. My concern was and remains with the core features of the occupational culture, from which various styles of work depart. Schutz's theory of relevance encourages the mapping of structures of meaning, especially the manner in which knowledge of space and time is ordered. There is no suggestion in his writings or in my work that the occupational culture is monochrone or a 'Flatland', retaining the same level of commitment from all officers.

Peter Manning's publications posed the questions that I have outlined and a good deal of the analysis of my data led me to write a critique of his work (Holdaway, 1977). One aspect of that critique is concerned with the conceptualisation of a professional police as a symbol of competence and status (Holdaway, 1983), which is a view that feeds into Manning's separation of the symbolic and instrumental dimensions of police work.

A critical analysis of the seminal American literature, notably Westley's and Skolnick's work found their foundations of evidence to be very weak. In particular, Westley's data do not support his thesis of reciprocal hostility between Westville's police and the public of that town. His evidence suggests that the police view of public hostility is a highly selective one and the strategies of force that he documents are an equally selective assemblage. The theoretical perspectives I worked with are able to cope with Westley's data and with the contradictions that can be found in Skolnick's analysis.

The essential features of the police occupational culture are a perception of the world as a place that is always on the verge of chaos, held back from devastation by a police presence. People are naive and potentially disorderly in all situations; control, ideally absolute control, is the fundamental police task. My interest in how this perception of potential social disorder affects police work led me to document the range of police strategies and tactics presented in Inside the British police. The significance of phenomena of relevance to police work is derived from these central axes of meaning, which underpin the reality of police work as it is perceived by the rank-and-file.

My attempt to separate the central and more peripheral features of the occupational culture is not clearly spelt out in the brevity of Inside the British police, neither is the Schutzian framework discussed in detail, which has led to some misunderstandings (for example, Jefferson and Grimshaw, 1984, p.185). A clearer feature of my work is probably the documentation of the traditions of the occupational culture that run a cultural thread through Cain's work on a force with a different patrol system and managerial ideology to the one I researched. There is a temptation to argue that very little change has taken place in the occupational culture during the last twenty years; the Policy Studies Institute's report on the Metropolitan Police adds credence to this view. In fact, I think that change is constantly taking place and we need to document its boundaries and its substantial content. Nevertheless, we can now confidently argue that, to parody Cain's phrase, the occupational culture is one ingredient that makes, 'the cake of policing possible', and we have some understanding of how police technology, law, policy and narrative are employed in the construction and maintenance of its central and peripheral structures.

The features of the occupational culture that I have identified extend our knowledge to police perceptions of the local population, strategies and tactics of control, work in the charge room and the questioning of 'prisoners', and the meaning of time and space – all of these being analysed in terms of Schutz's theory of relevance. The system of panda patrol that I observed and the laws that officers used were further materials that the lower ranks moulded to sustain the occupational culture. Critics who suggest that students of the occupational culture pay no attention to law or formal policy seem to miss the point that is being made. Law and policy are not obliterated within the occupational culture but re-worked, refracted in one direction or another as they do or do not resonate with the themes of the occupational culture. In my papers on a robbery squad, on accountability and on police community relations I have tried to demonstrate how policy, reworked though it is, is implemented by lower ranking officers (James, 1979; Holdaway, 1978 and 1982). But law and policy remain as some of the materials with which the occupational culture is re-created and sustained.

This point begs another theme of my own and Peter Manning's research. In an early paper I suggested that a yawning gap exists between managerial and rank-and-file policies (Holdaway, 1977). I had reason to revise that view in my paper on a street robbery squad, where the senior officer in charge of the squad appeared to absolve himself from control of his staff (James, op.cit.). Similarly, in Inside the British police there is a small amount of evidence to tie the division's senior officers into the work of the lower ranks.

My work differs from Chatterton's because its primary research focus is the meanings of phenomena which form the occupational culture; I am not so interested in the study of rules. Peter Manning's work is concerned with rules and meanings but I am rather sceptical about some of the structural divisions he identifies within the occupational culture and am probably more concerned with ethnography.

Before moving to consider the Policy Studies Institute report I want to mention briefly a number of other studies that add to our knowledge of the occupational culture. Baldwin and Kinsey (1982) stress the importance attached to intelligence gathering by the constables they observed in a British force, which is probably related to the distinct dominant crime focus of the occupational culture. Mervyn Jones (1980) has published some rather different data about perceptions of officers who choose to spend their working life on routine beat patrol. Jones' documentation of the contradiction between the rhetoric of a chief constable and his actions is clearly important, adding to our knowledge of the relationship between the police ranks and the manner in which the occupational culture is sustained.

A change in policy

In this section I attempt to excavate the sociological foundations upon which studies of the police occupational culture have been constructed. Time and again emphasis has been placed on the distinct sociological underpinnings of the available studies; their attempt to analyse social relationships and their intended and unintended consequences. Any analytical purchase they have on policy arises precisely from these same sociological foundations.

Research about the occupational culture is now oriented in a rather different direction. Universities are increasingly dependent upon external funding for their research work and are partly evaluated by the University Grants Committee according to the ability of their staff to attract research grants from external sources. Understandably, scholars now spend increasing amounts of time writing research proposals. 'Relevance', 'evaluation' and 'monitoring' form the sacred canopy of this academic age.

The Royal Commission on Criminal Procedure and Lord Scarman's report on the 1981 riots have added a stimulus to 'relevant research'. Chief officers who have fostered a high public profile have often provoked the researcher's imagination and done so at a time when crime and policing are key issues for the major political parties, so helping to frame the new foundation of work that I describe.

Although the impact of this re-orientation of research is not yet easy to discern, along with the benefits to be gained from it, there is surely some worry that we could find ourselves with increased amounts of information about the occupational culture but very small, disproportionate increases in knowledge. Analytical questions arising from sociology may well be dissolved away as the virtual exclusive policy focus, pragmatism, cursory theoretical concern and inter-disciplinary assumptions which form the content of the new intellectual framework are strengthened.

The Policy Studies Institute's report on the Metropolitan Police is in many ways an indication of this changing direction of research. When it was published, amidst attention from the national press, it seemed that new evidence about British policing was to be presented. When one casts an eye over the main headings covered in Volume IV, The police in action, they include 'figures', 'dominance and not losing face', 'punishment and retribution', and so on. Many potential trails to a range of previously published work are laid but never traced. The report is written without reference to previously published material on the occupational culture or on the police per se. Some new data are to be found in the report: about sexism, the police use of alcohol and about racial prejudice within the police. Many fascinating ideas and questions about the internal structure of the occupational culture are implicit in the text; the variety of supporting methods of research used in the study bear close inspection. These and other novel features are, nevertheless, not discussed with any consideration of the sociological knowledge we possess about the police.

These reservations are not about a piece of work that claims new knowledge but disregards the existing literature. My disappointment lies in the lack of recognition afforded the sociological foundations upon which the study is constructed. Perhaps another researcher will have to undertake this task, with an attendant risk of driving a false distinction between policy oriented and therefore 'relevant research', and more sociologically based or theoretical work. No doubt an explanation of this matter lies in the fact that the report was commissioned by and written for the Commissioner of the Metropolitan Police, which really only adds credence to my general argument that it is now police policy that tends to set the tenor of research.

Taking stock and some future directions

Our knowledge about the occupational culture remains somewhat slight; far too slight for any complacency about its breadth of coverage or its depth of analytical insight. It would certainly be unwise to heed the advice of a number of sociologists who argue, as Cain does, that we now know enough about the occupational culture and should therefore shift our attention to a rather different level of analysis; or, in Reiner's case, to retain the view that Skolnick's thesis of the 'working personality' is the locus classicus for British work, glossing over the tenuous link between British and American studies; or, in Jefferson's case, to characterise studies of the occupational culture as being within 'the sociological tradition - interactionism - that currently dominates sociological research into the police', thereby advocating the need to direct research attention to another paradigm. All of these claims are ill-founded.

Any characterisation of work on the occupational culture as a homogenous corpus of interactionist sociology is especially misleading. I have documented the existing, diverse approaches to the study of the occupational culture which include Durkheimian theory, role and reference group theory, Bittner's conceptualisation of an organisation, Goffman's dramatism, semiotics, Berger and Luckman's thesis and Schutzian phenomenology. Does this pot pourri add up to a dominance of the interactionist tradition? I do not think so. Some common ground between researchers is recognisable but everyone has tended to work their own ticket. Ken Plummer's comments about misunderstandings of the labelling perspective are equally instructive for research about the occupational culture. He writes that, 'lack of self recognition by labelling theorists and their diverse theoretical concerns for the labelling perspective has only emerged from diverse theoretical projects. They are united by some common substantive problems but not some common theories' (Plummer, 1979). Interestingly, the problems that Plummer cites as common ground for labelling theorists are also relevant to the future study of the occupational culture – the tension between the structural and the situational; between phenomenalism and essentialism; and between formalism and verstehen.

Rules and meanings

Following Bittner, Michael Chatterton has delineated some of the working rules that guide routine rank-and-file police work. Working rules, he argues, are to be related to their contexts of use, which, in some views, distinguishes them from laws. We therefore find in Chatterton's work the notion of policing as a situationally specific activity; a rule is worked and re-worked to meet the unfolding meaning of a situation of some police service. In his detailed documentation of the use of assault charges, where peace-keeping and law enforcement tactics remain constant options within the contexts from which the charge arises, the separation between working and formal rules is secured. Manning's analysis is somewhat similar to this.

If the working rules of policing are to be analysed in their contexts of use and then contrasted with the formal rules they vie with and yield to, an adequate documentation presumably requires a statement of the rule, or principle as Manning calls it, and detailed evidence of the rule being put to work in context. The research strategy of 'tracking' could presumably identify the focal rule and chart it through a potentially infinite number of contexts. Adequate research is accomplished when a naive user can read the sociological description and employ the rule with competence.

I can find some benefits and some drawbacks in this approach. Further research might select a particular law or written policy and trace it through the occupational culture, charting its flux and flow as it is employed in a range of contexts of police work. Successive studies could presumably chart a map of the essential and phenomenal features of rules, providing a valuable addition to our knowledge of the occupational culture.

My own preference is for a rather different approach. Rather than etch a map of rules that are said to structure the occupational culture, I think that Chatterton's approach is more likely to lead to a listing of primary rules and a documentation of the potentially vast range of settings within which they are contextualised, together with an explanation of the relationship between the primary and the contextual use of the rule. If a rule is contextualised in a vast range of settings of police work, what is the status of the primary rule? Is it an essential feature of the occupational culture from which its phenomenal use is derived? Or is the essentiality of a rule not clearly formulated in the rank-and-file mind, being a sort of survival that is so dimly perceived that it hardly warrants the ascription and status of a rule?

Issues like these lead me to consider the meanings or, more adequately, the typifications of the phenomena towards which rules guide action. Rules are analytically separable but they are also and perhaps more adequately analysed if they are placed within the 'world view' of the police lower ranks, which is structured around the relevance of typifications. If the emphasis of research shifts to typifications it becomes more possible to understand the inter-related structure of the occupational culture and thereby to move away from the study of discrete rules. It also becomes possible to give attention to the expressive features of policing, which tend to be neglected in the rule-based perspective.

For example, take the context of the questioning of a 'prisoner' in a police station where we are led from the rules governing, say, the use of appropriate force during the process of questioning to typifications of prisoners, to the meaning of solicitors and other people who might enter the charge room and cell areas, to the meaning of appropriate charges, to the meaning of figures of arrest, and so on. If this line of argument is sustained we are not led back to a primary rule or to an imperative for action as much as we are to an axial typification of a world on the edge of chaos which begs police control.

This very brief discussion does no more than raise the need to separate the rule-based and typification-based notions of the occupational culture. We should debate arguments from either side; research on the same subject from both perspectives could help us to learn about their respective limitations and advantages. We could develop our knowledge of the internal structure of the occupational culture and begin to understand how change might be achieved amongst the lower ranks. Importantly, this work will lead us to a more realistic appraisal of the sociological foundations upon which we work.

Symbolism and instrumentalism

In his discussion of the public presentations of police work, Peter Manning lays store by his appreciation of the vivid symbolism of policing. He makes a clear distinction between symbolism and instrumentalism which, in a rather similar manner to the rule-based notion of culture that I have just questioned, sets limits on our knowledge. There is no doubt that Manning's use of the dramaturgical perspective has brilliantly revealed new knowledge. But I wonder if this separation between symbolism and instrumentalism is somewhat misleading?

I have documented a range of vividly symbolic techniques of control which officers employed when making an arrest and during the subsequent process of investigation. A good number of these strategies and tactics symbolise police authority but they also serve an instrumental objective of securing a confession of guilt. I have also documented arrests that are performed with all the symbolism and drama that it is possible to wring out of them but the material reference point of the arrests is an instrumentally based increase in overtime payments through court attendance. In turn, arrests serving symbolic and instrumental objectives are later transposed to symbolise dramatically the organisational effectiveness of police policy, namely the accompanying instrumental attraction of increased public funding. This relationship between the symbolic and instrumental dimensions of policing is neglected in Manning's work.

Secondly, symbols are connotative and denotative. An arrest might symbolise police authority and control throughout a sub-division and beyond its boundaries. Here the symbol is connotative. The same symbol can be denotative, concerned with the punishment or 'education' of a prisoner. Any datum can therefore be analysed in terms of its symbolic and instrumental and associated connotative and denotative dimensions. Once the richness of the occupational culture is grasped by researchers a 'Flatland' conceptualisation of its terrain will be rejected (Rock, 1973 and 1974).

We need to develop our analysis of symbols and, if my critique of Manning is correct, to give more attention to the work of social anthropologists than has been the case in the past. Victor Turner's study of Ndembu ritual offers one guide through what he calls 'the forest of symbols', dealing with methodological and analytical problems (Turner, 1967 and 1974). I would like to see his ideas, which encompass the exoteric and esoteric interpretation of symbols and the flow of interpretation from the societal to the individual levels of meaning, brought to a consideration of the existing data on the occupational culture. Only then will we be able to unravel the various dimensions of analysis that I have described and preserve the richness of the occupational culture. We might also be saved from a criticism I have faced, namely that I use a datum to make a number of different points of analysis. Only a disenchanted academic world, with its cold instrumentalism could surely countenance such a fundamentalist 'Flatland'.

Centre and periphery

Taking up some of the themes of Schutz's phenomenology, Paul Rock has argued that the 'life world' should be analysed by 'a progressive stripping away of layers of meaning in an attempt to lay bare the physiology of a moral system. It should proceed on the assumption that it is possible to discover tiers and clusters of meaning, each with its own contours and each related to some larger principles of stratification' (Rock, 1974). The life world is not a 'Flatland' but finely contoured, importantly along spatial and temporal lines. We do not know enough about the lines such contours take or about the relationship between the principle and the derived, secondary structures of meaning.

If the spatial contouring of the police 'life world' is taken as an illustrative example, it is possible to understand how Rock's argument can be given empirical content. Our knowledge of the police use of space requires us to consider some of the American literature but, broadly speaking, it divides between a description of the spatial area within which the police work as a 'Flatland' of danger and hostility and the view that every street calls out its own meaning. Westley's work is an example of the first view; Rubinstein's of the second. Rubinstein describes an officer on patrol in police vehicle: 'Once he has named a place his opinion assumes precedence in determining what is going on there. He cares less about who is there than where they are. He does not make evaluations of the people at each corner every time he cruises past, but makes assumptions about them based on his conception of the place' (Rubinstein, 1973, p.65). Having charted these diverse meanings of space, Rubinstein does not relate them to some 'larger principle of stratification' which structures them.

Are the central meanings those of a naive population and the world as a place on the edge of chaos? If they are, how do particular meanings of area and place relate to them? Schutz's writing provides a more than adequate starting point for the mapping of the life world and an analysis of its central and peripheral meanings. Future research could build upon the available data to enhance our analysis of the internal structure of the occupational culture.

Culture and environment

A quest for some 'larger, internal principle of stratification' could be a misleading exercise. Some scholars argue that much more attention should be given to the social structures that transcend the occupational culture. Far too little attention has been given to researching the relationship between the occupational culture, the police organisation and the wider social structure. Sociologists who have concerned themselves with an analysis of the police within the structures of class and domination in our society have also neglected this question, save by dint of a deductive sociology that assumes an adequacy of explanation at all analytical levels (Jefferson and Grimshaw, 1984; and Brogden, 1982).

In his research about the occupational culture Peter Manning has explored Katz's thesis that working class allegiance to employment within bureaucratic settings is retained through an implicit domain of freedom afforded to a work force by managers (Manning, 1979). Some aspects of working class culture are thereby imported into the culture of a factory, relieving the monotony of repetitious work. A reading of my own data about the hedonistic use of police cars and the creation of action prompts comparisons with ethnographic studies of juvenile delinquency, where the linking theme is the construction of a world that is vibrant with excitement and action to enliven its mundane and quiet reality.

Some of the PSI data deal with a description of the manner in which male officers characterise women and the effects of this characterisation on female officers. The PSI researchers go as far as to argue that the constables display considerable anxiety about their sexual identity. Jokes and police banter generally define and affirm notions of male dominance within the police, with the associated masculine traits of aggression and strength. Similarly, the PSI team has presented evidence of racial prejudice articulated by officers and some data on racial discrimination (see also Southgate, 1982; and Willis, 1983). The use of alcohol to relieve the pressure of work is also given attention which, with other features of the occupational culture that I have reviewed, are clearly related to wider societal structures.

Research needs to tackle just what aspects of the occupational culture are 'under' or 'over determined' by external structures. For example, the sexism that has been documented by the PSI team is obviously related to societal relationships of gender. But why are these broader structural relationships amplified within the police? The same question might be asked about the expression of racial prejudice within the police. Attempts to map the 'police specific' and other linking structural features which mould it – inequalities of class, race and gender, for example, could help us to find greater understanding across the barriers erected by competing sociological perspectives and make inroads into the old debates about the relationship between 'macro' and 'micro' sociology. Other features could be combined in such an analysis – the ecological structure of the organisation, promotion and personnel policies, managerial ideologies, and so on. At the moment we do not understand how these so-called internal and external structures are related to each other and we need studies that attempt to differentiate them.

Ranks and American imports

An important aspect of the type of research that I have outlined would also tackle the relationship between the senior and junior ranks. The Iannis' have written about a management culture and a contrasting 'cop culture' in an American force (Ianni and Ianni, 1983). In Police work Peter Manning details the police administrative theory but some of its features seem to be absent from British police management policies. I have tried to make the distinction between 'managerial professionalism' and 'practical professionalism', though I have some reservations about the rather clear separation that I have drawn between them (James, 1979). Is there a management culture within the British police? How is the content of this culture related to the occupational culture of the lower ranks? Is it a defence, an accomodation or does it have elements of real conflict within its structures? I have the impression, and it is only that, of a growing change amongst the managerial ranks who are keen to reform the lower ranks' culture and who may draw on a common source of knowledge to formulate their ideas and the strategies to effect reform. We need to know much more about relationships between the managerial and lower ranks.

Having mentioned American research, I want to end this section with renewed emphasis on the need for cross-cultural studies. I have criticised Westley's and Skolnick's data and their research conclusions. We can, however, draw on their documentation of the danger that American officers perceive throughout their environment. A reading of Rubinstein's ethnography makes plain how this perception of danger has implications for an officer's demeanour, his level of eye gaze, the manner in which he makes arrests. In Britain the perception is one of potential disorder and a different range of techniques of work.

Although cross-cultural research is fraught with methodological and analytical problems it could bear fruitful studies and hopefully assist us to be increasingly aware of the distinctive and the shared characteristics of the British and American police occupational cultures. Detailed comparative analysis of ethnographic data should sharpen our documentation of the occupational culture and tease apart any notion of Anglo-American policing.

Conclusion

One implication of my analysis of research is the recognition of benefits to be gained from re-kindling interest in and appreciation of the sociological foundations that have structured studies of the occupational culture. A retention of these interests sounds plain enough but is not easy to sustain within the present climate of research, with its many pressures and incentives for us to lurch from one research project to another. Theoretical questions and the longer term work of consolidating research findings take second place to the primary task of the analysis of contemporary policies, with a view towards the pragmatic relevance of research results.

If this reading of the contemporary research context is no more than half correct, sociological studies of the occupational culture may face substantial erosion. A residue of knowledge will remain, submerged in an academic 'as if' world. Here, references are cited 'as if' they sign-post a series of studies that have similar intentions, are exhaustively analytical and are documented on the basis of solid evidence. I hope to have set out an argument to demystify any such 'as if' world.

We need to delineate the contours of the occupational culture with greater precision; to analyse the relationship between what might be called the internal cultural, the formal organisational and the external social structures. The axes of meaning or, perhaps, the axes of rules around which various styles of policing, specialisms and moralities depart can also be more clearly documented in this work. Cross-cultural studies will lead to an understanding of how different police organisations and social structures frame the American and British police occupational culture.

Why bother with these proposals for future research? What is their value? This is not the place to exhort the university as the institution within which knowledge is appreciated for its own sake. Neither am I arguing for a radical separation of sociological research from policy studies, with an attendant sorting of researchers into sheep or goats. Any bifurcation of sociology for and sociology of the police is misleading.

The sharp edge of policy analysis fashioned from the sociological studies of the occupational culture will be kept bright by a constant awareness of the theories that have informed them. All of the sociological work that I have discussed assists us to understand how the lower ranks' culture might be reformed, if that be an objective for the police. The concern for change within the police, which forms a central feature of the contemporary context of enquiry, is good; but its sharp edge of analysis will be made blunt if the sociological foundations of research are eroded.

References

Atkinson, M.J., (1971) 'Societal reactions to suicide: the role of coroners' definitions', in Cohen, S., (ed.), Images of deviance, Penguin, Harmondsworth
Baldwin, R. and Kinsey, R., (1982) Police powers and politics, Quartet Books, London
Banton, M., (1964) The policeman in the community, Tavistock, London
Banton, M., (1971) 'The sociology of the police', The Police Journal, XLIV, 3, 227-43
Banton, M., (1973) 'The sociology of the police II', The Police Journal, XLVI, 4, 341-62
Banton, M., (1975) 'The sociology of the police III', The Police Journal, XLVIII, 4, 299-315
Berger, P. and Luckman, T., (1966) The social construction of reality, Allen Lane, Penguin Press, London
Bittner, E., (1965) 'The concept of organisation', Social Research, 32, 239-55
Bittner, E., (1967) 'The police on skid-row: a study of peace-keeping', American Sociological Review, 32, 5, 699-715
Brogden, M., (1982) The police: autonomy and consent, Academic Press, London
Cain, M.E., (1968) 'Some links between role and reference group analysis', British Journal of Sociology, 19, 2, 191-205
Cain, M.E., (1973) Society and the policeman's role, Routledge and Kegan Paul, London
Cain, M.E., (1979) 'Trends in the sociology of police work', International Journal of the Sociology of Law, 7, 2, 143-67
Chatterton, M.R., (1975) Organisational relationships and processes in police work: a case study of urban policing, PhD thesis, University of Manchester
Chatterton, M.R., (1976) 'The police and social control', in King, J. (ed.), Control without custody, Cropwood Conference Series No.7, Institute of Criminology, Cambridge

Chatterton, M.R., (1979) 'The supervision of patrol work under the fixed points system', in Holdaway, S. (ed.), The British police, Edward Arnold, London

Chatterton, M.R., (1981) 'Practical coppers, oarsmen and administrators: front line supervisory styles in police organisations', unpublished paper presented to annual meeting of the ISA research committee on sociology of law, Oxford

Chatterton, M.R., (1983) 'Police work and assault charges', in Punch, M. (ed.), Control in the police organisation, MIT Press, Cambridge, Mass

Cohen, S., (1974) 'Criminology and the sociology of deviance in Britain', in Rock, P. and McIntosh, M. (eds), Deviance and social control, Tavistock, London

Cumming, E., Cumming, I. and Edell, L., (1964) 'Policeman as philosopher, guide and friend', Social Problems, 12, 276-86

Goffman, E., (1969) The presentation of self in everyday life, Penguin, Harmondsworth

Holdaway, S., (1977) 'Changes in urban policing', British Journal of Sociology, 28, 2, 119-37

Holdaway, S., (1978) 'The reality of police race relations: towards an effective community relations policy', New Community, 6, 3, 258-67

Holdaway, S., (1979) 'Introduction', in Holdaway, S., (ed.), The British police, Edward Arnold, London

Holdaway, S., (1980) The occupational culture of urban policing: an ethnographic study, PhD thesis, University of Sheffield

Holdaway, S., (1982) 'Police accountability: a current issue', Public Administration, 60, 84-9

Holdaway, S., (1983) Inside the British police: a force at work, Basil Blackwell, Oxford

Homans, G.C., (1951) The human group, Routledge and Kegan Paul, London

Hughes, E.C., (1953) Men and their work, Free Press, New York

Ianni, E.R. and Ianni, R., (1983) 'Street cops and management cops', in Punch, M. (ed.), Control in the police organisation, MIT Press, Cambridge, Mass

James, D., (1979) 'Police-black relations: the professional solution', in Holdaway, S., (ed.), The British police, Edward Arnold, London

Jefferson, T. and Grimshaw, R., (1984) Controlling the constable, Muller, London

Jones, M.J., (1980) Organisational aspects of police behaviour, Gower, Farnborough

Manning, P.K., (1972) 'Observing the police: deviants, respectables, and the law', in Douglas, J. (ed.), Research on deviance, Random House, New York

Manning, P.K., (1977) Police work: the social organisation of policing, MIT Press, Cambridge, Mass

Manning, P.K., (1979) 'The social control of police work', in Holdaway, S. (ed.), The British police, Edward Arnold, London

Manning, P.K., (1980) The narcs' game: organisational and informational limits to drug law enforcement, MIT Press, Cambridge, Mass

Manning, P.K., (1982) 'Organisational work', British Journal of Sociology, 33, 1, 118-34

Martin, J. and Wilson, G., (1969) The police: a study in manpower, Heinemann, London

Matza, D., (1969) Becoming deviant, Prentice Hall, Englewood Cliffs

Plummer, K., (1979) 'Misunderstanding labelling perspectives', in Downes, D. and Rock, P. (eds), Deviant interpretations, Martin Robertson, London

Policy Studies Institute (1983) Police and people in London, Vols.I-IV, Smith, D.J., Gray, J. and Small, S., London

Punch, M. and Naylor, T., (1973) 'The police: a social service', New Society, 17 May, 358-61

Reiner, R., (1978) The blue-coated worker: a sociological study of police unionism, Cambridge University Press, Cambridge

Rock, P., (1973) 'Phenomenalism and essentialism in deviancy theory', Sociology, 7, 1, 17-29

Rock, P., (1974) 'Conceptions of moral order', British Journal of Criminology, 14, 2, 139-49

Rock, P., (1979) 'The sociology of crime, symbolic interactionism and some problematic qualities of radical criminology', in Downes, D. and Rock, P. (eds), Deviant interpretations, Martin Robertson, London

Rubinstein, J., (1973) City police, Ballantine, New York

Schutz, A., (1974) Structures of the life world, Heinemann Educational Books, London

Silverman, D., (1970) The theory of organisations, Heinemann, London

Skolnick, J.H., (1966) Justice without trial: law enforcement in democratic society, Wiley, New York

Southgate, P., (1982) Police probationer training in race relations, Research and Planning Unit Paper 8, Home Office, London

Taylor, I., Walton, P. and Young, J., (1974) The new criminology, Routledge and Kegan Paul, London

Taylor, I., Walton, P. and Young, J., (eds), (1975) Critical criminology, Routledge and Kegan Paul, London

Turner, V., (1967) The forest of symbols, Cornell University Press, Ithaca, New York

Turner, V., (1974) The ritual process, Penguin, Harmondsworth

Westley, W., (1970) Violence and the police: a sociological study of law, custom and morality, MIT Press, Cambridge, Mass

Willis, C., (1983) The use, effectiveness and impact of police stop and search powers, Research and Planning Unit Paper 15, Home Office, London

Young, J., (1971) 'The role of the police as amplifiers of deviancy, negotiations of reality and translators of fantasy', in Cohen, S. (ed.), Images of deviance, Penguin, Harmondsworth

Young, J., (1975) 'Working class criminology', in Taylor, I., Walton, P. and Young, J. (eds), Critical criminology, Routledge and Kegan Paul, London

6 Police culture and police practice

NIGEL G. FIELDING

For understandable reasons the earliest and most abiding concern in analysis of the police has been the character of on-the-street police/public encounters. The matter is both amenable to direct study by straightforward research methods and immediately pertinent to the visible character of law enforcement as experienced by ordinary people. The development of our understanding of the police institution and organisation now calls for a different focus, using different methods to pursue the determinants of on-the-street policing within the organisation and in the relation of police to other social and state institutions. It is sensible to consider what the previous concentration of research on the routine police/public encounter can tell us to account for the course of such encounters. It may be that the evolution of thought on that matter bears implications for emergent perspectives on police work and the police organisation off the street, in station, courtroom and headquarters offices.

Social science, legal and behavioural science analyses of routine police/public encounters have proposed several broad mechanisms to account for the course of police/public interaction. Their emergence has overlapped, in the way of all scholarly work, but hindsight permits the perception of a sequential pattern. An initial concentration on the disjunction between legal and social reality implicated police officers as obstacles to the implementation of the rule of law. A preoccupation with bias and prejudice in urban policing led to research seeking to document, predict and extinguish a pathological 'police personality'. The law was impartial, citizens were the passive objects of police bullying and brutality. While work in this area progressed, the analytic distinction between formal and informal organisation, and a growing sophistication of method pointed to an alternative perspective. Attention shifted from the psychology of individual officers, each bearing discrete (and measurable) elements of 'pathology', to the social and reference groups by which they coped with the work. The 'occupational culture' was the redoubt and resource of basic grade officers, the means

77

by which patterned adaptations to the role could be legitimated, and by which pathological adaptations (from the citizen's perspective) could be maintained. In a recent variant, it is argued that these occupational cultures are somewhat rank-specific, at least in that 'street' and 'management' police cultures can be discerned.

In order to appreciate routine police/public interaction, one must consider the degree of analytic purchase of these frameworks. This may be done by considering the implications of the theory of organisation for the study of occupational cultures, the mechanism of socialisation into culture, and the means by which culture members validate performance of the work that is distinctively theirs. The approach here self-consciously holds on one side the macro-level, socio-political forces which may impinge on police/public interaction by, for example, changes in the political economy of police resources arising from public pressure, changes in law and/or changes in the political sensitivities and projects of governing politicians. This is not to deny that these do have an impact, even on the practice of basic grade officers in the relatively autonomous setting of beat patrol. Where they resonate with such practice in a form that is empirically manifest, they must be acknowledged, but it would be retrograde to embark once again on the discovery of posited mental categories in the fashion of naive pathology models. In brief, the argument will be that the analytic frameworks mentioned above provide grounds for the postulation of plausible alternative interpretations of police/public interaction which (i) often work co-terminously; and (ii) can only be validated or dismissed in relation to concrete empirical episodes of practice.

Organisation theory and occupational culture

There is a fruitful analytic distinction to be made between formal and informal aspects of organisation. The fact that formal models do not square with what members actually do has led to descriptions of the informal organisation as a patchwork of unofficial work practices and norms (Blau and Scott, 1963). Formal rules have been shown to be the product of bargaining and conflict, and apparently rigid hierarchies of authority have been revealed as notional in the face of their circumvention by members granted various degrees of discretion. The rigidity of organisation charts reflects neither the reality of decision-making nor of supervision.

Yet is is also known that whether or not formal tenets pertain, they are thought to do so by members and clients. The rules may not always be followed, but this does not mean that action is not oriented to them. The range of accounts and interpretations members may draw on to validate action under the organisation is constrained by its explicit, formal 'charter'. Charter issues are implicit in and observably affect the numerous decisions on the exercise of discretion made by constables. Charters limit the legitimation of action by restricting the range of legitimisable discourse; only certain motives, justifications and kinds of evidence may be used. This function is evident on ceremonial occasions, in personnel evaluations, and when there are complaints against members. More pertinent to routine practice, organisational success is much to do with ability to think up accepted justifications for action, and control over the interpretation of charters and discourse expressing their meaning may be used to disbar particular motives, justifications and inferences. Nor is this merely a cynical perspective. It can be shown that officers invest meaning in the symbolism and imagery of the organisation. The imagery attaching to enforcement not only communicates instrumental messages but 'also expresses selves' (Manning, 1980, p.xii).

These points oblige one to consider the most fruitful way of understanding an organisation. Organisations essentially are to be understood as creations of their members and clients. In Bittner's approach the organisation's essence lies in its acting as a repository of approved vocabularies to permit organisational action: 'formal organisational designs are schemes of interpretation that competent and entitled users can invoke in yet unknown ways whenever it suits their purposes' (Bittner, 1965, pp.249-50). In Garfinkel's work, organisation is characterised as a set of ideas which enables one to think about the ways in which patterns of social action are related. The observable or palpable signs of the character of the organisation are the methodical procedures members use to organise their action in structurally meaningful units. 'Formal' and 'informal' organisation have life only in the member's usage. Structure is seen as changing and partial rather than absolute, people as creative choice-makers assessing meaning within a situated context, and conflict and change as enduring. The organisation is not a chart-like, rigid structure, but a set of symbols attributed by members to the collection of actions under it.

The guiding metaphor for the organisation's internal cohesion is 'loose coupling', indicating the inexact nature of relationships between intentions, actions and outcomes. However, members effectively reify their own positions within the organisation by playing roles oriented to various internal and external audiences. '[I]n attempting to maintain power and authority, they act as if the organisation and their positions within it are concrete' (Manning, 1980, p.20). This somewhat extends the perspective suggested by considering charter issues. Weick's notion of the 'enacted environment' refers not only to what is 'seen' but to the structure by which such a vision is possible (Weick, 1969).

The implication for understanding police/public encounters is that a sub-stantial system for assigning meaning and warranting action stands offstage, representing the officer as organisation member whose latitude for action is facilitated by some aspects of the organisation and inhibited by others. While some influences apply to all officers and can be mediated by occupational culture, others are matters of individual officers' biographies and career. That is, what dictates courses of action varies unpredictably; the key influence on a given occasion may lie with the organisation's rule for presenting and/or processing an intervention, or with the values of the officer, or with the officer's orientation to the occupational culture, or with the dictates of the situation at hand. Such lists are plausible but not exhaustive; mixed explanations, or the serial influence of several of them, or new influences altogether, may be germane.

Socialisation to culture

Van Maanen's terms for the stages of organisational socialisation are respect-ively 'choice', 'introduction', 'encounter' and 'metamorphosis', and it is important that the last stage is concerned with 'continuance' rather than the achievement of some end-state (van Maanen, 1974). For some time the key to police action was seen to lie in the informal culture of occupational reference groups, and its rising influence was documented during training. The power of attraction of police reference groups was particularly emphasised by Harris (1973). Novices were impelled towards other recruits for guidance and support in the face of 'administrative and job-related depersonalisation'. The recruit peer group helped them resist their conversion from individuals into 'personnel'. A second motivator was the ambiguity and ambivalence of the formal messages about the police role. The near-cosmic breadth of the role was daunting, while training concentrated on legal, not social, reality. Third, the reference group was a redoubt to assuage feelings of isolation, danger and low esteem generated by encounters with the public at its worst. Yet despite these plausible attractions, it is known that recruit peer groups are not maintained after training, or even throughout probation. Data from my study [1] of police training in Derbyshire, in which probationers were interviewed and completed survey questionnaires at induction, after 12 months and at the end of the probationary period (24 months), show that the influence of groups formed at regional training centre, force training establishment, and relationships with tutor constables all fade during probation, as experience increases (Fielding, 1987).

Further, in Reuss-Ianni's view, socialisation is but one of four 'domains' which pattern precinct-level social relations, each of which may serve as a node for the assembly of distinctive sub-cultures. The 'socialisation structure' is a mechanism for learning what the job is about in a particular command. Additionally, an 'authority/power structure' organises authority relations through the levels of the organisation, while a 'peer group structure' imparts culturally-sanctioned rules for peer mediated behaviour 'in street cop culture generally and in the specific variance of what culture found in different units' in the precinct. Finally, 'cross group structures' regulate inter-level interaction, including defining 'mediator roles' (Reuss-Ianni, 1983, p.9).

These considerations are important if one accepts that members do not treat their situation as something unique but use organising categories which are imported into it and which relate to the wider social context. Police are not disembodied and culture-free but are more, or less, imbued with values and norms evident in their milieux. The values and practices prevalent in police sub-cultures are not to be dismissed as false consciousness decanted into passive vessels but, in keeping with Cohen's original formulation, should be regarded as an adaptation to the circumstances of police work (Cohen, 1965). As Reiner asserts, recruits 'do not imbibe [sub-cultural values] like parrots but because it makes sense of their experiences' (Reiner, 1985, p.186). It is necessary not only to specify how recruits derive and modify that stock of cultural knowledge but how it is contextually produced. Culture is not a static entity. For example, gross changes in recruitment will manifest in changes in culture; this is clear if one considers the transformation of American urban policing by the large-scale recruitment of ethnic minority officers.

Cultures are not themselves encountered in fieldwork. Culture is the organisation which people share and that their activities constitute. One should not assume that cultures are integrated and distinct sets of rules investing action with meaning. Rather, one must demonstrate it. This must be done by reference to different instances of practice. The demonstration of culture hinges on the idea that members have no privileged status but can be treated as 'enquirers' into their cultural settings. Members must be treated as interpretive actors in their own right. The reach and play of culture varies.

Thus, one cannot 'read off' action from agencies of socialisation or from 'the occupational culture'. For example, van Maanen emphasises the impact of the recruit's first enforcement-related encounter, an occasion nearly every officer remembers (van Maanen, 1975). He suggests that the outcome of the encounter increases the salience of police reference groups. It acts as a catalyst that makes 'structural' factors, like social isolation, danger, role ambiguity, public hostility, depersonalisation and conflict with other agencies suddenly real and important. Yet it also increases the salience of situational features, alerting officers to the need to attune action to context. Indeed, these 'structural factors' are manifest only in a situated context. The more we acknowledge the volatile influence of situational context, the less 'structural' these factors seem. Any occupational culture acting as a buffer to cope with these role problems has to be plastic to adapt to the shifting context of police work. Then 'occupational culture' becomes such a slippery concept as to be analytically unhelpful, or the disjunction between its gross values and the nuances of on-street practice becomes so great that one must question its ability to bind.

The concept of occupational culture may be taken further, by arguing that the occupational culture is not itself undifferentiated but comprises several cultures formed around adjustments to the job. Thus the initial conception of a coherent source of formal socialisation and a solidary occupational culture supplying alternative, informal influences, may be refined. Data from my Derbyshire study of police training show the resilience of recruits and their capacity to resist as well as embrace the influences arising from informal and formal sources. The variety of adaptations to the bearing of this occupational role may be emphasised. For example, at induction some recruits showed awareness of a conflict between analytic and enforcement-related approaches to crime. Similar responses were recorded at induction, at year 1 and at year 2 to the idea that some offenders belong in hospitals not prisons, with about 40 per cent agreement and 40 per cent disagreement. One recruit commented:

> Vandalism and stuff like that is an odd thing. If you've got a mob of kids who go round smashing things up, get the same kids on their own and it's a different thing altogether. I'm not a sociologist sort of wallah, who says "it's the society" but you've got to realise . . . an element of it's true . . . I think their thinking's . . . gone too far one way . . . and somehow you've got to combine the two. It's difficult because it's all these different factions fighting against each other instead of helping. You've got the sociologists and the social workers at one end of the scale, and there's never any getting together and both sides admitting that there might be a centre point.

In analysing changes in job perspectives the sense of contingency should be preserved. The occupation presents a range of conflicting influences, from formal rules to the core values of occupational culture, but the officer is the final arbiter.

Van Maanen and others argue that, rather than their background, the chief influence on recruits is their current experience of the work, and especially the culture generated by the police to cope with it. 'Consequently the police culture can be viewed as molding the attitudes - with numbing regularity - of virtually all who enter' (van Maanen, 1975, p.215). Whether the 'molding of attitudes' necessarily results in a patterning of all the officer's subsequent action is another matter. All that the emphasis on work-based culture implies is that priority is given to influences arising from the work setting rather than the officer's biography. Indeed, decisions made on individual grounds, divergent from the values of occupational culture, are necessarily less visible. They are likely to be taken when the officer is alone. It is relatively easy to document the influence of others on an individual's action but perhaps only from reflexive eye-witness accounts, like those by police-turned-researchers, does one get a sense of the individual standing against the prevailing norms of the occupational culture.

There is certainly a disparity between the work police draw on for occupational imagery and the mundane reality of police work. Manning and van Maanen note 'the police are evaluated, and evaluate themselves, against functions they rarely perform (arrest and crime control), deny the reality of functions they frequently perform, and do not take credit for many of their functions which are very significant to their public' (Manning and van Maanen, 1978, pp.5-6). When Cruse and Rubin observed 1,059 police/citizen interactions they found 'a wide difference between attitude and behaviour, particularly in racial differences and attitudes. That is, while policemen might express highly prejudiced attitudes, they were rated as having behaved in an even-handed fashion with citizens' (Cruse and Rubin, 1973).

There is no doubt that police hold strong views on many issues, but the nub of the matter is their relevance to actual behaviour. Both the old arguments about the (pathological) police personality and the current conventional logic that the occupational culture limits in a quite rigid way what officers 'may' think, err in favouring a form of determinism that belittles the importance of the person's experience of the work. Individuals' interpretive efforts, seeking to resolve the lessons of experience against a backcloth of occupational culture and the particular station and shift they work, are too little acknowledged.

This is to emphasise that officers experience the organisation and its work differently. The situations to which they respond according to their resources of motivation and commitment vary both by their location in the organisation and in different regions having different communities making different demands on the police. The picture is more complicated still. The circumstances that call forth particular performances by officers are explicable only by reference to the situated context of the discrete episodes of practice in which they occur. What makes for 'competence' in a given situation depends on the perspective of the audience regarding the episode (Fielding, 1984). The officer's orientation to the most significant audience having regard to the specific features of that occasion closely affects the conduct of the episode. Because of the paradox of discretion in police work (those lowest in the organisation have most discretion), that audience is often citizens and other beat officers, not supervisors.

Social scientists no longer characterise police as belonging to a discrete personality category; the ghost of the 'police personality' has more or less been laid. However, some consistencies of practice are discernible. The result has been the generation of 'typologies' of police adaptations to the role. These are of undoubted analytic utility. Officers do display features of a consistent adaptation to their status in the (local) organisation, and they do bear attitudes in a coherent fashion over time. The problem with typologies is that people tend to convert the categories into stereotypes. Systematicity can rigidify the types and actually narrow the accuracy of one's perception. It is unwise to expect that the 'types' specified will behave the same way in regard to comparable interventions time and again, because of the volatility of the context-bound situations with which they are dealing. To allude to one famous typology (Reiner, 1978), there will be occasions when even the 'uniform carrier' will take positive action and when even the 'new centurion' will refrain from action. The typologies so far proposed may be adequate in their reference to officers' adaptation to their role and status intra-organisationally but may not bear so directly on their action on the street.

Culture and accounts of practice

Constraints on one's ability to understand police/public encounters either from the perspective of formal organisation, legal reality, police personality or occupational culture have been indicated. The present approach to culture, and the method for studying it, imply that regarding the matter from the stance of officers themselves may be helpful. It is from this perspective that one might appreciate the rhetorical practices of officers in accounting for their work. If it is accepted that officers are the arbiters of the various potential influences on their action in encounters with citizens, analysis of the rhetoric they employ in describing it offers insight into the sense of option and constraint they bear. During training these matters are explicit and immediately pertinent to novice officers.

Officers' ability to achieve unremarked use of rhetoric appropriate to particular situations relies on their range of experience. They have to sense the kinds of actions and justifications appropriate on the experiential basis of those they have already met. As operational service increases, the influence of formal training recedes and the importance of knowing how to proceed behaviourally in public encounters becomes a central preoccupation. Officers recognise that gaps in their knowledge of law can be compensated by adroitness in handling citizens within the confines of the encounter itself.

Guided by the dictates of the moment to control the situation and if possible resolve it, the police are encouraged by their wide responsibilities to intervene. These contingencies make an ability to maintain the propriety of an intervention a crucial skill, relevant both intra-organisationally and in dealing with the public. Officers' training obliges them to recognise they cannot expect to learn all the law there is to know and that full enforcement is not a realistic prospect. Beginning from an assumption of selectivity encourages officers to see law as the final resource, to secure compliance when efforts to resolve the situation within its own terms fail. Enforcement is interpretive work, and even the strongest 'by the book' officer cannot escape the large measure of negotiation fundamental to it.

These negotiated features do not deny the element of power that police can deploy in encounters with the public. But there is evidence that even probationers become sensitive to the need to use power in an under-stated, finely tuned way:

> You try and be nice to the yobs and then they start. Everyone does it, they go out onto the beat and instead of telling these yobs to get out they talk to them and the next night they take it out of you . . . They've got over you, they've beaten your authority down . . . With most people, being polite you see, having a bit of respect for them does work, they have respect for you back. But some of them just take advantage of you being pleasant to them . . . You try to help them out almost, but if they rebuke you there's nothing further you can do and then you have to talk a bit more firmer than you usually would to get them back into line. (Interview at 12 month stage.)

The extract displays an orientation to an incremental escalation in the use of physical force.

Youths pose a particularly troublesome group to probationers. Adolescent youths can be puzzling for probationers barely older than they are. Youth provides no automatic insight into youth, and a strict upbringing can actually blind the officer to comprehension of youths' perspective. Further, unlike blacks, the case of white youths obliges young officers to confront the fact that similarity does not necessarily make for insight. It forces them to confront the social consequences of going into uniform:

> Whether they're delinquents or not, some people you speak to, especially juveniles and young persons, they've no respect whatsoever . . . You can't do anything about it. It often makes me think if they are like that what's the point in taking them home to their parents . . . I wasn't like that you see, and my parents were never disrespectful. I can only reflect on how my life was and my parents brought me up. My father, he never brought me up with a rod of iron but he let it be known that if I ever brought trouble home I'd be for it. (Interview at 12 month stage.)

One has better information on oneself from a knowledge of one's own biography than about anyone else. Insight into one's own motives and how these are best realised by pursuing particular interactional strategies in a situated context can initiate learning of the skill of making plausible interpretations. The ability to orient one's own performance to what are perceived as the dictates of the situation is the initial step in appreciating the influence of how one proceeds on the outcome of encounters with citizens. Accurate short or long-term prediction relies on the adequacy of one's analysis of the situation. This interpretive project is continually being refined by officers, on and off the job. It is not just to do with regulating order but with gleaning information and cultivating contacts. The novice's becoming alert to and refining these matters of deportment, conversational style and interpretive insight is dictated by practical requirements of the everyday working situation as well as the goal of securing confirmation as a constable. This process having been begun, it is a much more straightforward and immediate corollary also to become interested in how other parties to interaction proceed.

Readily endorsed in the rhetoric, but also genuinely emphasised, is a willingness to receive information and cultivate local contacts. Its appeal is demonstrably genuine because it is not only a continually-expressed motive in joining but the corollary of uniformed patrol's preventive function, receiving support from supervisors, occupational culture, and contemporary managerial rhetoric. Crime prevention, the officer's personal security and the cultivation of amiable, informative local contacts are interrelated. A former military policeman recruited to Derbyshire declared:

> No, [police work is] not just [to do] with crime. You've still got your building up a good relationship with the public . . . Good example is Northern Ireland, where the RUC wouldn't go into the Republican estates, we [military police] would. We would stop and talk to the people, we would gain their confidence and therefore we got respect off them where the RUC didn't. ᐯA lot of the work is public relations for the man on the beat. (Interview at induction.)

The officer's sense of 'public relations' bears little resemblance to the work of public relations officers but addresses goals and techniques the recruit's cultural apparatus gives him no other way of expressing.

This image of the work is strong enough to countermand the predilection to control by force one might anticipate on the part of recruits:

> The British policeman has got a reputation throughout the world. He's respected and he's admired basically because he's not armed. He depends a great deal on his tact and diplomacy. It doesn't always work and there's times when he must be armed for his own safety and the safety of

others . . . I dread the day when a superior officer says "You will be armed". (Interview at induction.)

Insight into the centrality of this 'public relations' element of the work generally arises from considering one's own performance of police duties in relation to one's own biography, often drawing on one's early experiences of the police. At induction 39 per cent of recruits picked 'military' as most like policing, with 'public relations officer' a close second at 36 per cent. 'Social worker' was seen as most like policing by 17 per cent, but 'teacher' claimed only two per cent of responses. However, at the 12 month stage, 'public relations' maintained a leading position, followed by 'military' (which fell to 29 per cent), while 'social worker' fell to eight per cent and 'teacher' rose to twelve per cent. As experience increases, the importance of 'public relations' undergoes a translation of emphasis. It becomes more subtly defined, more specific, and the novice begins to distinguish accomplished skills from those yet to be achieved. 'Public relations' is no longer a generalised catchphrase but a term for the clever performance of routine interaction. Officers come to appreciate the need to recognise that people have different perspectives and interpretive frames:

> That comes from realising that there's people and they've got to be thought of. You learn that, and that's quite a basic training, strangely enough. You learn that there's a way of talking to people, and attitudes, and fortunately I had some of it and I picked some of it up very quickly. Some of the younger ones don't. (Interview at 12 month stage.)

Officers also become aware that the cooperation of the public cannot be assumed but depends on the officer's personal qualities, the character of local law enforcement and so on. Probationers observably express the idea of 'balance' in relation to their enforcement efforts:

> Sometimes (where) you "do" a traffic offence they think "Why do the police bother with this?" so sometimes it gets through to you. You think it's not very good public relations, not really what you're there for in one sense . . . You're trying to get through to the public and ask them to help you and then you put a ticket on somebody's car and you think "Are they going to help me if I'm getting some hassle over the road or are they going to accept it as part of your job?" (Interview at 24 month stage.)

What the officer does here is to regard his own image as 'constable' by casting it in the eyes of members of the public. Recognising that some people resent enforcement, he seriously examines the consequences for his own role image of their view of the situation. The gain from public support may exceed that from 'by the book' enforcement. Such views chart a growing awareness that police work is not only reliant on good information but involves a reciprocal relationship. The favours the constable can give are considerable, from acting as sympathetic listener to ignoring certain infractions.

After doing the work during their probationary service, constables are demonstrably able to specify the way that interaction with the public can bear desired results if it is skilfully managed. In this case a constable retails his version of the ploy of pretending to a little information to get a big return, which he describes as one of the most satisfying aspects of the work:

> If you bring a chap in and you're on a wing and a prayer, you don't know if you've got a case, and blow me, he tells you everything that you didn't ever dream existed, you didn't even know it happened . . . that is a great deal of satisfaction. Knowing that in spite of your lack of equipment and, come to that, your educational qualifications, you cleared this one up . . . that is the best part of the job. (Interview at 12 month stage.)

85

The constable derives satisfaction from subtle skills of impression-management, interpretation and communication.

Yet the satisfactions from engaging in the kind of enforcement work that can be carried out if one has the 'in' afforded by good local knowledge are bought at the expense of sustaining the reciprocal relationship. Not only is there effort in servicing the relationship, work is generated by one's calculated approachability:

> I get bombarded with questions on law and "How do I solve this problem?" every time I go for a drink. It's like if you're a dentist or a doctor. But by the same token, three or four weeks later they'll come up to me and say "Here, have you heard this?" And people are almost naughty, they're worse than policemen actually - "Mrs Jones' [car] tax has run out. Did you know?" Now I tend to use this on occasions, I'll be honest. If it's necessary I take some course of action, but by people knowing who you are they can choose whether they drink with you or not. And you gain a lot that you wouldn't gain otherwise . . . But the only other thing is that you gain pressure as well. (ibid.)

It is also relevant that officers recognise that these skills take time to achieve. Those who seek this expertise explicitly orient their activity to the stance of those who represent the desirable skills:

> A chap that's done seven years . . . has got not just the knowledge of the law which the chap in the college would have got, but the application of it to the practical situation and even the small duty of talking to people, communicating. It's not quite the same as in the classroom. You talk to all sorts of different characters and after the years you get to judge what somebody's like after you've had just two or three sentences with him, and yet, as well as just listening to them, you [are] . . . thinking of what you are going to ask him next . . . It's all this as well as the application of the law, thinking about the law and bringing it out like that, [in] which you need some practical experience. (Interview at 12 month stage.)

Officers' talk about competent practice reveals their awareness that it requires socialisation not only to formal rules but to situated knowledge and to linguistic and para-linguistic devices which facilitate interaction. The origin of the warrant for action is not just in the occupational culture, nor the formal rules rendered by means of a structure of supervision. A naive emphasis on the autonomy of police constables, based in analyses of the assuredly great discretion of the ranks, ignores the manner in which adequate justifications for courses of action are embedded in the dialectic between formal definitions of legitimate practice and informal work practices. The organisation affords members a semiotic system which is available for creative use, but the vagueness of the linkage between environment and organisation implies that external events and formal structures cannot account for 'behavioural output'. Rather, the prevailing environment can be known only as an image which is perceived or enacted in the rhetoric and practices of members. The strategic data are therefore in the moments of officers' discourse where they proffer accounts of action oriented to the achievement of specific goals. Lawyers sometimes mutter that hard cases make bad law. Social scientists cannot afford to take the same stance towards the complexity of empirical data. Appreciation of the course of police/public interactions enjoins an analytic framework sensitive to the delicate and continual interplay of formal organisational charter, local variants of occupational culture, and officers' own experience.

Note

[1]   The research was funded by the Economic and Social Research Council (ESRC) (reference number: C/00/23/008/1). The author is grateful for comments on earlier drafts by Professors Michael Agar and Peter Manning.

References

Bittner, E., (1965) 'The concept of organisation', Social Research, 32, 239-55
Blau, P. and Scott, M., (1963) Formal organisations: a comparative approach, Routledge and Kegan Paul, London
Cohen, A., (1965) Delinquent boys, Prentice Hall, New Jersey
Cruse, D. and Rubin, J., (1973) 'Police behaviour: part I', Journal of Psychiatry and Law, 1, 18-19
Fielding, N.G., (1984) 'Police socialisation and police competence', British Journal of Sociology, 35, 4, 568-90
Fielding, N.G., (1987) Joining forces: police training, socialisation and occupational competence, Tavistock, London
Harris, R., (1973) The police academy: an inside view, Wiley, New York
Manning, P.K., (1980) The narcs' game, MIT Press, Cambridge, Mass
Manning, P.K. and van Maanen, J., (1978) 'Background to policing', in Manning, P.K. and van Maanen, J. (eds), Policing: a view from the streets, Goodyear, Santa Monica, California
Reiner, R., (1978) The blue-coated worker, Cambridge University Press, Cambridge
Reiner, R., (1985) 'Police and race relations', in Baxter, J. and Koffman, L., Police. The constitution and the community, Professional Books, Abingdon
Reuss-Ianni, E., (1983) Two cultures of policing, Transaction, London
van Maanen, J., (1974) 'Working the street: a developmental view of police behaviour', in Jacobs, H. (ed.), The potential for reform of criminal justice, Sage, Beverly Hills
van Maanen, J., (1975) 'Police socialization: a longitudinal examination of job attitudes in an urban police department', Admin.Science Quarterly, 20, 207- 28
Weick, K., (1969) The social psychology of organising, Addison Wesley, Reading

7 Avoiding trouble: the patrol officer's perception of encounters with the public

CLIVE NORRIS

Introduction

It is the contention of this paper that to understand and explain police behaviour it is necessary to examine how the police patrol task is constructed by the organisational actors. This approach implies a partial rejection of much of the sociology of police work. Like sociology in general, a significant part of the sociology of the police has taken as its raison d'etre the discovery of law-like generalisations to explain the effect of invidual police officer decisions, particularly in relation to the decision to arrest.

Previous research has focused in the main on three sets of variables which were presumed to explain officer behaviour. These can be categorised as individual, situational and organisational explanations (Friedrich, 1977). At the individual level, officer characteristics have been presumed important in the determination of arrest practice. Therefore age, sex, race, class, educational attainment and length of service have all been analysed in relation to the decision to arrest (Forst, Lucianovic and Cox, 1977; Friedrich, 1977; White and Bloch, 1975; Policy Studies Institute (PSI), 1983 vol.III). At the situational level, location, legal seriousness, suspect's characteristics, the presence or absence of bystanders, and whether the police were acting reactively or proactively have all been measured as determinants of arrest practice (Black, 1980; Black and Reiss, 1967; Bogomolny, 1976; Lundman, 1974; Friedrich, 1977; Pilliavin and Briar, 1964; Smith and Visher, 1981). Organisational factors such as the style of policing in an area, the nature of the patrol organisation and the nature of supervision have been analysed in relation to arrest behaviours, detection rate, and the police use of force (Toch, Grant and Galvin, 1975; Kelling et al., 1974; Fyfe, 1982).

One problem with these studies of police/public interaction has been their lack of explanatory power (cf Sherman, 1980). Part of this is due to the lack of methodological sophistication, with many studies testing only for bivariate relationships. However, even Friedrich's sophisticated analysis, based on the Black/Reiss data and using regression to measure the effect of more than one variable on arrest decisions, could only account for 25 per cent of the variance.

One of the key problems with the above studies is that they fail to appreciate organisational and occupational constraints which shape decision-making. The decisions taken by a patrol officer when dealing with the people involved in an incident are not based on a neutral reading of the classical sociological variables of age, sex, race and class, or indeed more relevant variables such as suspect's demeanour or the legal seriousness of the offence. Instead they are filtered through an occupational lens, which refocuses the patrol officer's perspective on more immediately relevant and practical concerns.

But if quantitative sociology has failed to explain officer behaviour, so too have the interactionists. The interactionists may have uncovered the occupational and organisational milieu of policing but, with the exception of Chatterton (1983), there has been little systematic attempt to widen the perspective and to indicate how this affects relationships on the street. While quantitative sociology has not appreciated the relevance and inter-relatedness of these factors, qualitative sociology has failed to exploit them. What goes on in the street cannot be divorced from what happens within the station, particularly how supervisory officers and peers constrain and sanction various actions. It is therefore necessary to examine both the organisational and occupational milieux in which the task of policing is constructed, and it is to this that we now turn.

Culture and autonomy

The patrol task is structured and ordered through the interaction between the organisation, occupation and environment in which it is located, which give rise to the peculiar configuration of working rules that are contained in the occupational culture. The ascendancy of the occupational culture over other forms of influence arises from the paradox that, in police work, discretion tends to increase towards the bottom of the hierarchy. Indeed, the perennial problem for the police manager is how to control the lower ranks. Even under the 'fixed point' system discussed by Chatterton (1979), there were considerable opportunities for easing behaviour which, as he illustrated, were tolerated as long as officers were covered by a 'good story' if something should go wrong and they should be called to account. James' study (1979) illustrated how senior managers responded to rising levels of street crime by setting up a specialist squad to operate in accordance with the professional ethos of senior management. Within a matter of months, however, the squad had managed to subvert the organisational goal of professional policing and replace it with practical policing.

Patrol officers' autonomy is compounded by three factors outlined in the PSI report. First, frontline supervisors do not see it as their job to interfere on the level of the street activities of their officers. Second, senior managers, i.e. inspectors and above, rarely stay at a station for more than two years so that there is little time to build up a team, comprehensive objectives and personnel management. Third, PCs are therefore taught by other PCs and informal work practices are passed on through the peer group rather than the organisation. (Policy Studies Institute, 1983, vol.IV, p.274ff.)

The problem of supervision is not just a technical matter, but relates to the legal position of the constable. Police constables are legally autonomous and therefore their immediate superiors cannot instruct them as to precisely what to do in a given situation, since discretion is an integral part of the office. Supervisors can and do suggest to their officers that they deal with a situation in a particular way, they can recommend and cajole and they can threaten officers with formal and informal organisational sanctions. However, as Chatterton has shown, 'a PC could legitimately respond, "Sorry, Sergeant. That may be your way of dealing with such an incident but the way I did it was just as good"' (Chatterton, 1981, p.26).

Finally, the ascendancy of the occupational culture is given further weight by the nature of the work that officers deal with. Most situations are not one-dimensional, but are ambiguous and confusing, open to various interpretations. Police work is always situationally contingent. This is reflected in the organisational mandate. There are rules about dress, courtesy, conduct, etc., but these do not dictate how officers should or should not act in a given situation. Police work continually involves discretion (Lambert, 1970), and the practice of policing evolves as the structure of each particular interaction unfolds (van Maanen, 1978, p.224ff).

Culture and uncertainty

The patrol officer's decision to act in particular circumstances is therefore affected by a situationally informed, culturally defined reading of organisation-ally and legally prescribed 'rules'. The principal concern of the officer is the avoidance of negative sanctions, either from the organisation, in the form of disciplinary proceedings or the loss of perks; or from the public, in terms of challenges to authority which entail physical or psychological harm. Skolnick brilliantly integrated police culture with the level of psychological motivation in his chapter on the working personality of the police officer (Skolnick, 1966). He relates this to two principal variables: 'danger and authority which should be interpreted in the light of a constant pressure to appear efficient' (op.cit., p.44).

Following Skolnick, Chatterton argues that the two primary concerns of officers when dealing with a specific incident are the avoidance of 'within-the-job' trouble and 'on-the-job' trouble (Chatterton, 1978, 1981). Within-the-job trouble 'is bound up with the relationship between patrol personnel and their superiors in the organisation' (Chatterton, 1978, p.49), such that the lower ranks are 'concerned that any information about them received by higher level officers project[s] a favourable impression and at least [does] not damage their reputa-tions' (Chatterton, 1983, p.201). On-the-job trouble, on the other hand, arises from the environment that patrol officers police and the relationship between themselves and the various publics on a division that they encounter. As Chatterton notes:

> The decisions and actions taken at incidents reflect the concern to control relationships between themselves and the various publics on a division, to maintain their capacity to intervene authoritatively in any incident and to preserve their own and others' beliefs that they were 'on top of the area'. (Chatterton, 1981, p.208)

In reactive policing especially, this problem of control is heightened by informational uncertainty. A 'fight' to which a patrol officer is sent may be youthful pranks; a 'domestic' usually involves only tongues, but sometimes knives.

On arrival at the incident a message has to be situationally reinterpreted with reference to location, the actors involved and other available sense data.

One of the consequences of such informational uncertainty is the perceptual heightening of the threat of danger and violence related to on-the-job trouble. It gives rise to what Manning (1977) has termed the 'threat-danger-hero' notion of police work and the development of a set of working rules which classifies various groups and classes as more dangerous than others. In Skolnick's terms, police officers develop a shorthand classification of people who represent 'symbolic assailants'. Thus he writes:

> The policeman, because his work requires him to be occupied continually with potential violence develops a perceptual shorthand to identify certain types of people as symbolic assailants, that is persons who use gesture, language and attire that the policeman has come to recognise as a prelude to violence. (Skolnick, 1966, p.45)

As Holdaway has shown, in Britain the category of 'symbolic assailant' is extended to include not just those who threaten the police with potential violence but also those who, because of their authority or status, can challenge or disarm police authority (Holdaway, 1983, ch.6). Lawyers, doctors and social workers fall into the category of 'challengers', while women and children are 'disarmers'.

The consequences and correlates of uncertainty relate to the problem of on-the-job trouble that the patrol officer faces. It is arguable, however, that the most important aspect of uncertainty facing the patrol officer stems from the internal organisation of policing rather than the external environment. Within-the-job trouble primarily results from the fact that the police officer 'can never be absolutely certain that the action taken in a particular situation will later prove to be the most effective way of handling the situation' (Chatterton, 1978, p.49). As the PSI report makes plain, within the organisation rules operate in an almost entirely negative fashion: they are inhibitory rules. However, due to the nature of supervision, the enforcement of such rules is almost entirely retrospective. It is related to paperwork, or the account of action, rather than the action itself. Inhibitory rules are not 'internalised but are taken into account when deciding how to act in case they should be caught and the rule invoked against them (Policy Studies Institute, 1983, vol.IV, p.171).

Proverbially, the lower ranks' assertion that 'You can't police by the book' results in the fact that 'You're always in the shit'. While the organisation is prepared to condone rule breaking as long as everything goes smoothly, if a complaint is received or something should go wrong then a multitude of inhibitory rules can be used to bring someone to account.

This uncertainty is increased rather than decreased by the contradiction between the rhetoric and the reality of law and police operational guidelines laid down in the Judges' Rules. In practice the law often favours crime control rather than due process (McBarnet, 1979, 1981). Thus, while many police researchers have described the rule-breaking and illegality of the rank-and-file practices, McBarnet carefully illustrates how such practices are enshrined in ad hoc case law (McBarnet, 1981, ch.3). The consequence is that:

> Front men like the police become the 'fall guys' of the criminal justice system taking the blame for any injustices in the operation of law, both in theory and . . . indeed in law. The law holds individual policemen personally responsible for the contraventions of legality that are successfully sued,

while at the same time refusing to make clear until after the event exactly what the police are supposed to do. (McBarnet, 1981, p.156)

The uncertainty faced by the lower ranks results in the need to control as much information as possible. Their freedom from direct supervision creates the climate where information management is made possible. Organisational sanction results primarily from indirect information in the form of paperwork, gossip, or a public complaint. By selectively filtering and laundering information, the patrol officer is able to lessen the risk of in-the-job trouble.

The control of information has various ramifications. If the police organisation both condemns and condones primary deviations, the result is to engender secondary deviations in the form of peer group solidarity which makes secrecy and the control of information possible. Thus the solidarity which results from the external aspects of the job (cf Westley, 1970, ch.3), for example the threat of physical harm, is strengthened by internal contradictions. Peer group solidarity is directed as much against the organisation as the environment. In Westley's, admittedly small, sample of 15 officers, 11 would not 'shop' another officer for stealing and 10 would perjure themselves to protect the offender.

Culture and socialisation

As with all organisations, the factor which separates the new recruit from the old-timer is the ability to articulate actions in the light of a situationally relevant reading of organisational rules and procedures. Organisational rules are not merely transposed from theory to practice, they are mediated at various levels which transform their meaning and import. While the formal organisation gives rise to a set of rules for both practice and justification, the appropriate invocation of rules requires a second-order system. There must be rules for using the rules. This second-order rule system derives from the organisational culture and is transmitted during a period of occupational socialisation which new recruits must undergo to gain the social knowledge and skills necessary to assume an organisational role (van Maanen and Schien, 1979, p.211). This requires a particular reading of organisational life because, implicitly, it places the concept of culture as the central feature of organisational analysis (Astley and van de Ven, 1983). Culture is a universal human phenomenon. However, its particular configuration results from the peculiar problems that differing social groups face. As Ford (1942) suggests, 'culture is a traditional way of solving problems' or a 'learned solution to problems', and a major application of this perspective has been recent organisational studies. Smircich (1983a) illustrates that organisational analysis has been influenced by five major perspectives of culture. In a later paper, she proposes the following definition of organisational cultures:

> The emergence of social organisations depends on the emergence of shared interpretive schemas, expressed in language and other symbolic constructions that develop through social interaction. Such schemas provide the basis for shared systems of meaning that allow day to day activities to become routinized or taken for granted. (Smircich, 1983b, p.160)

Organisational reality is then constructed individually and through social interaction and members actively participate in the creation and recreation of meaning. In the light of this, Smircich reminds us that 'human actors do not know or perceive the world, but know and perceive their world through the medium of culturally specific frames of reference' (Smircich, 1983b, p.161). It cannot be assumed that the organisation has homogeneous structures of meaning which inform and guide action. Organisational managers, for instance, do not have a monopoly on the development of meaning, although they often act as if they do. Others in the organisation are also active in producing and shaping organisational reality through the meanings and interpretations that they bring to their work world. Indeed, in hierarchical organisations there is a greater likelihood of a disjunction between the two: 'Thus the organisational strategy favoured by a dominant coalition may be countered by rival frames of reference and poorly implemented by accident or design (ibid.). This is highly pertinent to police organisations and it is therefore necessary to examine the way in which the peculiar problems faced by the lower ranks gives rise to a patterned and culturally held solution which informs the everyday practice of policing.

Language and culture

The occupational relevances of patrol officers cannot be derived from the organisational rhetoric of crime fighting since the latter is of limited applicability to the reality of routine patrol. Nor can they be derived from the organisational rule-book. To uncover such meanings it is necessary to examine 'the variety of practices and mundane considerations involved in the determination of the occupational meaning and situational relevance of policies and procedures for ongoing, everyday organisational activities' (Zimmerman, 1970, p.222).

It is here that the category of language provides a useful tool for the grounding of a shared meaning system. If a vocabulary has wide acceptance within a particular segment of an organisation, then it can give very strong clues as to the key concerns of the members of that segment. Sacks' (1963) and Garfinkle's (1967) work is relevant here. For organisational members to be able to use a vocabulary correctly, it is necessary for them to understand the rules that occasion its use. Successful communication requires a shared frame of reference. Manning, following Cicourel, puts it thus:

> The assumption that everybody knows the referent of certain categories and the means by which they are linked to a population is the basis of normal use and, by contrast, abnormal use. Both hearer and listener are able to put conversations together by means of these induced rules of conversations. (Manning, 1970, p.254)

Language provides the basis for the development of shared meaning systems and therefore reflects the situational relevances of particular groups. Within funeral directing (Unruh, 1979), the mining industry (Fitzpatrick, 1980) or medicine (Becker et al., 1961) there exists a specific occupational argot and, as Manning notes, it

> contains the information necessary for dealing with the problems of the organisation. As these are faced, role terms, role imputations and typifications arise and have with them sets of acceptable referents. (Manning, 1970, p.225)

Within any organisational language there is both a vocabulary and a grammar (cf Burke, 1945; Mills, 1940; Taylor, 1979). The vocabulary provides the distinct and discrete elements which locate people and behaviours that are occupationally and organisationally relevant. However, an organisational argot performs a wider role than merely the naming of things, it is also a vocabulary of motive. As Gerth and Mills argue:

> A motive is a term in a vocabulary which appears to the actor himself and/or to the observer to be an adequate reason for his conduct. This conception grasps the intrinsically social character of motivation: a

94

satisfactory or adequate motive is one that satisfies those who question some act or program, whether the actor questions his own or another's conduct. The words which may fulfil this function are limited to the vocabulary of motives acceptable for given situations by given social circles. (Gerth and Mills, 1965, p.116)

By focusing on the vocabulary which officers use to talk to each other about their work, we are thus able to explore the way in which patrol officers construct their everyday work world.

However it is necessary to move beyond merely analysing the content of the vocabulary and to articulate the grammar which provides the connection between the (sometimes) seemingly isolated items within the vocabulary. The task of the analyst is, therefore, both to record and describe the language in use in its natural setting and the behaviours which accompany it, and further to develop a meta-language which enables the researcher 'to talk about the language actors use to talk about their roles and the appropriate use within the setting' (Manning, 1970, p.256).

The terms of trouble

Within the police culture, there is a highly developed occupational vocabulary (part of which is reproduced below). It is apparent from an examination of the terms that they are derived from neither the legal discourse of judicial language nor from the formal concerns of the police organisation. Rather they have as their referents the practical and day-to-day problems which patrol officers face as a result of their routine interactions with the public.

At first sight, the terms seem little more than a colourful, yet rather vague and arbitrary slang:

'street justice'	'pear-shaped'	'umbrellas'
'come back at you'	'out of order'	'banana-shaped'
'went apeshit'	'over the top'	'bollocking'
'lost his bottle'	'a 612'	'Jackanory'
'a good kicking'	'bent'	'bottle'
'summary justice'	'stuck on'	'story-time'
'threw a wobbly'	'taking the mickey'	'griefy'

Most of the terms are not unique to the police; they are borrowed from the wider culture. However, their meaning and import is subtly reworked and transformed to provide a wide and rich vocabulary. While each term is interesting in its own right, taken as a whole, correct usage in the organisational setting is reliant on an underlying grammar which structures and orders the use of the vocabulary. For instance, what do 'over the top', 'story-time' and 'bent' have in common? Or, for that matter, 'taking the mickey', 'Jackanory' and 'griefy'? It is to an attempt to try and answer this question that I now want to turn.

If one takes seriously Chatterton's claim that the primary concern of patrol officers when dealing with an incident is the avoidance of 'within-the-job' and 'on-the-job' trouble, then it becomes readily apparent what the terms are referring to. They are all actions on the part of the police or the public that are related to the problem of 'trouble'. Furthermore, the terms can be broken down into three distinct categories: those that refer to behaviours that are indicative of trouble; the strategies that officers use to avoid on-the-job and in-the-job trouble; and the organisational consequences of not avoiding trouble. Thus:

The vocabulary and grammar of trouble

Behaviours	Strategies	Consequences
went apeshit	umbrellas	pear-shaped
threw a wobbly	Jackanory	banana-shaped
taking the mickey	story-time	bent
over the top	bottle	griefy
lost his bottle	street justice	bollocking
out of order	summary justice	come back at you
	a good kicking	a 612
		stuck on

It is now necessary to examine each of the terms separately, to unpack their meaning and show how they frame officers' perceptions of the people and incidents that they deal with. The discussion will draw on fieldwork I undertook between March 1983 and December 1984 in three contrasting police divisions in one metropolitan and one county force. Over 40 officers were accompanied on patrol in cars and on foot.

Behaviours that are indicative of trouble

The terms 'throwing a wobbly' and 'going apeshit' refer to those behaviours that are potentially the most troublesome for officers. They do not refer to the rough and tumble of the ordinary street tussle or of someone trying to resist arrest by being aggressive or non-cooperative. Rather, they refer to uncontrolled violent behaviour, such as frenzied kicking, biting, scratching, punching and flailing, which necessitates the use of force to quell. When people are in such a state it is extremely difficult to control them. Consider the following example of a woman who is being arrested after going berserk in a public library and smashing up the reception area.

> The woman was dragged to the back of the van, still struggling and screaming. A crowd of about fifteen or twenty people had gathered loosely around the forecourt of the library. The distance from the ground to the back of the van is some two feet, and it was extremely difficult to get the struggling woman into the back. The four of us (three PCs and myself) held her and forced her into the back of the van. She sprang out again. She was held by the neck, arms and middle, lifted up into the air, struggling all the way, and pushed further into the van. PC A and PC B collapsed around her to stop her struggling in the confines of the van. 'Don't you bite me!' ordered PC B as he grabbed her hair to avert the sinking teeth. 'Get some cuffs' suggested B. 'I haven't got any', replied A, still trying to contain the writhing body. 'Take them off me then'. B was restraining her legs, A her arms and I her middle. A managed to retrieve the handcuffs from B's belt. The woman started to scream and thrash hysterically as A struggled to get the handcuffs on her. Finally they were securely on, and she remained in an ungainly heap on the floor of the van with three pairs of hands restraining her movements.

Such behaviours present officers with several inter-related problems with regard to competent practice. It is generally understood by their sergeants and peers that people go 'completely apeshit' for no apparent reason. However, it is equally recognised that successful policing requires the handling of such situations so that officers maintain their control without recourse to excessive force.

When a person goes 'apeshit', this represents the officer's loss of control. Although it is to be expected in isolated incidents, if officers have a reputation for prisoners going 'apeshit' on them, then questions will be raised about their ability to handle people. Officers are keenly aware that seemingly trivial incidents and comments can provoke a prisoner and make him or her less amenable to control:

> After arresting three shoplifters, and having placed them in the back of the Panda, PC C called back to the station to report to the sergeant that he had 'three coming in'. He explained to me later that he never calls them 'prisoners, 'cos that really winds them up'.

Not only does someone 'going apeshit' represent a threat to officers' competence, but also to their physical well-being. As the first example showed, when people go berserk they mobilise enormous reserves of strength. Indeed, during my first week of fieldwork, a station sergeant was questioning a prisoner who 'threw a wobbly'. In the ensuing fracas the sergeant was seriously injured and hospitalised for three weeks. In spite of the occupational necessity of controlling violent and aggressive people, the police are not routinely taught how to control berserk people. Generally, if someone does go berserk, particularly in the station, everybody 'bundles in'. The principle seems to be that sheer weight of numbers will literally crush opposition.

The problem with such a strategy is that it is unpredictable in its outcome. The prisoner may suffer injuries which could result in the need for hospitalisation and possibly result in the officers being charged with assault.

If 'throwing a wobbly' and 'going apeshit' represent physical challenges to the officer's authority, then 'taking the mickey' is the term for symbolic resistance. For instance, when an officer has warned someone to desist from an activity such as playing very loud music in the street, if they then increase the volume rather than turn it down, this would represent 'taking the mickey'. Although such incidents raise problems for officers, particularly what Muir terms the 'paradox of face' (Muir, 1977, ch.2), they can be handled so that there are no ramifications beyond the encounter itself.

Manning points out that patrol officers' work rarely leads to a satisfactory outcome for them (Manning, 1982, p.127) In the following example, the officer had obtained what initially seemed to be 'a good pinch', but a satisfactory outcome was undermined by the offender continuing to use a stolen cheque book while on bail. Furthermore, the officer's competence was called into question by his failing initially to recover the cheque book.

> I got this bloke for cheque fraud, he'd really been living it up, £800 in four days. Anyway I got him and charged him. He was granted bail for the weekend before going to court on the Monday when he was sent down. But do you know what that bastard did? While he was out on bail he got the cheque book, which was never recovered, and did another £400 over the weekend. That's really taking the mickey, that is. It's only just come to light and I've got to go down to ...... prison and interview him. He ain't half going to get a good kicking when I get him on my own.

Behaviours which are indicative of trouble for police officers are not always the result of an encounter with a member of the public. There are several terms which usually, although not exclusively, refer to police behaviours which are harbingers of trouble: specifically, 'over the top', 'out of order' and 'lost his bottle'.

When used to describe the behaviour of members of the public, 'out of order' is similar in meaning to 'taking the mickey', although it does not imply the deliberate and intentional disobedience to police instruction. For instance, driving a car down a one-way street could be 'out of order' since the term implies a flagrant abuse of a legal or normative standard. When used to refer to the behaviours of police officers, however, its meaning is more specific:

> After a violent pub fight, which had resulted in over ten arrests and injuries to several of the prisoners, the canteen was busy with the chatter of the night's events. There seemed to be an uneasy feeling that some of the violence had been caused by the inspector's heavy-handed behaviour. As one PC expressed it, 'He was out of order'. And as another officer suggested, 'When he's got the cavalry behind him, he gets into strong-arm tactics, pushing and kicking people'.

The criticism of the inspector was not based upon his use of force per se; not sanctioning the use of force when required would have exposed him to the criticism that he had 'lost his bottle'. Rather, it was implicit in the criticism that the amount of force was situationally unjustified. As such, it is based not on a concern with the legal niceties of minimum force but with the occupational desire to lie low and stay out of trouble. Such 'heavy-handed tactics' raise the possibility of awkward questions having to be answered and put in jeopardy the security of the relief. If they have to stage a cover-up, there is always the chance that they will be discovered.

'Bottle' and its corollary 'lost his bottle' have wide currency within the police argot, but are elusive concepts to pin down. Powis (1977) defines it thus:

> Courage, forceful character or nerve. 'He has plenty of bottle' or 'He has lost his bottle'. A variation is where something of no value moral or material is said to have 'no bottle'.

Drivers are often said to have 'bottle' when they indulge in high speed chases. Squeezing through a gap between a stationary car and oncoming traffic while travelling at 80 miles per hour is a sign of 'having bottle'. Conversely, the driver who always plays it safe, never taking any undue chances, is considered to have 'no bottle'.

The risks are not only confined to driving but to dealing with potentially violent interactions in a forceful and decisive manner. In this way senior officers are often said to have 'lost their bottle', since their concerns with legality and due process temper the more practical impulses of the relief. For instance, a senior officer was said to have 'lost his bottle' because he would not authorise the breaking down of a suspect's door without a warrant. In this example, 'bottle' is not just related to physical risk-taking, but to being prepared to take personal and organisational risks which might endanger one's career.

Strategies for dealing with trouble

If 'losing one's bottle' presents officers with problems, then 'having bottle' helps to prevent them. In this sense, 'bottle' relates to the origin of the term, which is slightly more subtle than current everyday usage. 'Bottle' is cockney rhyming slang for 'Bottle and glass: class'. The class being alluded to is that of a boxer. In boxing, 'class' does not refer just to the strong man who hits and punches his way through a bout, but also to the fighter who can duck and weave, tiring his opponent. Similarly in police usage, 'bottle' refers to the ability to keep one's nerve in a situation which is potentially violent and, with skilful use of talk and bluff, calm it down without recourse to force.

Having 'bottle' is one way of avoiding trouble in a situation, but another strategy exists which is primarily related to the use of organisationally derived rhetorics to justify action retrospectively. The vehicle for such a device is paperwork. In general, police officers hate paperwork. They see their job as over-run by it and paperwork as diverting them from the real task of policing. In one way, however, the mastery of organisational report writing, although viewed as unnecessary, can be used as a key device for staying out of trouble.

The centrality of paperwork, the written report on various incidents, is accentuated by the relative isolation of the patrol officer's task. Most incidents are dealt with either alone or with one other officer, and there is very little supervision of actual incidents. Thus, the written report often becomes the sole criterion for making judgements about whether an incident has been correctly dealt with (cf Policy Studies Institute, 1983, vol.IV). In this respect, the pocket book is important, for several reasons. It is supposed to provide the first record of an incident, written up soon after the event. As such, it is presumed to be an accurate record of what took place during an incident, undistorted by memory or other factors. This has particular salience for court appearances, which are often months after the event, and as a basis for generating other written reports at a much later date.

Other reasons for using the pocket book are concerned not with organisational efficiency but with occupational survival. They are directed at the possibility that something might go 'bent' or 'griefy' on an officer. Such strategies are called 'umbrellas' or 'covering'. As one PC explained:

> If something should go wrong, a complaint against you or something like that, if you've got it written in your pocket book it can be used as evidence to support you. For instance, say you arrested someone in a fight and there was a delay in getting them to the station because the van had broken down. You must write down what the delay was, why it occurred, as accurate as possible. Otherwise the man's lawyer could say you'd taken him up to the common and beat him up. Unless you've got it in your pocket book and it can be justified to your sergeant, and the courts, you're going to be in the shit.

But as Manning notes:

> Incidents as recorded in formal reports bear a problematic relationship to the actual event. The incident record and the behavioural record are two phenomenologically independent matters, they are two parallel but slightly disjointed strips of experience. (Manning, 1982, p.126)

Officers are aware that the reports are not reproductions of incidents but reconstructions. The reconstructions are for a particular audience and therefore they are written in a style and manner which is framed by organisational expectations. For patrol officers, the crucial concern is to try and ensure that only information which portrays them in a favourable light reaches senior managers. On the other hand, senior managers are more concerned with ensuring that the correct administrative and legal procedures have been adhered to. Such reconstructions are often used as stylistic devices. For instance:

> Two officers sat in the canteen trying to get their reports straight. They had arrested two men and were trying to reconstruct the events. 'I said to

him, "Would you mind?'", one officer read from his pocket book. 'Well, I didn't really, I said "Get your fucking arms against the wall", but you can't put that in a report, can you'.

The concern with presentation over accuracy can go further; this is no longer referred to as 'umbrellas' or 'covering' but 'story-time' or 'Jackanory', the latter often being alluded to by the singing of the signature tune of a popular children's television programme that bears the same name. For example, after rather hastily breaking down a door, two officers are presented with the problem of justification, as this extract indicates:

> Back in the canteen, D and E are discussing what they should do about the paperwork. E has written his initial report. It reads: 'We searched the whole house and as we believed that the suspect was still on the premises there was only one room in which he could be and that was locked on the inside. I thought I heard a noise from inside the room and so broke the door down.' D adds with a smile, 'I heard the noise', and then suggests, 'If you like, you could add that the adjacent room was only separated by a thin partition wall and the noise you heard was another PC moving about in the room'. E added this, read through the report and thought that 'it would do'.

While such examples illustrate minor reconstructions primarily for the sake of organisational requirements, they are unlikely to compromise the officer legally. But such strategies can be used to substantiate a shaky legal position for an arrest. By falsifying the evidence, reasonable grounds can be provided for a course of action. 'Jackanories', then, move from being a question of style to one of perjury. For instance:

> The inspector came into the canteen and asked if someone 'wanted a body'. It was apparent that one of the prisoners had been arrested, but nobody knew who the arresting officer was. The inspector was looking at the team of ten or so officers present, hoping that one of them would volunteer. Nobody did. Instead they volunteered an officer: 'F will take it, sir'. Reluctantly, F got up to deal with the prisoner. 'I need a witness too'. This was awkward also, but after a few moments of silence, another officer volunteered. 'I'll be a witness, sir'. 'But you were round the back', came another voice. Nobody seemed to care. Somehow the reports would get sorted out.

By far the most controversial resource at the patrol officer's disposal for avoiding trouble is the use of extra-legal violence. Within the culture such behaviour is termed 'summary justice', 'street justice', 'a good kicking' or 'a good hiding'. The extent of such behaviour is enormously difficult to gauge. This is not just a problem of 'observer effect'. A lone observer, even working for lengthy periods in the field, is unlikely to come across many situations where any force is necessary, let alone extra-legal force. For instance, a prisoner is struggling and an officer has forced the man's arm behind his back. As the man continues to struggle, the officer pushes the man's arm further and further up behind his back. At what point, if any, does the force used become 'excessive'?

The PSI researchers, Smith and Gray (Policy Studies Institute, 1983, vol.IV) witnessed eight separate incidents during which, in their opinion, excessive force was used. Excessive force is not the same as 'street justice'. It may result from an officer 'going over the top' or losing his or her temper. 'Street justice' or 'summary justice', on the other hand, have a more specific meaning referring to extra-legal violence used as punishment or retribution. The following story told by an officer illustrates well this more exclusive meaning.

The desk sergeant also told G of the fight that had occurred the night before in the charge room. The station sergeant had been questioning a large West Indian suspect when the suspect suddenly went berserk and attacked the sergeant who was alone with the prisoner. It took four officers to restrain the man. The sergeant had been knocked unconscious and had to be taken to hospital. The desk sergeant ended the story with: 'But they got him later, right between the bollocks.'

Stories like these are frequently related by officers, detailing how they eventually got the upper hand and taught a violent or cheeky offender a lesson. Thus 'summary justice' can be used to reinstate lost authority on the street. During a conversation about the level of hostility shown by young West Indian males, an officer from another division stated:

I'd fucking nick 'em. Even if you can't do 'em then because of the numbers, I'd get them later when nobody was around. I don't forget a face, you know.

A rather subtle variation of this process was indicated in the following story which illustrates how 'summary justice' can be seen as making up for what is perceived as a deficiency of the legal system, which is too lenient on offenders:

A prisoner had started to complain of feeling ill, stomach pains and the lot. A doctor was called who said there was nothing wrong with him and left the station. The prisoner continued to display the symptoms with more intensity and the doctor was called again. The doctor still did not believe that the symptoms were real, but decided to play safe and had the man admitted to hospital. The hospital doctor could find nothing wrong with the man either. He then asked what the man had done. 'I told him all about his violent crimes, and on hearing this the doctor said with a wry smile "Well, I think we'll have to have his appendix after all"'. The PC chuckled with glee at the justice of it all.

'Summary justice' and the use of extra-legal force were not just evidenced by the use of stories. On three separate occasions I witnessed behaviour which, in my opinion, constituted the extra-legal use of force and on two occasions was definitely related to retribution:

The inspector started to move the crowd to the outside of the pub. He pushed on towards the door and the lad started to struggle. He was grabbed by three officers and dragged outside, still struggling. More officers joined in until there was a circle with the man on the ground in the middle being kicked. Later I heard that the man had lost his front teeth.

The consequences of trouble

As with the use of paperwork for a covering device, the use of summary justice presents the officer with the possibility of organisational and legal sanction. Officers are well aware that such behaviour, as well as less questionable actions, can result in incidents going 'bent', 'griefy', 'pear-shaped' or 'banana-shaped' on them. When this occurs, there is always a possibility of being 'stuck on' for an infraction of the discipline code or of a 612 (formal complaint) being issued against them.

These, then, are the organisational consequences of something 'coming back at you'. It means that an officer's work has become the subject of official scrutiny and negative evaluation. At best, he or she will receive a 'bollocking' from a superior officer; at worst, formal discipline proceedings will be undertaken. In cases of serious misconduct, this could result in the matter being referred to the Director of Public Prosecutions and legal action being instigated.

From the patrol officer's point of view, the discipline code represents the most pervasive reminder that any incident, however trivial, can be troublesome, since the code covers working practice, the relations of deference and demeanour between ranks and peers, and the private lives of officers. Its power lies not so much in the explicit nature of what is sanctionable, but in its being sufficiently vague to rely heavily on interpretation and in being all-embracing. For example, how can the discretionary power of the constable be reconciled with that section of the discipline code which specifies that police officers will be neglecting their duty if they 'fail to report anything that is their duty to report'? Similarly, what constitutes 'any unnecessary violence to any prisoner or other person with whom he may be brought into contact in the execution of his duty'? As Chatterton illustrates, such issues are not merely academic; sergeants do threaten their officers with neglect of duty if they fail to exercise discretion in a particular way (Chatterton, 1981).

However, these more serious breaches of the discipline code, because of the difficulty of detection, provide a scant resource but a powerful reminder of the problem of keeping clear of the code, or - more important - of the host of minor and less substantial rules, the infringement of which can result in being 'stuck on'. For instance, an officer is in breach of the discipline code if he or she gossips while on duty; is uncivil to any member of the public; is insubordinate by word, act or demeanour; omits to make any necessary entry in an official document or book; or directly or indirectly solicits any gratuity, present or subscription without the consent of the Commissioner.

The crucial point about the discipline code is that in the main it is neither observed nor enforced. Officers regularly receive free and discounted food and refreshment at local cafes, fail to record stops, leave their beats, fail to put on their hats when leaving the patrol car, fail to report damage to a police vehicle, and - perhaps more importantly but less frequently - sign false statements, make false, misleading and inaccurate statements, both with and without the approval of supervisory officers.

Of the 57 separate points contained within the discipline code (Police Federation, 1965, pp.69-72), my fieldnotes document 30 separate and different infractions, many of them routine. In addition to the ones listed above, they include drinking on duty; being absent without leave; using unnecessary force; and being rude to members of the public. Many infringements of the discipline code are informally sanctioned by supervisory officers. Consider the following example.

> It was an extremely cold morning. Although we had been posted to Beat 2, H had decided to walk to the other side of Beat 3 and see if we could get a cup of tea at a well-known tea hole. We knocked on the window and were warmly welcomed as tea was duly made. Five minutes later J and K arrived, joked that they thought they would find us here, and joined us for early morning tea. Shortly afterwards, L arrived. The entire sub-divisional foot patrol was now ensconced in the warmth of the tea hole. 'Oh shit', declared H, as the sergeant's patrol car pulled up alongside the tea hole. Everyone looked a little uneasy as the sergeant got out of his car and entered. 'We're just off sarge', declared H. The sergeant gave a broad grin. 'It's all right, stay and finish your tea', he declared as he helped himself from the pot.

Or, as the following extract illustrates:

> The inspector was deploying his officers and asked one of the younger constables who was normally posted on foot patrol, 'Have you been out in a vehicle this week?' 'Yes, I was out last night', he replied. 'Officially, I mean', quipped the inspector, acknowledging the fact that even when posted to foot patrols, his officers would often be picked up by one of the mobile patrols and stay in the car or the van for the entire shift. 'It was, sir, but I don't mind going out again'.

Such toleration of discipline infraction has a double edge for relief officers. While it makes their job more pleasant, they realise that it can be used against them at any time if they get on the wrong side of a sergeant or inspector; and since the rules are all-pervasive, finding a justifiable reason would not be difficult.

Rather than using the discipline code to gain compliance, a more important strategy, which is recognised by both patrol officers and their supervisors, is using supervisory power to offer protection from the discipline code and thus ensure compliance with other, more valued norms. This is particularly the case for incidents on the street that have gone 'griefy'. Thus by 'losing paper', 'shutting one's eyes', sanctioning a false statement, 'putting in a good word', or providing written reports for disciplinary inquiries, a supervisory officer can lessen or avert the impact of disciplinary proceedings. This is no light incentive to stay on the right side of one's supervisors. As the PSI report revealed, 'within the past ten years the mean number of complaints per officer was 4.4' (Policy Studies Institute, 1983, vol.III, p.114). Therefore at some point or other a patrol officer will undoubtedly need such protection.

This dependency is double-edged. Sergeants and inspectors are sometimes guilty by deed, but more often by association. 'If the shit hits the fan', and they are called to account, they are equally dependent on the support of their officers to maintain their integrity.

Conclusions

The terms of trouble represent a culturally derived solution to the organisational and environmental problems posed by the practice of policing. While it is true that most encounters police officers have with the public are essentially trouble-free, officers are aware that these encounters have the potential to go 'griefy' on them. The result of this awareness is to highlight the officers' need to establish control over incidents, by creating the conditions under which their authority to define and determine resolutions is upheld. The issue of control is not confined to on-the-job matters, there is a spill-over effect from incidents on the street to events in the station. A satisfactory termination of an encounter does not just depend on the resolution reached at the incident, but on the organisational resolution. Unless the paperwork is written with reference to acceptable organisational rhetorics, then the incident can still go 'bent'.

In essence, what the terms of trouble describe is what the new recruit has to learn to become a competent organisational member from the perspective of the occupational culture. This approach takes seriously Fielding's argument (1984) that we must define competent practice by reference to occupational rather than organisational criteria, and that there is a considerable disjunction between the rhetoric of training and the reality of police work (Fielding, forthcoming). If this disjunction is to be bridged, then training must take account of how patrol work is actually performed. In so doing, training will also have to address the problem of dubious and illegal practice. This does not mean that it has to sanction it, but recognises that acknowledging the situation is the first step in doing something to change it.

Note

The research on which this chapter is based was supported by two Economic and Social Research Council (ESRC) (formerly Social Science Research Council) studentships, award numbers S82117305 and G00428325065.

I would like to thank Malcolm Hibberd, Barrie Irving and Jon Willmore of the Police Foundation who helped me gain access to police forces; Nigel Fielding of the University of Surrey, who provided moral support throughout the entire project and made extensive comments on an earlier draft of this paper; and the officers from all three research sites who allowed me the privilege of watching them work.

References

Astley, W.G. and van de Ven, (1983) 'Central perspectives and debates in organisation theory', Administrative Science Quarterly, 28, 245-73

Becker, H.S., Geer, B., Hughes, E.C. and Strauss, A.L., (1961) Boys in white: student culture in medical school, University of Chicago Press, Chicago

Black, D., (1980) The manners and customs of the police, Academic Press, London

Black, D. and Reiss, A., (1967) 'Patterns of behaviour in police citizen transactions', in President's Commission on Law Enforcement and Administration of Justice, Studies of crime and law enforcement in major metropolitan areas, Field Surveys III, vol.2. US Government Printing Office, Washington DC

Bogomolny, R., (1976) 'Street patrol: the decision to stop a citizen', Criminal Law Bulletin, 12, 5, 544-82

Burke, K., (1945) A grammar of motives, Prentice Hall, New York

Chatterton, M.R., (1975) Organisational relationships and processes in police work: a case study of urban policing, PhD thesis, University of Manchester

Chatterton, M.R., (1978) 'The police in social control', in Baldwin, R. and Bottomley, A.K. (eds), Criminal justice, Martin Robertson, London

Chatterton, M.R., (1979) 'The supervision of patrol work under the fixed point system', in Holdaway, S. (ed.), The British police, Edward Arnold, London

Chatterton, M.R., (1981) Practical coppers, oarsmen and administrators: front-line supervisory styles in police organisations, unpublished paper presented to ISA research committee on the sociology of law, Oxford

Chatterton, M.R., (1983) 'Police work and assault charges, in Punch M. (ed.), Control in the police organisation, MIT Press, Cambridge, Mass

Fielding, N., (1984) 'Police socialisation and police competence', British Journal of Sociology, 35, 4

Fielding, N., (forthcoming) 'Competence and culture in the police', Sociology

Fitzpatrick, J., (1980) 'Adapting to danger: a participant observation study of an underground mine', Sociology of Work and Occupations, 7, 2, 131-58

Ford, C.S., (1942) 'Culture and human behaviour', Scientific Monthly, 44, 546-57

Forst, B., Lucianovic, J. and Cox, S., (1977) What happens after arrest? Institute for Law and Social Research, Washington DC

Friedrich, R.J., (1977) The impact of organisational, individual and situational factors on police behavior, PhD dissertation, State University of New York at Albany

Fyfe, J.J., (1982) 'Blind justice: police shootings in Memphis', Journal of Criminal Law and Criminology, 73, 2, 707-22

Garfinkle, H., (1967) Studies in ethnomethodology, Prentice Hall, New Jersey

Gerth, H. and Mills, C.W. (1965) Character and social structure, Routledge and Kegan Paul, London

Holdaway, S., (1983) Inside the British police, Basil Blackwell, Oxford

James, D., (1979) 'Black-police relations: the professional solution', in Holdaway, S. (ed.), The British police, Edward Arnold, London

Kelling, G., Pate, T., Dieckman, D. and Brown, C., (1974) The Kansas City preventive patrol experiment, Police Foundation, Washington DC

Lambert, J., (1970) Crime, police and race relations, Oxford University Press, Oxford

Lundman, R., (1974) 'Routine police arrest practices', Social Problems, 22

McBarnet, D., (1979) 'Arrest, the legal context of policing', in Holdaway, S., (ed.), The British police, Edward Arnold, London

McBarnet, D., (1981) Conviction, Macmillan, London

Manning, P.K., (1970) 'Talk and becoming: a view of organisational socialisation', in Douglas, J. (ed.), Understanding everyday life, Routledge and Kegal Paul, London

Manning, P.K., (1977) Police work, MIT Press, Cambridge, Mass

Manning, P.K., (1982) 'Organisational work: structuration of the environment', British Journal of Sociology, 33, 188-239

Mills, C. Wright, (1940) 'Situated actions and vocabularies of motive', American Sociological Review, 5, 4, 904-13

Muir, W.K., (1977) Police: streetcorner politicians, University of Chicago Press, Chicago

Piliavin, I. and Briar, S., (1964) 'Police encounters with juveniles', American Journal of Sociology, 70, 206-14

Police Federation (1965) A handbook of police discipline, London

Policy Studies Institute, (1983) Police and people in London, vols I-IV, Smith, D.J., Gray, J. and Small, S., London

Powis, D., (1977) The signs of crime, McGraw Hill, Maidenhead

Sacks, H., (1963) 'Sociological description', Berkeley Journal of Sociology, 8, 1-19

Sherman, L., (1980) 'The causes of police behaviour: the current state of quantitative research', Journal of Research into Crime and Delinquency, 17, 1

Skolnick, J., (1966) Justice without trial, Wiley, New York

Smircich, L., (1983a) 'Concepts of culture and organizational analysis', in Administrative Science Quarterly, 28, 330-358

Smircich, L., (1983b) 'Studying organizations as cultures', in Morgan, G. (ed.), Beyond method: strategies for social research, Sage, Beverley Hills

Smith, D. and Visher, C., (1981) 'Street-level justice: situational determinants of police arrest decisions', Social Problems, 29, 2

Taylor, L., (1979) 'Vocabularies, rhetorics and grammar: problems in the sociology of motivation', in Downes, D. and Rock, P. (eds), Deviant interpretations, Martin Robertson, Oxford

Toch, H., Grant D. and Galvin, R., (1975) Agents of change: a study in police reform, Schenkman, Cambridge, Mass

Unruh, D., (1979) 'Doing funeral directing', Urban Life, 8, 2, 247-63

van Maanen, J., (1978) 'Police socialisation', Administrative Science Quarterly, 20, 207-28

van Maanen, J. and Schein, (1979) 'Towards a theory of organisational socialisation', Research in organisational behavior, 1, 209-64

Westley, W., (1970) <u>Violence and the police</u>, MIT Press, Cambridge, Mass

White, T. and Bloch, P., (1975) <u>Police officer height and selected aspects of performance</u>, Police Foundation, Washington DC

Zimmerman, D., (1970) 'The practicalities of rule use', in Douglas, J. (ed.), <u>Understanding everyday life</u>, Routledge and Kegan Paul, London

8 Managing paperwork
MICHAEL R. CHATTERTON

Although police officers spend a considerable amount of time on paperwork, little attention has been paid to it in studies of policing. The Policy Studies Institute research on the Metropolitan Police and Kinsey's work in Merseyside reveal that a large proportion of duty time is spent on police premises and that a significant slice of this time is accounted for by paperwork and administration (Policy Studies Institute, 1983, vol.III; Kinsey, 1985). Yet these studies pay hardly any attention to the activities which are covered by these terms, the processes involved and the types of paperwork produced.

One can confidently predict that more attention will be given to this subject in the future. With the current emphasis on efficiency and effectiveness and the drive to put more police officers out on the streets, the time spent producing items of paperwork will need to be scrutinised more carefully and streamlining introduced where possible (Home Office Circular 114/1983). The better we understand the processes involved in the production of paperwork and what significance these have for the organisation and the people in it, the more effective such changes are likely to be. This chapter is aimed at opening up this previously neglected area of research enquiry.

An interesting – but as yet unexplored – paradox reveals the need for a closer examination of this area of policing. The attitudes of police officers to paperwork are complex and appear to be contradictory. They speak disparagingly about it yet they also treat is as important and use it to promote their own ends. Although they denigrate administrative posts which remove people from the streets, and refer to police personnel who 'push' paper using derogatory terms like 'plastics', they also hold in esteem colleagues who can produce prosecution files and 'pen' good reports with relative ease.

Action-seeking and the value attached to activities that generate excitement and interest also figure prominently in accounts of policing provided by researchers. As Holdaway has convincingly demonstrated, such accounts help to sustain a construction of policing in which central place is given to high speed car chases, fights, and the apprehension and constraining of 'good prisoners' and 'challengers' who threaten the control officers seek to maintain over their territory (Holdaway, 1983; Policy Studies Institute, 1983, vol.III). A central organisational goal of taking 'good prisoners' for robbery and burglary by self-initiated means conspires with the practical concerns of the lower ranks to support this action orientation.

By contrast, paperwork appears monotonous and routine and evokes all the negative connotations of 'bureaucracy'. Because it is less salient, researchers and police officers alike have tended to present it as a residual activity. Field workers will recall how tempting it is, when a constable they are accompanying states he is going into the police station to write reports, to switch over to someone else who is remaining out on patrol, where the action is and where 'real police work' is done.

As a consequence of the high profile given to action-oriented police activities and 'thief-taking', the subterranean value placed upon paperwork, the different types of items produced, the various uses made of them and their significance to different segments within the organisation have been overlooked. This is also surprising given the fact that we know these organisational segments have distinctive interests and concerns to protect and to promote (Manning, 1977; Punch, 1983). Do these various segments use items of paperwork for their own ends? Which items do they use, to what ends and with what consequences?

Manning was the first to draw our attention to the contrast between 'real, action policing' and paperwork. 'Paper is the defining characteristic of formal operations; but is rejected as irrelevant [by the lower ranks]. In this way paper becomes the negative or contrasting conception, against which real police work is measured' (Manning, 1980, p.221).

The narcotics agents Manning studied regard paperwork as 'dirty work' in Hughes' sense of that term: beneath their dignity and potentially disgusting. It was regarded as irrelevant to what they were trying to achieve in their work. The 'reality' they presented in their written accounts was in some ways removed from 'street reality'. Reports which they submitted on their activities and on what they had achieved, were pejoratively referred to as 'scandal sheets' or 'lie sheets', implying that they were 'mannered misrepresentations of the actual activities of officers' (Manning, op.cit., p.226).

Manning summarises an attitude towards paperwork which, he claims, pervades the whole of the organisation:

> There is a sense in which the organisation discounts and dismisses its own records as accurate portrayals of its work. When they are required, they are done grudgingly, are not trusted, and are set aside as beside the point when discussing what is being done, what will be done, and how well it has been done (ibid.).

Manning's observations on paperwork need to be developed further and explored in the context of British policing. In his study, paradoxes and contradictions similar to those I have been discussing are brought to light.

Although paperwork had low status, had residual importance and might be a misrepresentation of the truth, he demonstrates that its use by senior management did control how the lower ranks performed and influenced what they produced.

In one of the two departments he studied, paperwork was used to monitor the work of the detectives. Reports were used by supervision to track the progress of information as it was processed through the various stages of an investigation. The grounds for decisions were recorded and were thus more visible in the department. The time it took a detective to close a case was more easily checked and, on the whole, detectives were more accountable than their colleagues in the other departments in the study. The use of paperwork in this manner was tied in with the type of control system operating in the department. Manning describes this as an organisation-centred model. The detectives working in this department consequently put more effort into the cultivation of informants, surveillance work and the investigation of cases. They produced more arrests and charged more people with hard drug offences. In the investigator-centred model, on the other hand, sources of information and complaints were not recorded and hence supervisors could not monitor them or decide who should be assigned to investigate them. The paperwork produced by detectives did not enable their supervisors to monitor their work in any detail. Thus the number, type, promise and current developments in a given investigation may be known only by the investigator (Manning, op.cit., p.88).

Below I shall try to demonstrate the general applicability of these two models and use them with reference to the two sub-divisions in the study described below. The amount and type of paperwork produced, the procedures designed to check on quantity and quality, as well as the speed with which enquiries were 'closed', will prove to be significant indicators of the type of managerial control systems operating on those sub-divisions.

Earlier studies suggest that just as senior management may attempt to use paper to monitor and control their subordinates, they in turn also use it to preserve their own areas of autonomy and for self-protection. The lower ranks need to be able to filter, and thereby control, the information which the higher ranks obtain about their decisions and activities if they are to be able to continue to exercise their discretion. As I noted in an earlier study, 'the context of low visibility which has been recognised as a feature of police work, is as much an achievement of of the lower ranks as it is an intrinsic feature of the environment in which they work' (Chatterton, 1983, p.202).

'Practical coppers', skilled practitioners of the craft of policing know how to work paper as well as work a beat. Learning the job involves knowing when you need to submit paper and when you need not bother, what you must include in the account and what it is imperative to leave out to avoid creating more work and trouble for yourself. In other words, knowing how to cover your back by producing the appropriate paperwork is just as essential as having the skills of street work. Constables and their first-line supervisors may produce and check paperwork grudgingly but they appreciate its importance. They are aware of the consequences which stem from getting it wrong and use paperwork to cover their backs. The same occupational culture which highlights the action-orientation is also, if less dramatically, concerned with techniques of paperwork production. Paradoxically, in view of its low status and the derogatory comments made about it, paperwork is central to the core concern of the lower ranks with avoiding 'within-the-job' trouble (Chatterton, 1976, 1983; van Maanen, 1983).

This suggests that when the lower ranks complain about paperwork, they may actually be complaining about the fact that they have it to do, i.e. that they are accountable to others for their actions and must explain these on paper. However, such derisory comments should not be interpreted to mean that the lower ranks regard paperwork as unimportant. On the contrary, they need to be able to work paper competently to adapt effectively to the fact that they are accountable.

Paperwork is not only relevant to the core concerns of the lower ranks because it is defensive work. The contradictions in the attitudes of officers to paperwork are further highlighted by the fact that whilst they claim to despise it, they use paper to achieve the results they want. It is through the work done in their reports, for instance, that officers persuade the higher ranks that no purpose is to be served by taking certain enquiries any further. Conversely, through their work in file preparation, they hope to produce a file which will persuade the higher ranks and the prosecutors that a case is worth prosecuting, and the courts that the defendant is guilty.

The time spent in the police station recording interviews, taking statements, drawing sketch plans, etc. produces the cases which enable the police organisation to interface with the courts and other organisations. Events, incidents and encounters out on the streets are shaped, ordered and transformed through this paperwork into recognisable, typical cases of 'due care and attention', 'Section 18', 'TWOCs' (taking without consent), 'affrays', etc. (Cicourel, 1968). Because paperwork has been neglected in our studies of policing, such activities have tended to remain hidden.

I have argued elsewhere that insufficient attention has been paid to the fact that not all incidents or cases are closed after the officer has responded to the original call and taken immediate action at the scene (Chatterton, 1985). The post-attendance procedures and the paperwork they produce are as constitutive of real police work as the more familiar beat work. Police officers recognise that there is little point in engaging in the chase, the scuffle, etc. if the case is to be lost subsequently because the officer concerned incompetently executes the post-attendance procedures and prepares a poor case file.

Even at the most mundane level, the gap in our knowledge about the meanings and uses of paper and paperworking is revealed. Paperwork can provide a welcome relief from a boring, wet, uneventful shift - a form of 'official easing' (Cain, 1973). Time out with a mug of tea, in a warm police station, temporarily released from the demands of the personal radio, can be legitimised by the reports which the sergeant has insisted must be completed before the end of that tour of duty!

In this chapter I shall explore some of the contradictions I have just outlined. I shall focus specifically upon the issues which sergeants face in supervising the way their constables deal with paper, the uses that the higher ranks make of it and what this, in turn, entails for the sergeants. Particular attention will be paid to sergeants' attitudes to paperwork processes, to the way in which they manage them and the organisational factors which assist or hinder their supervision and management of paperwork.

110

The project [1]

The research was carried out between February 1983 and April 1985 on two sub-divisions of a large territorial division of an eastern midlands police force. The two sub-divisions, Central and East, were organised on different lines, so an opportunity was provided to examine the work of patrol sergeants in two contrasting organisational settings.

Central sub-division was divided into two separate sections, which I shall call City and Chadd. Four groups, each comprising twelve patrolling constables, a patrol sergeant, a patrol inspector, together with a station sergeant and a communications room sergeant, made up the City section. On Chadd each of the four groups comprised a sergeant and eight constables. One inspector was responsible for the Chadd section. On City, the patrol inspector, sergeant and constables worked together as a group, half of them working the base shifts 0600-1400, 1400-2200 and 2200-0600 hours, and the other half, overlapping shifts of 0900-1700, 1400-2200 and 0600-1400 hours. East sub-division was also organised on the section principle. The area was divided into four sections, each comprising three or four sergeants and between 18 and 30 constables, depending on the size of the area and the population policed. The principal difference from Central was that the constables on each section were not organised into distinctive groups with their own sergeant and inspector. The constables came on duty in twos and threes at various times on each section during the 24-hour period. These were normally at 0600, 0800, 1000, 1400, 1600, 1800 and 2200 hours. The sergeants also chose their own starting times from these alternatives. An inspector was responsible for a section, as at Chadd, and he would choose his shifts accordingly. Normally there was a sergeant, and usually an inspector, working with a specific group of constables on City section and invariably a sergeant working with a specific group of constables on Chadd. However, on East sub-division constables regularly came on duty and worked for several hours before a sergeant or an inspector came on duty on their section. An East constable, working a tour from 0600 to 1400 hours, could work half that tour, and sometimes the whole of it, without seeing a sergeant or inspector. If he needed to consult a supervisor he might try to contact a sergeant working on one of the other three sections, but there was no guarantee that a sergeant would be on duty on that section at that time.

Another difference between the two sub-divisions was that there were no group briefings on East, except on the night shift, whereas on Central sub-division at the beginning of each of the base shifts the groups were briefed by the patrol inspector. Occasionally a formal parade was held with the officers standing to attention to be inspected by the patrol inspector. On East sub-division constables were expected to brief themselves at the beginning of each tour.

Central sub-division represents the traditional model of 'group', 'block' or 'scale' organisation, with a modified shift system to provide more cover between the hours of 0900 and 0200. The East system on the other hand was intended to grant more autonomy to members of each rank who were expected to accept a greater amount of responsibility than in the past. A force working party, in outlining the system to be operated on that sub-division, had recognised the additional burden of responsibility which sergeants in particular would have to carry: 'There will obviously be occasions when the sergeant will be the highest rank in the area and will have to shoulder the responsibilities of the inspector' (Woodall, Newton and Hannaford, 1982, p.49). The working party also foresaw the rank of constable developing in a similar fashion: 'There will be

111

minimal supervision and a consequent need for this rank to become more self-reliant and more accountable than they have been used to' (ibid.).

During the first ten months of the project I undertook an observational study of patrol sergeants on Central sub-division. Towards the latter part of this period, sufficient rapport had been established to enable me to record in detail and contemporaneously all activities, decisions and interactions of the sergeants during a tour of duty. In the second year of the project a research assistant was appointed, the observations and the detailed recording continued and the research was extended to East sub-division.

Two main sources of quantitative data were used to supplement the qualitative material. A structured observation schedule comprising 154 variables was used to code detailed field notes relating to 152 tours of duty. This figure was made up of 21 tours on City section during 1983, 47 tours on City section during 1984, 47 tours on East sub-division during 1984 and 37 tours on the Chadd section. During the last four months of the study, 46 sergeants were interviewed. They included all the sergeants with whom we had worked during the course of the project and five sergeants from another, adjacent sub-division. Some of the 41 sergeants from East and Central were sergeants who had moved elsewhere during the course of the study. Some experienced acting sergeants were also included. Nineteen of the sergeants had worked or were working on East sub-division, 22 on Central sub-division.

The observation schedule provided a systematic work activity analysis of the 152 tours of duty. The schedules mapped the patterns of interaction, the decisions and the types of advice given by sergeants during those tours. In the interviews sergeants were asked about their own views of their role. They were then asked what they thought the views of their sub-divisional superintendent would be. The aim was to establish what they considered to be legitimate role expectations and to ascertain how much control they had over factors which we knew from our fieldwork directly influenced their capacity to exercise their responsibilities effectively.

Sergeants' attitude to paperwork

The negative attitudes towards paperwork were partly a response to the fact that these sergeants, like their counterparts elsewhere, found that it prevented them from spending the time they needed out on the streets. The analysis of the 152 tours revealed that on nine per cent of these tours the patrol sergeants did not get out onto the streets at all, at any time during the tour. On over two-thirds of tours the maximum amount of time spent on patrolling and attending incidents was two and a half hours. On many tours it was a lot less.

Sergeants blamed paperwork for this situation. In the interviews, 89 per cent agreed with the statement 'Because of the amount of paperwork I have to do, I spend too much time in the office'. Of these, 98 per cent reported that they found this frustrating in varying degrees: 26 per cent stated it was 'very frustrating'; 48 per cent found it 'frustrating'; and 24 per cent found it 'a bit frustrating'. No significant difference was revealed between the sergeants on the two sub-divisions on this issue. About a quarter of the East and Central sergeants found being office-bound 'very frustrating'; 37 per cent of East sergeants and 46 per cent of Central sergeants found this 'frustrating'; and 21 per cent of sergeants on East and 18 per cent of sergeants on Central found it 'a bit frustrating'.

112

Yet the contradictions in police attitudes to paperwork, which I noted above, are apparent in these data. The sergeants were asked to give their own views on the level of responsibility a patrol sergeant should accept for certain matters. The levels of responsibility ranged from 'total', through 'a good deal' and 'a small part' to 'no responsibility'.

Most sergeants knew they were held responsible for their constables' paperwork and accepted that responsibility themselves, even thought it kept them tied to the office.

In response to the question, 'How much responsibility do you think you should accept for ensuring that your PCs' files are of good quality?', the majority of the sergeants stated that they accepted 'total responsibility' (50 per cent) or 'a good deal of responsibility' (46 per cent). Only a very small minority said they should not carry much responsibility for the quality of paperwork production.

Asked to consider what their sub-divisional commanders expected of them and how they thought sub-divisional commanders would answer the question, an even higher percentage of sergeants elected for 'total responsibility' (63 per cent) and the remainder all stated they were expected to carry 'a good deal of responsibility'.

The time subordinates take to close a case, i.e. to complete the necessary paperwork and then pass it onto the next relevant stage in the process, is an aspect of the paperwork production which management can try closely to control (Manning, 1980). The sergeants were asked, therefore, about the level of responsibility they thought they should accept for ensuring their constables' paperwork was submitted on time. Again, most of them were prepared to accept this as a legitimate role expectation. Sixty-one per cent said that they accepted 'total responsibility' for the punctual submission of paperwork; 33 per cent accepted 'a good deal of responsibility'. Only seven per cent thought they should have to accept only 'a small amount of responsibility'. Even higher numbers believed that their bosses expected them to be 'totally responsible' for this (78 per cent). The remainder all believed they were expected to carry 'a good deal of the responsibility' and would carry the can if paperwork was put in late.

Ensuring that they fulfilled these responsibilities not only kept the sergeants office-bound. It also meant that they had to allow their constables time in the station as well, so they could complete their paperwork, take advice and make any necessary telephone enquiries. This exposed the patrol sergeants to criticism because they were also responsible for making sure that constables spent most of their duty time out on the streets.

In answer to the question, 'As a patrol sergeant, how much responsibility do you think you should accept for ensuring that your PCs spend most of their duty time out on the streets?', most sergeants accepted this as one of their key responsibilities. Forty-one per cent said they accepted 'total responsibility' for this, 50 per cent 'a good deal of responsibility' and a mere four per cent thought they should take only 'a small part of the responsibility'. Another four per cent thought they should have to carry 'no responsibility at all'. Their views of what the higher ranks expected predictably led more of them to elect for 'total responsibility' (67 per cent) and 'a good deal of the responsibility' (33 per cent).

The competing demands of street work and paperwork presented these sergeants with a classic role conflict situation (Biddle and Thomas, 1966; Gross et al., 1964; Preiss and Ehrlich, 1966). However, the extent to which this caused them difficulties, frustration and stress depended upon the amount of autonomy and room for manoeuvre available to them to strike the necessary compromise. The sergeants were asked their views on the statement, 'Although my bosses want PCs out on the streets they also expect them to keep up with their paper, so I have to work out a compromise and I carry the can if it comes unstuck'. The majority of the sergeants agreed with this statement. Only seven per cent disagreed with this view, whereas 44 per cent 'strongly agreed' with it. Three-quarters of the sergeants experienced some frustration over this conflict, although the level of frustration was generally not particularly high; seven per cent found it 'very frustrating', 30 per cent 'frustrating' and 37 per cent 'a bit frustrating'.

Summarising our findings so far, although sergeants were frustrated and annoyed by the fact that their paperwork commitments kept them tied up for too long in the police station, they still considered that it was legitimate for senior officers to hold them responsible for ensuring that paperwork was of a good quality and that it was submitted punctually. However, when it came to reconciling the competing demands made upon their constables' time by beat work and paperwork, sergeants could cope more easily with that, provided they were allowed to work out the compromise. This was where the situation of the sergeants on the two sub-divisions was so different. Sergeants working on Central sub-division experienced the conflict between these two sets of expectations more acutely than their colleagues on East sub-division did.

Although almost all the sergeants recognised that the demands were in conflict, it is striking that 47 per cent of the sergeants on East, compared with only nine per cent on Central, reported that they did not find the conflict in the slightest bit frustrating. Whereas 14 per cent of the sergeants on Central experienced this conflict as 'very frustrating', none on East did. This difference suggests that East sergeants had more autonomy in this area. They found that the conflict between both demands could be managed and that a compromise could be struck without too much difficulty. This is the first clue to the difference that existed between the management structures of the two sub-divisions.

Control over the production processes

Studies of supervisory positions in industrial settings have paid particular attention to the degree to which supervisors are able to influence factors which affect the operations of the units for which they are responsible. For example, Child and Partridge report:

> The decisions for which supervisors had little or no authority concern matters which determine the main parameters of operations within their sections. This is a significant comment on whether these supervisors can be said to have managerial control over their sections and it recalls the long-term decline that has taken place in their authority. (Child and Partridge, 1982, p.46)

Does the antipathy of sergeants towards paperwork stem from the fact that they, like supervisors in other organisations, did not have the control they felt they needed over this vital area of production? Were they able to 'close' cases confidently? Could they pass items of paperwork into the system and accurately predict the outcome? Were their decisions supported by those who reviewed them further along the line? If the supervision and checking of paperwork is viewed as a quality control function (and I would argue that it should be) then in order to perform this function, sergeants minimally need to know the criteria others will use to assess the adequacy of a report or prosecution file. They also need to be able to ensure that those who inspect an item at a later stage will rectify any defects or omissions which, for whatever reason, they are unable to do anything about at the time the item is put forward. Unless these conditions apply, sergeants can be said to have only limited control over processes which are of paramount importance to their constables, senior officers and themselves. Unless they have this control, a constant stream of items of paperwork will loop back, threatening to block the system and making management and organisation of paperwork extremely difficult. Where this happens with regularity, it obviously also has serious status implications for the rank of sergeant. PCs are bound to raise questions about their sergeant's status when the paperwork he has 'certified' comes back for more corrections, more enquiries to be made, more evidence to be found, etc. Unless the reasons for this are carefully explained, PCs may also question the sergeant's competence.

Sergeants on both sub-divisions were observed to complain bitterly and angrily on many occasions during the course of the fieldwork when personnel in other parts of the system returned items of paperwork for work to be done which these personnel could just as easily have done themselves. The time spent by these personnel typing out a message, or, more usually, filling out a form instructing the sergeant or constables what was required, further infuriated the sergeants. In many instances these personnel could have utilised that time to obtain the item of information themselves.

Sergeants were asked whether they agreed that too much paperwork was unnecessarily returned to them because minor items had been left out. Just over two-thirds agreed with the statement and 15 per cent 'strongly agreed' with it. Twenty-two per cent reported they found the returning of paperwork to fill in minor gaps 'very frustrating' when it happened. A further 28 per cent found it 'frustrating' and 44 per cent found it 'a bit frustrating'.

There was no difference between Central and East sub-divisional sergeants on this issue. On each sub-division 68 per cent of the sergeants agreed with the statement and they experienced similar degrees of frustration when it happened. One of the most frustrating examples we observed was when a file was returned by the prosecutions department to the Chadd section. The prosecutions department was based within divisional headquarters where the photocopier was also housed. Yet the file was returned with instructions to have a photocopy made. This entailed an officer from the Chadd section driving down to headquarters to take the photocopy.

This was an exceptionally blatant example of the misuse of the time of patrol personnel by other departments. The more usual type of occurrence was more minor but still irritating and cumulatively more expensive of time. The statement of the charge, for instance, might omit to say which parts of an offending vehicle were in a dangerous condition and even though the officer's statement on file contained this information, the file was invariably returned to the sergeant to have the PC add the item in the appropriate place. This type of case was very common. The following additional examples, chosen at random from the fieldwork notes, should serve to make the point.

'What was the lighting-up time on the day in question?' (request from the County Prosecuting Solicitor's Department). 'What speed was the offending vehicle doing and what was the method of checking?' (request from the prosecutions department; the information was in the file). 'Add "intoximeter" where indicated' (request from prosecutions department). One of the higher ranks on the division returned the papers regarding a firearms certificate enquiry, listing a number of questions which the PC had to answer in a separate report, yet all the information was already provided in the papers originally submitted to him. There were many other instances, too numerous to mention. A quick rummage through the afternoon sergeant's tray any day after the incoming correspondence has been delivered would, I predict, provide several further examples.

The returning of paperwork in this way hit the sergeants in several vulnerable areas. It was obviously time-wasting: each returned file had to be logged back into the system, the constable had to be pulled off other work to do it and it meant that the file was further delayed. Most significant of all, these cases signified to sergeants their marginal position in the management structure and their inability to resist these demands on their most precious commodity - time. It illustrated their limited capacity to change things, which may in part explain why so many sergeants agreed with the statement that there was little they could do to change the things which their PCs had legitimate grievances about.

Two other indicators of a sergeant's ability to manage paperwork processes were specifically aimed at the quality control function.

One question asked them about the influence they thought they had over decisions regarding the taking of legal proceedings. Did sergeants consider that enough notice was taken of what they recommended, i.e. prosecution, caution or no further action? How much say a sergeant has in this area indicates whether he can shape the outcome of the file preparation sequence and whether his efforts, and those of his constables, achieve their desired objectives. In this sense each of the three types of decision and recommendation is important. However, the 'no further action' decision is especially important because it relates directly to the sergeant's capacity to influence how his constables are utilised. It relates to the management and deployment of personnel as well as to the control he exercises over the paper production processes. If a sergeant is empowered at an early stage to decide that there is no point in initiating a lengthy and time-consuming investigation into an incident, he can save his constables a considerable amount of time and release them for other tasks.

During the course of the research, sergeants were heard to complain frequently about having to require a full, detailed file from their PCs on road traffic accidents, when they and the constables knew that these cases would ultimately result in a 'no further action' decision. Too often, in their opinion, the PCs had to 'go through the motions', making appointments to see witnesses, taking statements, drawing sketch plans of the incidents, and in the process consuming a great deal of time on cases which, as they had predicted at the outset, did not result in a prosecution.

The sergeants were asked whether they agreed with the statement, 'I think more notice should be taken of my recommendations regarding prosecution decisions'. Almost half agreed (48 per cent); the others disagreed. These opinions again proved to be divided along sub-divisional lines. Over two-thirds of the sergeants on Central sub-division thought the influence they had over the final outcome of their files and reports was too limited. Over a quarter of them felt sufficiently keenly about this to state that they 'strongly agreed' with the statement. In marked contrast, a large number of the East sergeants said they 'disagreed' with the statement (76 per cent). They considered that their views

116

were noted and, more often than not, they agreed with the decision taken regarding legal proceedings.

The second statement aimed to elicit from the sergeants whether they were confident that they knew what the ultimate decision-makers expected and could, therefore, dispose of their paperwork knowing that it satisfied those requirements. They were asked their opinion on the statement, 'It is difficult to predict whether the files which I pass up will go straight through the system, or come back for further enquiries to be made'. The absence of a consensus on this question (48 per cent of the sergeants agreeing with it) again reflects a divergence between the views on Central and East sub-divisions. Only 26 per cent of the East sergeants agreed with the statement, whereas 64 per cent of Central sergeants agreed, 28 per cent of them 'strongly'.

These data serve to reinforce the impression gathered earlier that East sergeants experienced more autonomy and control over the paperwork process. This partly stemmed from the relationship East sergeants had with the 'decision-makers' on their sub-division, which was very different from the relationship Central sergeants had with theirs.

Halfway through the course of the project the force introduced a new system for handling paperwork which was designed to improve liaison between the originator of an item (usually a PC), the checker (usually a sergeant) and the decision-maker, an inspector who was responsible for the sub-divisional administrative support unit and who made the final decision about whether legal proceedings would be invoked. On East sub-division, patrol sergeants regularly approached the inspector in the administrative support unit and discussed cases with him. Through these contacts they were more directly involved in the decision-making process than their colleagues on Central. These discussions enabled them to state their own opinions; they learned the views of the decision-maker and what he expected and they helped the decision-maker to arrive at decisions regarding their items of paperwork., No amount of paper can record all the details about incidents. Often in these direct, face-to-face discussions, the 'feel' for a case that had led a sergeant to propose a certain course of action was conveyed to the inspector and the inspector's initial impressions of a case were altered. On other occasions the inspector would explain why he thought that a certain recommended course of action was not viable, in much greater detail than would have been possible had he commented on the decision in writing.

On Central sub-division this kind of liaison between patrol sergeants and the decision-maker did not exist. The sergeants considered they had little say in influencing prosecution decisions and the criteria used to assess the adequacy of a file seemed to be changing constantly.

Regulating the flow of paperwork

In this section I propose to examine other pressures on Central sergeants and again compare these with the position of the East sergeants. I shall explore how the emphasis on a speedy return of paperwork was sustained and how the sergeants on Central adapted to these demands.

As they pass through different stages of paperwork processing, items of paperwork can be held up or go astray. At one extreme, an item of paperwork may not be produced at all because the officers have forgotten to make a report. At the other extreme, an item can go permanently missing and if this is a file a great deal of work has to be redone, provided witnesses are prepared to be reinterviewed and the loss of face is justified. (One cannot begin to speculate on the number of times no proceedings or a caution have resulted because case papers have been irretrievably lost or mislaid.) Management therefore needs to track the progress of paperwork in order that the last person to handle a lost item can be identified and to ensure that the time between initiation and completion is reasonably short. Management's policies on this varied according to the type of item, the ease with which it could be completed, and the urgency with which the information it contained was needed by the system, another police force or a non-police agency.

Reports of crime had to be submitted before the end of the tour of duty in which the complaint was received. A top copy and two 'bottom' copies were despatched to different destinations in the system. One was retained by the sergeant and either passed to the CID for investigation (the East system) or returned to the uniformed officer, usually the reporting officer. Normally, the constable was expected to return the report within seven days of allocation, furnishing additional information which was not available initially and reporting on the enquiries undertaken and any success achieved.

The timetable for road traffic accident reports where someone had sustained an injury was different. These had to be completed and put forward into the system 'as soon as possible' and within 48 hours of the accident. 'Non-injury' accidents were reported on a different form which had to be submitted at the end of the appropriate tour of duty, or as soon as possible thereafter.

Enquiries from other police forces and other divisions within the research force also had to be completed as expeditiously as possible. If a report was delayed and the other force had to send a follow-up request, this reflected badly on the effectiveness of the force and sergeants were therefore expected to ensure that the number of such repeat requests was kept to a minimum.

Where the investigating officer had to make appointments with and interview several witnesses and contact members of other agencies and police forces, the timetable of the investigation was under his control only to a limited extent. He was dependent upon witnesses' availability, the speed with which other agencies provided the information he needed and the time he had free from other commitments, attending calls for service, etc., to arrange to conduct these enquiries. For different types of offences there are statutory time limits, outside which it is not possible to bring a prosecution. Before these are reached, sergeants can expect to receive several reminders from the prosecutions department – colloquially known as 'chaser-memos'. If the paperwork reaches these destinations close to the deadlines, the sergeants can expect a critical report to be generated.

An organisation-centred system of control will rigorously check the progress made with paperwork, requiring constables to complete items within specified time periods and exerting an unremitting pressure when items are being processed too slowly. This was certainly the case on Central sub-division. The time limits imposed served no other purpose, as far as I could see, than that of ensuring a more rapid turnover of items than occurred on East sub-division.

The same 'tracking' system for paperwork was adopted on both sub-divisions. On each section a record was kept of every piece of paperwork each PC was allocated or produced. Printed forms, known as IC sheets, were used for this purpose and the heading on these sheets indicate how often the sergeants were expected to check their PCs' progress in processing the listed items. At the top of each IC sheet was printed 'Weekly check of inward correspondence and outstanding files'. This was followed by the constable's section, name and number. Beneath the heading the sheet was divided into columns with headings as follows: 'Date', 'Reference No.', IC No.', 'Brief details of enquiry', 'File to be submitted by', 'Court on', 'Date submitted' and 'Initials'.

All the sheets for each section were kept in a binder, referred to as that particular section's IC register. Every time a PC was allocated a piece of paperwork, the sergeant turned to that PC's part of the register and recorded under the last entry the details of the new item, following the format just described. The sergeants would periodically carry out IC checks which entailed going through the listed items with their PCs. Although the frequency of such checks varied across the two sub-divisions, all patrol sergeants did them. They also checked with their constables on any self-initiated work they had done which had produced paperwork that would need to be processed. Sergeants needed to keep track of self-initiated work as well and relied upon their constables to keep them up to date about it.

Where the two sub-divisions differed was in the amount of care the sergeants exercised to maintain a constant check on their constables' paperwork.

It is no exaggeration to state that Central sergeants could describe precisely what paperwork each of their PCs was carrying in his case load at any moment. Without reference to the IC register, they were able to recall from memory all the important pieces of work. For example, on night shift I once worked with a patrol sergeant on Central who had just returned from a period of annual leave. This was his first night back on duty. When we went out on patrol he arranged to meet each of his PCs out on foot patrol and walked with them for a while, enquiring from memory about various pieces of paperwork which had been outstanding when he went on leave and whether any progress had been made on them.

If one walked into the patrol sergeant's office at City or Chadd, particularly on the afternoon shift after the incoming correspondence had been delivered, one would invariably find the IC register open on the sergeant's desk and, more often than not, the sergeant would be checking items and recording the work he was allocating to the PCs. If he was out of the office, the IC register would be open on his desk as if to signify that a temporary diversion had taken him away from one of the key tasks he performed.

Individual versus collective responsibility

When I first arrived on Central sub-division I was immediately struck by the amount of attention given to recording work in the IC registers and to monitoring the progress constables were making on outstanding items. At first, I thought the sergeants were being particularly fastidious about these checks because a PC on the sub-division had recently been served discipline papers for not submitting a file on time. His sergeant had also been interviewed and it was generally believed that disciplinary action would also be taken against him. However, the concern persisted, sustained by procedures which led the sergeants constantly to assert that a sergeant who wanted to avoid trouble had to keep a very close watch on each of his PC's paperwork.

119

Although it does not explain the emphasis placed upon the quick turnover of paperwork on Central, the accountability of the patrol sergeants there was accentuated by the group system of working, which meant that they were each personally responsible for a specific group of identifiable PCs. Even though constables on a particular group would overlap with the base shift of another group when they were working on the 0900-1700, 1400-2200 and 1800-0200 shifts, they were still regarded as the responsibility of 'their own' sergeant and inspector. Any paperwork they submitted during the overlap period was left for 'their' sergeant when he came on duty.

The sergeants on each of the sections on East sub-division were not responsible for a specific number of constables. As I explained earlier, the PCs worked different tours with different sergeants, depending upon which sergeant's duties coincided with theirs. Hence a sergeant might work two or three consecutive tours with the same PCs and then not see them again for a week, even longer. What this meant in terms of the responsibility for paperwork was that the sergeant on duty would check the files and reports which were lying in the sergeant's basket when he came on duty and any reports submitted during that tour of duty. He would also allocate any paperwork awaiting distribution. It is important to note that in a large number of instances the sergeant would not have known about these incidents before reading and checking the reports and the files on them. By the same token, he might never be consulted about or check again the incidents and items of paperwork about which he gave advice that shift.

Some sections had recognised the problems this lack of continuity created and had adopted informal measures of alleviating them. One section had recently nominated one sergeant as the 'IC sergeant' whose specific responsibility was to check the IC registers at regular intervals. On another, one PC had been given the responsibility for all the enquiries from other police forces.

Generally speaking, however, the collective responsibility of East sergeants meant that no sergeant there could easily be held personally responsible if a specific item of paper was submitted late or was mislaid. This was reasonable because it would have been very difficult for these sergeants to keep up to date with all the paperwork of each and every PC on the section. It was much easier on Central to hold sergeants responsible for the speedy processing of paperwork because of the 'group system' of supervision. More to the point, however, was the fact that the East sergeants did not find it necessary to keep such a close check on their PCs' paperwork, as did their colleagues on Central. This was evident during the NUM dispute when there were fewer PCs working on the sub-division. At this time sergeants had more opportunity to discover what paper particular PCs were working on, yet the East sergeants were less well acquainted with it than their colleagues on Central.

There were other factors, too, which sustained the emphasis on paperwork on Central sub-division.

Additional IC register checks

One of the most significant differences between the two sub-divisions was the extent to which the higher ranks on Central also 'tracked' the flow of paperwork. At frequent intervals the patrol inspectors would check through the IC sheets of each PC in their sections. If they were not happy about the length of time the preparation of a particular item was taking, they would draw the attention of the patrol sergeant to that item by writing a note under the last entry on the IC sheet, advising him to ensure that the item was expedited immediately. In addition, the sub-divisional chief inspector and superintendent would check the IC sheets at frequent intervals, and record their observations about any delays.

Even if the inspectors and the higher ranks found the work on the sheets to be in order, they would write the date and their signature underneath the last entry, thus declaring that they had carried out the check. This was seen by the lower ranks as a protective gambit and sustained the emphasis upon paperwork. Even the higher ranks had to protect themselves from any future criticism by recording their checks. When the higher ranks had occasion to comment upon a particular item, this meant that if anything went wrong with the processing of the item later, then there was written proof that the PC and sergeant had both been warned. They would be culpable but the higher ranks would be exonerated.

On East sub-division only the sergeants were responsible for the IC registers. With the exception of one inspector who had transferred from Central sub-division, we could find no entries on the IC sheets of East officers by inspectors, the chief inspector or superintendent. The sergeants were entrusted with ensuring punctual submission of paperwork, as were their constables. In view of the close system of monitoring by the higher ranks on Central, on the other hand, it is not surprising that patrol sergeants there gave paperwork such a high priority.

There were other indicators, too, of this pressure and of the organisation-centred model sustained by it.

The significance of the CS book

The sergeants on Central used a back-up system to the IC registers in the shape of the CS book. In it they recorded every report and file which left them on its way to another part of the system. It was their 'insurance policy' when an allegation was made that they were to blame because an item of paperwork had been delayed or mislaid. When this happened the sergeant could immediately check the entries in the CS book. If the item had left his section, he would be able to quote the reference number in the CS book and, more important, the date when it had been put forward. By this stage, of course, there would have been a large number of subsequent entries in the book and as each item had a consecutive number, no-one could accuse the sergeant of making a retrospective entry. This was one of the crucial differences between the CS book and the IC registers. I asked sergeants why they duplicated information by recording the date the item was put forward on both the IC sheet and in the CS book. The answer was that the CS book afforded greater protection. Whereas it might be asserted that a sergeant had made out a new IC sheet, he would be protected from the accusation that he had made a late entry in the CS book.

The existence of the CS book provided concrete evidence that Central patrol sergeants believed that other units to which they despatched paper would sometimes delay the processing of the item or even lose it and would then try to blame patrol sergeants by suggesting that they had received the item late, or had not received it at all. The CS book symbolised their responsibility for paperwork ('the buck stops here'), their vulnerability to criticism and blame, and their lack of confidence in personnel in other departments who were quick to criticise them for inefficiency but whose own administrative systems left a great deal to be desired. When items of paperwork went astray, they would try to 'pass the buck' onto the patrol sergeant and his PCs.

Significantly, the patrol sergeants on East sub-division did not use a CS book or any other form of additional record. They could see no point in the CS book system when it was explained to them by us and by sergeants from Central. Yet, as we have already seen, the majority of sergeants, irrespective of the sub-divisions they worked on, were quite ready to accept a high level of responsibility for their PCs' paperwork. East sergeants were no different from the Central sergeants in that respect. We can conclude from this paradox that the latter were more vulnerable to allegations of incompetence and carelessness in the administration of paperwork. When reports were received late, files delayed, etc., an issue was made of it. The sergeants were called to account and that was when they needed to marshal all the evidence they could, to prove they were not at fault. The East sergeants did not need the additional record. They did not regularly face this inquisitorial, blame-ascriptive process and therefore they did not find it necessary to be so well defended.

This vulnerability and consequent defensiveness of the Central sergeants was evident in another, related practice. Several Central sergeants kept their own personal records of the serial numbers of the fixed penalty tickets issued by their PCs. This private record, which they kept locked away, was immediately available to them. Although it duplicated information in the IC registers, it enabled quicker retrieval and offered another method of protecting themselves and the PC if a ticket went astray.

Although we witnessed no instances where the sergeant's personal record of fixed penalty tickets issued was used, sergeants used the CS book a great deal when personal callers came into the office or telephoned. Sometimes a sergeant used it to check an item on behalf of a colleague from another section who was not on duty at the time.

The 'chaser memo'

One of the most common reasons for checking the CS book was the receipt of a memorandum from another department about a piece of paperwork. Although I cannot claim that the instances we observed were representative, on a large number of occasions the memos proved to be inaccurate because, as the CS book showed, the file or report had gone forward. This occurred with sufficient frequency to explain why the sergeants had so little confidence in the records and reliability of these other departments. This system of sending memos also constantly sustained the impression that paperwork was important. In one case I observed, a Central sergeant examined a memo which had arrived that afternoon. It had been sent by the prosecutions department and was enquiring about a file regarding a road traffic accident case. The sergeant commented that he would 'put money on the fact that the file had been put forward'. He checked the CS book and was proved correct. He then showed me the IC sheet of the PC in the case. The file had been submitted 24 days earlier, within 15 days of the accident being reported. He wrote a polite message on the memo to that effect. Another Central sergeant, after going through a similar process, commented with a wry smile, 'It's called keeping you on your toes'.

On other occasions, when a file did prove to be in the possession of a PC because enquiries were still continuing, the sergeant would simply endorse the memo with some standard phrase like 'enquiries continuing' or 'awaiting statement from outside force'. It was rarely the case that the memo led the sergeant to discuss the case with the PC. Few discussions of files and reports resulted from the receipt of such memos.

Despite the fact that memos from other departments did not threaten the sergeants, the Central sergeants often became very angry when they received them. Why was this? In their view the memo system served no useful purpose for them or for the PCs. It was seen instead as a protective gambit, used by the higher ranks or other departments who wanted to protect themselves in case something did ultimately go wrong. If it did, they would then produce the memorandum with the sergeant's reply recorded on it, to confirm that a warning had been issued and ignored. The Central sergeants recognised that the memo was used as part of the same game and for the same reason that they used the CS book: self-protection.

What Central sergeants resented was the claim that the memos were issued to assist and advise them that one of their PCs was in danger of getting out of time or delayed. They maintained that they had the most up-to-date and reliable information about their PCs' paperwork and the amount of progress that had been made on it. Their anger stemmed from the fact that these memos, like the entries the higher ranks made in the IC registers, symbolised the fact that they were not trusted to manage and to control the processing of paperwork.

The following case provides a good example of a situation where the sergeant and PC decided on a way of dealing with a problem with a constable's paperwork but faced a constant barrage of questions on the IC sheet and memos. Together, this sergeant and constable worked out a set of priorities and a way of managing the enquiries. The sergeant resented the constant interference from the higher ranks and other departments and explicitly stated that he objected to being made to feel that he was finding excuses for his PC's 'failings'. On a particular date he had allocated a number of files to this PC, as the IC sheet testified. These were reallocated cases taken from a PC who had been transferred off the section. The PC had had his work cut out with these cases. Not only did they represent an addition to his workload, but two of the files were proving quite difficult to complete because of the unavailability of witnesses. 'Instead of coming down to see me they continued to send me silly chaser memos about these cases. The lad and I got fed up of it in the end', he complained. When he tried to explain the circumstances to the higher-ups, he was made to feel that he was just trying to defend his PC's incompetence.

Sergeants on East did not resent the memo system for the simple reason that it helped them to track their constables' paperwork. It provided an early warning system, reminding them of submission dates, some of which they might otherwise have overlooked. Their attitude reflects the fact that they were left to manage the system without interference and were grateful for the back-up facility provided by the memos. The likelihood of any oversights occurring on Central, of course, was very remote, given the regular checks made there by all ranks from sergeant upwards.

Accounting for delays in the submission of the paperwork

The attempt to regulate the processing of paperwork by imposing strict time limits on how long various items should take to produce is beset with difficulty. The amount of paperwork each constable is carrying at any one time can vary, and this obviously partly determines how much time he can give to each enquiry and when. A constable may have to suspend all his enquiries for a period because he is diverted to other duties which take him away from the section. Attendance on courses, court duty, relieving in the communications room, the charge office or enquiry office, together with leave, sickness and rest days, can result in no work being done on his files for several weeks (Chatterton and Ellis, 1986). Sergeants have little, if any, influence over the abstractions and extractions which rob their sections of personnel. Yet these ultimately determine their resource capability and how much time they can allow their constables off the streets, away from the demands of service, to write up their reports, etc. Ninety-four per cent of the sergeants said they found it a struggle to respond to all the calls for service because of these other commitments that regularly drained the strength of their sections. Seventy-eight per cent found it virtually impossible to plan a constable's work in any detail because of the many unexpected things that could crop up during the tour of duty. Account has also to be taken of the effects of the shift system because shifts differ in the opportunities they provide to interview members of the public. Such opportunities are restricted between certain times on the night and morning shifts. The times on these shifts when citizens are accessible are also the times when calls for service are at their heaviest (Chatterton, 1985).

The enquiries needed to prepare a file can be quite protracted because of other factors which are outside the constable's and sergeant's control. Any enquiry which involves the cooperation of another police force or another agency means that the management of the case moves outside the control of the investigating officer. A request for a witness statement has to be incorporated within a timetable over which the officer has no direct influence or control. Fixed-penalty enquiries can be very protracted if they involve the PC tracing back the owner of a vehicle which has changed ownership several times since the offence. In those cases where this involves people living outside the sub-division and several different force enquiries are necessitated, the months can easily roll by before the relevant owners are traced, if they ever are.

Enquiries involving the Driving Vehicle Licensing Centre invariably have to be made in writing. An officer who is awaiting authorisation to proceed on a no excise licence offence or some other information will tend to hold up submission of the file papers until the information arrives. This is not strictly necessary, and it is possible to put the file forward for action to be taken on other offences in the case. However, officers tend to delay until the relevant papers are available in preference to putting in an incomplete submission.

On other occasions, unavoidable delays occur because members of the public are slow either in obtaining the information the police need, or in passing it on. One recurring example of this is the case where the injured party has to obtain an estimate of the amount of damage or loss resulting from a crime.

Other accounts offered for delay are more particularised and less easily verified. They are therefore more dependent upon what the sergeant is prepared to believe. One sergeant explained that he expected a proportion of crime reports to entail enquiries beyond the seven days normally allowed for them. He believed delays arose because so many of the crimes his PCs were asked to investigate led nowhere, and they had no alternative but to submit with the usual standard references to having 'visited the scene', 'kept observations in the area where possible', 'carried out house-to-house enquiries', etc., but 'with negative results'. This eventually 'got to them' in his opinion, because they felt they were always reporting on their own failures. Consequently they occasionally held on to some of the reports in the desperate hope that they might be able to come up with something. Eventually some of these were even more delayed as paperwork received later took precedence.

These examples serve to make the point that the management of paperwork must be flexible enough to allow for the many, varied contingencies which can delay the submission of fully completed items. Despite this, sergeants on Central were put under constant pressure to keep the paper turning over within the time limits imposed by senior officers through their cryptic directives on the IC sheets. Sergeants were made to feel that the justifications they offered for delays were perceived by the higher ranks to be 'lame excuses' designed to protect constables with an aversion to paperwork.

On East sub-division, on the other hand, sergeants were given licence to manage the processing of paperwork. Because they were consequently put under much less pressure, they did not find it necessary to chase up items of paperwork all the time. They could afford to allow constables to give priority to other things where they considered this necessary. To a large extent they left their officers free to organise their own work, irrespective of whether this was street work or paperwork.

As a consequence, the time taken on East to complete an enquiry or to prepare the paperwork was far longer in the main than the higher ranks on Central would permit. Yet paperwork passed through the East system without any repercussions; even lengthy delays did not produce the kind of inquisitorial investigation that we observed on Central. For example, PSU duty during the NUM dispute provided an excuse for late paperwork. The general effects of the dispute, the long hours on duty and under-staffing took their toll. No-one could deny the relevance of PSU duties in mitigation, although some sergeants insisted that their PCs were able to take paperwork with them and do it while they were on standby. (Some PCs who used PSU duties as an excuse were caught out by the sergeants later when they boasted of the money they had won playing cards whilst on standby!) One sergeant commented that he was not worried about submitting a file for a shoplifting offence from four months earlier because he would blame the delay on the effects of the dispute in the unlikely event that someone asked him to explain it. Not unexpectedly, this was an East sub-divisional sergeant. We came across other delays of this magnitude on East. Crime reports which were returned after enquiries three months on from the original incident were not uncommon, and there were cases of crime reports being delayed for five months. Such delays were accepted on East sub-division and PCs were not disciplined. This may have been due to the NUM dispute or it may not. The point is that the sergeants believed that this account would be acceptable to their superiors.

The situation was very different on Central. There were several cases during the period of the dispute where a PC was disciplined because of the amount of time taken to prepare a file. This suggests that it was not the dispute but the prevailing ethos on the two divisions which explains how delays were defined and the concern to avoid them.

Although the law places statutory time limits within which notices of intended prosecution must be served and proceedings commenced, these are far more generous than the time limits imposed by the higher ranks on Central sub-division. The fact that the East system allowed sergeants and their constables more time and harassed them less also suggests that departments and systems outside the division were not responsible for the pressure.

The use of the Central IC registers by the higher ranks, the defensive gambits of the sergeants evident in their use of the CS book, and the frustration and annoyance expressed by sergeants when they received the memoranda which they describe as 'chasing' them are all manifestations of an organisation-centred approach to paperworking. The approach is a component of a general managerial style operating on Central sub-division which aimed to control subordinates as closely as possible, to constrain their autonomy and to sharpen up the turn-round of paper as an indicator of both control and effectiveness. On East, the supervision and monitoring of paperwork production process reflected a different ethos - consistent with the principles enunciated in the policy statements of the working party quoted earlier.

Serial supervision and the quality of paperwork

As we learnt earlier, all the sergeants, irrespective of their sub-division, believed that they should accept responsibility for ensuring that PCs' files were of a good quality. This brings us back to the paradox discussed in the opening section. This aspect of paperworking, at least, is certainly not seen as 'dirty work'. Sergeants recognised that files were important and that they had a duty both to protect themselves and their constables from criticism and to promote their own ends and those of the organisation by trying to ensure that the preferred outcome was achieved through the medium of competent paperwork. How did sergeants discharge these responsibilities? How they monitored the quality of paperwork is particularly important, bearing in mind the amount of time they spent in the police station. Were there any differences in this respect between East and Central sergeants?

Constables clearly expected sergeants to be available when they needed advice about the files they were working on. During every tour of duty some discussions took place about items of paperwork. In the in-depth analysis of the sample tours, the reasons for these discussions were examined. Just under half of all the discussions that took place concerning items of paperwork were consultations that occurred prior to the item being submitted (see Table 1). Another interesting point is that on Central sub-division there was every chance that the sergeant and the constable would have discussed that particular item at least once before (Table 2). Twenty-one per cent of the discussions on Central were about items that had already been the subject of discussion during that tour of duty. A further 30 per cent of the discussions related to items of paperwork about which there had been consultation between the two during the previous tour. (This pattern of consultation was also noted with respect to incidents and enquiries before they reached the paperwork stage.)

Table 2 refers to 'serial supervision', i.e. consultation taking place at several stages during the process of preparing a file. One could actually see a file taking shape as the PC returned with a new piece of recorded evidence which the sergeant had earlier directed him to seek. This form of supervision seems to be an alternative to sergeants working in company with their PCs which station-based patrol sergeants had been forced to adopt and had trained their PCs to use.

On East sub-division there appears to have been less serial supervision with respect to paperwork. The percentage of discussions relating to items about which there had been previous discussion was much lower; 75 per cent of the discussions concerned items that were new to that sergeant. However, this reflects the system of collective responsibility operating on East sub-division and the difference in the sergeant's and constable's shift patterns which were

Table 1
Reasons why discussions of paperwork items occurred
(Number of discussions for particular reasons shown as a percentage
of all discussions of paperwork on each unit)

	Central 1983		Central 1984		East 1984	
	No.	%	No.	%	No.	%
Sergeant had returned the item	37	23	109	24	21	10
Someone else had returned the item	18	11	27	6	8	4
Discussion was part of an IC check with PC	20	13	73	16	55	27
Discussion followed receipt of a 'chaser memo'	-	-	8	2	7	4
PC consults sergeant before submitting item	77	49	218	48	100	49
Sergeant asks about item for no apparent reason	6	4	22	5	12	6
Totals	158	100	457	100	203	100

Table 2
Serial supervision – paperwork
(Whether an item had been discussed by the patrol sergeant and the
constable previously, shown as a percentage of all the discussed
items on each unit)

	Central 1983		Central 1984		East 1984	
	No.	%	No.	%	No.	%
Item had already been discussed that tour of duty	31	20	96	21	24	12
Item had been discussed during a previous tour of duty	36	23	137	30	26	13
Item had not been discussed before	91	58	224	49	153	75
Totals	158	100	457	100	203	100

Average number of items discussed each tour on each unit:
Central (1983): 7.5; Central (1984): 5.1; East (1984): 4.4

described earlier. Serial supervision did take place on East, but we would not have picked this up in the coding unless the same sergeant was consulted again by the constable. Returning to Table 1, we find additional evidence of the difference between the two sub-divisions. These differences are consistent with what we would expect given the different significance and uses of paperwork on the two sub-divisions.

For example, over 30 per cent of the discussions on Central in 1983 and 1984 related to items which the sergeants or someone else in the organisation had returned because they were unsatisfactory in some way. On East sub-division, only 14 per cent of the discussions were the result of an item being returned for more work to be done on it. This is also consistent with the finding that East sergeants were more confident about submitting paperwork, in the knowledge that it would not be returned to them.

Although the evidence is by no means conclusive, it is consistent with the interpretation that the pressure on the Central sergeants and, through them, on their PCs to expedite paperwork quickly, resulted in errors. These errors were picked up subsequently by the sergeants when they checked the items or by others later in the process who returned them. On East, the rate of turnover of paperwork was much slower, which meant there were more items to discuss during the less frequent IC checks. Many of these items would be discussed for the first time, given the infrequent checks of the IC registers and the system of collective responsibility.

The use of paperwork on self-initiated cases

The paperwork produced by constables obviously offers a means of assessing their writing skills and their ability to assemble evidence, collate facts, take statements, etc. However, it also gives some indication of the type of work the officers are involved in and, particularly, how frequently they involve themselves in incidents of their own volition. These incidents can be distinguished from those which they attend as a result of a request from members of the public. Traditionally, the number of arrests and the number of persons reported for offences which are self-initiated have been used within the police service as an indicator of a constable's motivation. Self-initiated work is an indirect method of tracing the pattern of work constables do on the streets where they are less visible to their supervisors.

The reader will correctly anticipate that the organisation-centred ethos on Central sub-division, with its emphasis on close monitoring and control of subordinates' work, resulted in it being the one where a great deal of importance was attached to self-initiated work and where constables experienced the greatest pressure to produce it.

'Red pen entries'

Proof of the importance of self-initiated work in the eyes of the higher ranks and of the way this emphasis was sustained was provided by the 'red pen entry'. Whenever the patrol sergeants on Central recorded reports or files referring to incidents their PCs had elected to be involved with, they entered them in the IC register in red ink, enabling anyone who cared to inspect the register to see at a glance how much self-initiated work each PC had produced. PCs would sometimes check with the sergeant that they had been credited with a 'red pen entry' for a particular file or report. Sometimes the sergeant would deny the request for such an entry, arguing that the item was not a piece of self-initiated work in the strict sense. In these exchanges, the limitations of the measure as an indicator of commitment and effort were highlighted, as well as the pressure put on the PCs to maintain their quota of self-initiated process. In one example, a PC argued that a report he had submitted on a dog owner for not possessing a licence should count as a piece of self-initiated work. The sergeant countered by arguing it was not, because it had started with a road traffic accident which had been reported by a member of the public. The PC detailed the enquiries he had made to trace the offending animal in connection with the accident enquiry and which had also resulted in the owner being found out for not possessing a licence. The sergeant refused and explained how one of the PC's colleagues had asked only a few weeks previously that a road traffic accident and 'breathalyser' case be considered as a piece of self-initiated work. The PC in question had conducted some painstaking and lengthy enquiries to locate witnesses to the incident. The sergeant had been impressed by the PC's argument that he had exercised initiative and followed up leads which were only discovered by virtue of his own efforts. The sergeant had sought the advice of one of the higher ranks who had refused to allow this as a true red pen entry. The example failed to placate the PC and only served to reinforce his view that the system was 'unfair and stupid'.

The importance of this kind of entry in the IC registers became more apparent when an appraisal was being prepared on a probationer constable or on a PC who had requested a transfer to a specialist unit. We observed several instances where the higher ranks on Central sub-division inspected the IC sheets to determine whether the PC 'deserved' the requested move. The converse also applied, with personnel in 'plum jobs' being expected to prove they deserved to remain in them by producing self-initiated work. The sheets of the Quick Response Vehicle drivers were examined, for example, and this resulted in several PCs being taken off the cars and replaced by others whose red pen entries justified a 'horizontal promotion'.

If the officer was a probationer constable, the pressure was more persistent and it increased as he moved closer to one of the periodic assessments and an interview with the divisional chief superintendent or his second-in-command. In one case, a sergeant met up with one of his probationers who was on a night foot patrol in the city centre. He reminded him of his impending assessment and interview with the second-in-command of the division and asked him whether he had generated any self-initiated work. The probationer assured him that he would have some by refreshment time. Later he produced four fixed-penalty tickets and when the sergeant accused him of 'hitting and running' (i.e. leaving them on the windscreens of unattended vehicles illegally parked), the PC retorted that on the contrary he was expecting a complaint to be made against him regarding one of them; he had offered the offender plenty of opportunity to move but had been given a load of abuse in return.

In another case, a sergeant explained that he was deliberately trying to create a competitive spirit and friendly rivalry between two of his probationers. Neither could afford to have anything negative said about their self-initiated work. Later in the shift one of them came into the office to have his self-initiated work recorded. All six cases related to defective lights on motor vehicles. He rationalised his actions by pointing out how bad the weather was that evening and how, with winter approaching, it was important that the owners fix the lights. The sergeant replied that he did not need to justify himself and asked him to tell the other probationer he wanted to see him in his office. He looked through the IC sheets and pointed out that the PC had not done much self-initiated work. The second probationer explained that over the previous month he had been away from the division quite a lot. The sergeant accused him of avoiding self-initiated work and the PC admitted he hated doing it. The sergeant advised him to look for different types of offences if the 'bread and butter' offences bothered him. He told him to use the collator's files to find out which disqualified drivers were still driving cars in the city centre and to go 'rooting' for them. The PC stated there was not enough time to do this, which was why his colleagues went for the easier ones. The sergeant proceeded to argue there was no disgrace in doing people for not having an excise licence. There was quite a bit of money involved and offenders were 'giving the two fingers to the law'. He promised to help the PC by telling the Quick Response Driver to take him out during the next two shifts. Jokingly he stated there was no excuse for the PC not finding the self-initiated work if he had his own driver.

Each of these cases which occurred on Central illustrates the pressure sergeants were under to get a quota of self-initiated cases from their constables. One probationer was warned that he should aim to achieve one 'knock-off' (reporting someone for an offence) and issue three cautions each tour during his probationary period if he wanted a favourable report.

Not every sergeant agreed with this emphasis. Most of the sergeants interviewed (65 per cent) agreed with the statement 'Bosses place too much emphasis on self-initiated work when they are assessing the capabilities of my PCs'. Just over one-third thought the use of self-initiated work provided a reasonable measure of performance and supported the emphasis placed upon it. Of those who objected to the emphasis, three per cent reported they found this 'very frustrating', another ten per cent thought it was 'frustrating', and 42 per cent found it 'a bit frustrating'. The remainder reported that although they did not agree with it they tried not to let it get to them and so experienced no frustration about it.

The differences between sergeants on the two sub-divisions are again interesting.

Although they were personally under less pressure than their colleagues on Central, the East sergeants knew that the deputy divisional commander was keen on self-initiated work and that it tended to be used as a performance indicator in the force generally. Many did not agree with this. Seventy-four per cent of the East sergeants agreed there was too much emphasis put on self-initiated work, 21 per cent of them strongly. On Central, only 55 per cent of the sergeants were in agreement with the statement; 11 per cent of them 'strongly agreed'.

Critics of the emphasis on self-initiated work cited its pettiness, the amount of extra paperwork it generated, which kept officers even longer in the station, and its adverse effect on relationships between the police and the public. In one instance, after wading through a large pile of fixed penalty tickets and other self-initiated paperwork, a Central patrol sergeant threw down his pen in disgust, stating that he was fed up with reports for 'tuppence ha'penny offences' like driving without a seat belt. Two PCs who were in the office at the time laughed. It was all right for them to laugh, he went on, but the whole thing was out of proportion. He had been forced to allow a PC who had reported a large number of such minor offences a whole tour of duty in which to catch up with his paperwork. He was going off on ten days leave and had generated so much self-initiated it had swamped him. At this point another PC entered the station and the sergeant enquired whether he had considered knocking off the local vicar for having a church clock which showed the wrong time!

East sergeants boasted about the fact that there were no red pen entries in their IC registers. They spoke scathingly about the system that operated on Central. One argued that the issuing of penalty tickets was a traffic warden's job! Others emphasised that they had to take into account the amount of service work and crime enquiries the PCs on East had to do which left little time for them to issue a fixed quota of cautions and knock-offs. Furthermore, on their sub-division a premium was placed on promoting good police-public relations. The Central system, they maintained, produced league tables and competition amongst PCs, resulting in the knock-offs for trivial offences which damaged the goodwill of the public.

Two forms and the different ways they were used on the two sub-divisions signify the difference in emphasis placed on self-initiated work and provide additional evidence of the contrasting management systems on East and Central. Both were officially printed forms carrying the constabulary crest and both related to various minor traffic offences. One advised offenders whose vehicles had been observed illegally parked without lights, for example, that they had committed an offence but that no further action beyond a warning was proposed. Significantly, the last sentence of the form stated that it was issued by the constabulary in the interests of road safety. East constables regularly used this warning form. On Central, on the other hand, because the emphasis was on the production of self-initiated work, such offences were more likely to be reported. In such circumstances, officers were likely to use a second form to explain to members of the public why they were justified in reporting them for an offence. This form set out the circumstances in which a vehicle could be parked without lights on a public highway. It contained a sketch plan showing the prohibited area for parking without lights near a road junction, and on the back were listed a number of other lighting requirements. These two forms were clearly designed for different purposes. One was explicitly advisory and educational in intent and epitomised a discretionary approach to law enforcement. The other signified a legalistic approach and provided the justification for the officer's actions. What is most relevant for our purposes is the fact that although we observed the first type of form in regular use on East, we never saw it used on Central sub-division. However, Central officers used the second type to explain to members of the public who complained, why they had been reported.

The higher ranks on the division soon realised the negative consequences of this performance indicator when the effects of a drive on self-initiated work on Chadd manifested themselves. About the time that the self-initiated work reached its peak, I was present when one of the higher ranks on the division spoke to a Chadd sergeant and in the course of the conversation mentioned a number of complaints which had been received and asked him to advise the PCs to 'curb their enthusiasm'. Feelings on this matter were running so high that there was a strong rumour circulating that sergeants who disapproved of the situation were advising irate members of the public who came in to the station to complain, to write to the chief constable and complain to him. However, I have no evidence that this was so.

Two models of sub-divisional management and supervision

Although they are two sub-divisions within the same division, and therefore operate under the same chief superintendent and deputy, at the time of the study

131

Central and East sub-divisions were so different that they could have been parts of two different forces. Some of these differences have been brought to light by this discussion of paperwork. If such differences can exist between two adjacent sub-divisions - a fact which has not previously received attention in the literature - how much variation is there nationally?

In this final section I shall briefly introduce other material from the study to illustrate that the two systems of control extended not only to paperwork but to other areas of activity as well.

Target setting by senior ranks

On Central, the sub-divisional commanders attended on numerous occasions the briefing sessions at the beginning of tours of duty. They directed the uniformed personnel to concentrate on certain offences - driving in bus lanes, ignoring 'no access' signs, riding bicycles on the pavement, etc. This never occurred on East sub-division during our time there.

Enforcement of discipline

Uniformed personnel were instructed that they were to travel to and from work either in full uniform or civilian clothes. They were warned that anyone wearing a plain jacket with a blue shirt and uniform-type trousers would be disciplined. East officers did not have this regulation imposed upon them and, to the frustration of colleagues in Central, were sometimes observed shopping in the city centre dressed in the proscribed manner. This rule was tightly enforced on Central personnel.

A force order permitted uniformed officers to patrol without a jacket until 2200 hours on hot summer evenings. On the division as a whole, officers were told that jackets would be worn after 2000 hours, but only on Central sub-division was this regulation strictly enforced.

Uses of other records

Like the IC registers, the cautions books were regularly inspected on Central by all supervisory ranks and used as a performance measure. At the briefings constables were reminded by their inspector and sometimes the higher ranks to record the names of offenders they had cautioned because insufficient numbers of entries were being made. On East, the same attention was not paid to the number of entries in the cautions books.

Sergeants were responsible for paying visits to licensed premises on their areas. On Central, a chart hung on the wall in the sergeant's office listing every public house in the area. Each sergeant was allocated several of these public houses and recorded each month which ones he had visited and on which dates. The sub-divisional commanders checked this chart regularly and upbraided any sergeant who failed to fulfil his complement of visits. On East sub-division, there were no such charts and sergeants were left to manage their time and fulfil this responsibility along with the others they carried.

Perceptions of supervisors' authority

The contrast between the two sub-divisions in the level of control sergeants perceived themselves as having over the processes of paperwork production was repeated in their views of the influence they carried in other areas.

Sixty-three per cent of the East sergeants agreed with the statement, 'The sergeant is the first line of management and is regarded as a manager in every respect' (cf. Child and Partridge, 1982, p.220). Only 41 per cent of Central sergeants agreed.

In response to the statement, 'The sergeant is really out on a limb - he's not one of the lads yet neither is he accepted by the bosses as one of them' (cf. Child and Partridge, op.cit.), 73 per cent of Central sergeants agreed. Only 47 per cent of East sergeants agreed.

Just as the East sergeants reported that they were more involved in decisions regarding paperwork, this extended to other aspects of their role. Whereas 52 per cent of Central sergeants agreed with the statement, 'Not enough notice is taken of what I recommend in my appraisals of PCs', only 17 per cent of those on East did. Similarly, the channels of communication between sergeants and the higher ranks which we found to be more open on East with regard to paperwork, also provided the sergeants there with more of the information they needed to do their job effectively in other areas. For example, crucial to future manpower planning is the advance notice sergeants receive about events which will involve their constables in shift changes, deviations from regular duties, etc. Status considerations are also bound up with this, because constables expect their sergeants to know about such changes and to tell them about them.

Sergeants were asked what they felt about the statement, 'Too often my bosses do not give me enough advance notice of future policing events and commitments which will affect my section'. Thirty-one per cent of East sergeants agreed with this; 77 per cent of the Central sergeants agreed with it.

These brief observations on the control structures of the two sub-divisions enable us to 'flesh out' the organisation-centred and the investigator-centred models identified in the analysis of the paperwork processes.

Central sub-division is the classic city or borough force structure, and the approach of senior officers and the defensive response of subordinates shared many similarities with the city force I studied between 1968 and 1971 (Chatterton, 1975). East was a deliberately designed 'experimental' sub-division on which an attempt was made to implement the contemporary policies of granting more status and autonomy to the lower ranks and promoting closer and harmonious police-public relationships through decentralisation and less legalistic enforcement policies. The great weakness of the East system lay in the fact that there were no performance measures. Consequently, it could easily appear to be too laissez faire and a system in which lazy officers and supervisors could get by with a minimum of effort. In Central, on the other hand, the superintendent could point to the IC registers, the red pen entries, the turnover of paperwork, the results of particular enforcement campaigns, the cautions book, the pub visits chart, and so on to demonstrate that he was able to monitor performance on the gound and to ensure that his policies were translated into action.

Conclusions and implications

One of the intentions of this chapter was to demonstrate that not all of the time spent on paperwork can be dismissed as time wasted on activities that do not constitute real police work. The analysis has also shown that police attitudes to paperwork are multi-faceted. What should now be clear is that how police

133

officers respond to survey questions on the issue of paperwork will depend very much upon the context in which they interpret them.

The lower ranks in the research division certainly regarded the completion of the forms which were returned unnecessarily by other departments as 'dirty work', and in this respect their attitudes were similar to those of their American counterparts. There are status issues involved in these complaints but a greater cause of frustration was the amount of time police officers had to spend in the police station performing mundane tasks.

On a practical note, it is clear that there is a tendency for administrative units (which in theory are supposed to act as a resource to operational officers) to develop their own departmental interests, agenda and timetables. This has to be closely watched. Otherwise the pursuit of segmental goals can have a detrimental effect on the availability for operational duties of members of the uniformed branch. Civilianising posts in these departments may make economic sense. But the price may be costly for operational policing unless civilian personnel in these units are able and prepared to recognise the demands made on operational police officers and to tailor their expectations and design their administrative systems and procedures around those needs, even if this is at some considerable inconvenience to themselves. This nettle needs to be grasped at chief officer level. Sergeants feel that they do not have the power to resist these demands without the clear unequivocal support of chief officers.

As a departure point, the principle should be enunciated that constables and their first line supervisors should have the right to decide how their time is utilised. Other units should not be able to make demands on that time without making a strong case for doing so. The system I have described on East subdivision represents a move in this direction by granting constables and sergeants greater autonomy and flexibility than they previously enjoyed.

For a similar reason, the time limits within which paperwork is required to be produced should be scrutinised and the rationale for these expectations examined. If they are reasonable, then it is important that the rationale is explained to operational personnel.

In a similar vein, the information constables record for statistical purposes and the uses to which this is put should be examined and the opportunity cost of this data collection considered. It is pertinent to ask how much feedback operational officers receive about the way these data are employed. For example, what use is actually made of the information they record on accident reports and how frequently is it utilised? Are operational officers told about these uses? If not, perhaps training courses should include periods on this topic. If the information on crime reports comes to be used more widely for crime pattern analysis in future, and if this is fed back to officers to enable them to target on problems, completing crime reports will become a task constables can see the point of doing. They will appreciate why reports need to be completed, and completed accurately, with as much relevant information as possible recorded.

These suggestions are based on the not unreasonable proposition that constables' negative attitudes to some paperwork stem partly from the fact that they are dictated by the needs and interests of other units and have no pay-off for them to compensate for the time and effort they put into submitting them.

Although it has not been possible within the space available here to discuss the paperwork which sergeants produce as part of the formal appraisal system, the section on self-initiated work raises the much wider issue of how police work is evaluated. We have noted the negative attitudes of many sergeants towards the uses of paperwork related to self-initiated law enforcement as a performance measure. The appraisal of police work and of police personnel and the devising of sensitive performance measures in policing which will not produce the kind of unintended, disfunctional consequences which we observed with the imposition of self-initiated quotas, must qualify as one of the most important issues for police researchers and managers to explore at the present time.

This analysis has shown that not all paperwork is viewed negatively. It has been argued that the lower ranks appreciate the importance of the paperwork which constitutes prosecution files and similar pieces of documentation, because this work is tied in with their own goals as well as those of the organisation. It has been shown that there are positive advantages arising from a system where the initiator, checker and decision-maker, and particularly the last two, are able to communicate regularly and through discussion develop a better appreciation of each other's expectations and approach to cases.

In the light of these findings it will be interesting to observe the effects of the Crown prosecution service on paperwork processes and for the other operational commitments of police officers. It is conceivable that the remoteness of Crown prosecutors from the operational policing context, spacially and experientially, may produce demands which first line supervisors will find difficult to reconcile with other pressures, e.g. for their constables to spend more time out on the streets.

Will the demands for value for money, efficiency and effectiveness rest easily alongside the expectations of the Crown prosecutors? Whose interests will dictate the length of time the preparation of a prosecution file should take? Will the pressures on operational personnel be taken into account when case papers are reviewed? The opportunity costs involved in obtaining additional statements, etc. will be difficult for anyone removed from the operational context to appreciate. The pressure which Central sergeants faced in adjusting to such competing demands could extend more widely in the future, and in this sense Central sub-division could represent a microcosm of the service in the future.

Notes

[1]   I would like to thank my research assistant, Gary Armstrong, for his tireless efforts in the field and for never needing to be chased for his paperwork. I am also indebted to the Economic and Social Research Council (ESRC) and the Crowd Behaviour Panel for supporting the research (reference number: GO 5250009). I would like to thank the editor for her helpful and detailed comments on the first draft of this chapter. Thanks are also owed to the chief constable and the personnel on D division who cooperated with the study.

References

Biddle, B.J. and Thomas, E.J., (1966) Role theory: concepts and research, Wiley, London

Cain, M., (1973) Society and the policeman's role, Routledge and Kegan Paul, London

Chatterton, M.R., (1975) Organisational relationships and processes in police work: a case study of urban policing, PhD thesis, University of Manchester

Chatterton, M.R., (1976) 'Police in social control', in King, J. (ed.), Control without custody, Cropwood Conference Series No.7, Institute of Criminology, Cambridge

Chatterton, M.R., (1983) 'Police work and assault charges', in Punch, M. (ed.), Control in the police organisation, MIT Press, Cambridge, Mass

Chatterton, M.R., (1985) 'Resource control: issues and prospects', Policing, 1, 4, 226-35

Chatterton, M.R. and Ellis, K.T., (1986) An investigation of the feasibility of a focused patrolling system, unpublished

Child, J. and Partridge, B., (1982) Lost managers. Supervisors in industry and society, Cambridge University Press, Cambridge

Cicourel, A., (1968) The social organisation of juvenile justice, Wiley, London

Gross, N., Mason, W.S. and McEachern, A.W., (1964) Explorations in role analysis: studies of the school superintendency role, Wiley, New York

Holdaway, S., (1983) Inside the British police, Basil Blackwell, Oxford

Home Office Circular 114/1983 Manpower, effectiveness and efficiency in the police service

Kinsey, R., (1985) Survey of Merseyside police officers, Merseyside County Council, Liverpool

Manning, P., (1977) Police work, MIT Press, Cambridge, Mass

Manning, P., (1980) The narcs' game, MIT Press, Cambridge, Mass

Policy Studies Institute (1983) Police and people in London. Vol.III. A survey of police officers, by Smith, D.J., London

Preiss, J.J. and Erlich, H.J., (1966) An examination of role theory. The case of the state police, University of Nebraska Press, Lincoln

Punch, M., (1983) Control in the police organisation, MIT Press, Cambridge, Mass

van Maanen, J., (1983) 'The boss: first-line supervision in an American police agency', in Punch, M., Control in the police organisation, MIT Press, Cambridge, Mass

Woodall, R., Newton, K. and Hannaford, C., (1982) A working party report on the feasibility of a return to traditional policing, Derbyshire Constabulary

PART III
REGULATING
THE POLICE

9 Police decision-making

PETER K. MANNING AND KEITH HAWKINS

Introduction

In this chapter we seek to discern some of the major characteristics of police decision-making in light of features common to the making of legal decisions in general. The chapter concludes with a discussion of some of the implications of the analysis and some suggestions for future research work.

Police research

Research into police work is now a tradition of long standing which reaches back to Westley's University of Chicago PhD dissertation of 1950 (published in 1970) and includes some of the most useful sources on the sociology of legal processes (for example, Banton, 1964; Skolnick, 1966; Wilson, 1968; Reiss, 1971; Black, 1980; Policy Studies Institute, 1983; see also Bordua, 1967; Rubinstein, 1973). One of the preoccupations (though more tacit than explicit) of these writers has been the question of how an individual police officer reaches a decision about whether, and how, to involve the law in encounters with suspected or alleged offenders. This emphasis is not surprising because the police control access to the criminal justice process, and the police officer's decision is important from this social policy point of view. Decision-making is also emphasised in routine police work of course, where the criminal law is very vividly seen to be in action.

One consequence of policing research in this tradition, however, has been to regard police decision behaviour as essentially a matter of making choices about how to process or dispose of discrete, isolated events or individuals on the street. In particular, the image of police decision-making tends to be one of discretion exercised by isolated individuals 'out there', working in rather low visibility settings (Goldstein, 1960), to a substantial extent unencumbered by organisational and legal controls on the exercise of their discretion. The focus of much of the work has been, therefore, upon police decision-making as a form of case-creating discretion, in which the key decision is one of gate-keeping about which individuals are to be screened in or out of the formal system of criminal justice. There has been much less attention to decisions made in the course of the further processing of cases, which might be regarded as case-handling discretion (Hawkins, 1984a), and virtually none to decisions made by police officials about how to decide about classes of cases or problems - about, in other words, the formulation of policing policy.

Another consequence of the focus upon case-creating discretion has been that in much of the existing work on police decision-making, the problem has tended to be framed as one of the selective enforcement of the law, or even the non-enforcement of the law (La Fave, 1966), or as one of the extent to which supervening moral and organisational constraints distort the lawyer's ideal of the even-handed and dispassionate enforcement of the law (Davis, 1969, 1975). Thus we have come to understand police decision-making as an enterprise in which individual behaviour is not only constrained to an extent by rules embodied in statements of the law and of organisational policy, but is also a product of morally informed, normal ways of responding to particular types of individual, event and setting. In understanding what shapes encounters with suspects, for example, we tend to regard organisational policy and resource constraints as disposing against full enforcement of the law. Instead, a major component in discriminating between those screened in or out of the criminal justice system is a commonsense, moral conception of an individual's desert. This leads to judgements about the reach and application of the criminal law being premised, often very substantially, upon interpreted signs such as the appropriateness of a suspect's demeanour, or the extent to which he or she appears to make claims to toughness, or to be anti-authority.(e.g. Piliavin and Briar, 1964).

We intend in this chapter to essay a broader focus and consider from a naturalistic perspective police decision-making as merely one species of legal decision-making. Naturalism assumes the necessity of examining decisions as they are made within organisations, and within the presuppositional framework of those who take them. Thus, experimental, rationalistic and logical studies of decision-making are rejected, and studies which highlight the collective, pheno-menological, and bounded nature of decisions are sought (Hawkins, 1986; Manning, 1986). In some important sense, our notion of decision rests upon an interest in decision-accounts, or what is explained or understood to be the nature of decisions taken. We are interested in the symbolisation of such matters within organisational contexts.

Because the symbolic forms of decisions within the criminal justice system contain a set of general traits, they can be compared. Indeed policing is, of course, only one form of law enforcement decision-making. Quite apart from an array of private policing and security systems, there is an enormous analogous apparatus of social control in the form of various regulatory agencies and inspectorates, whose activities until recently have largely escaped the attention of researchers (but see, for example, Carson, 1970a, 1970b; Cranston, 1979; Richardson et al., 1983; Hawkins, 1984b; Hutter, 1984; Jamieson, 1985). However, although studies of police work - our primary concern here - have been an important source, shaping the 'law in action' and sociology of law perspective within the social sciences, the research has not been understood within the context of the structure of decision-making generally within the criminal justice system. This system, which rationalises its mandate in terms of producing decisions based on law with a generalised moral character which are binding in theory on all citizens, is composed of several segments (citizens, police, prosecutors, defenders, courts, prisons, and probation and parole, cf Reiss, 1974). This overview of criminal justice decisions, as brief as it must be, requires that one selects characteristics of police decision-making as a kind of ideal type seen against alternatives rather than in light of description of current police practices. Of these, we possess a surfeit.

The aim of the following section is to discuss police decision-making within the criminal justice system in terms of four criterial features: consequentiality, degree of generality (case vs. policy focus), visibility, and complexity of the task. Variation within policing is discussed in a subsequent section.

Criterial features

Consequentiality As we have already suggested, one of the obvious characteristics of police decisions is that they are extremely consequential for the individuals who are the subject of decision. Police officers screen people and events for further processing, that is, a decision is made which differentiates between people, leading either to a decision to do nothing or a decision to proceed further in some way. This conception inelegantly groups together an array of different consequences. From an organisational point of view, screening is demanded as a means of controlling access to the scarce resource of criminal justice processing, thereby preventing or at least making more manageable an overloading of the organisation's capacity to continue to do its job. In this respect the organisational constraints upon policing resemble those which are to be observed in other public service organisations (Lipsky, 1980). From the individual enforcement agent's point of view, screening is a necessary moral task which serves to weed out the essentially undeserving to protect them from the potentially harsh rigours of the criminal process. As Reiss and Bordua pointed out (1967), the police officer's conception of justice is satisfied when such an offender is let off.

So far as the suspect is concerned, the screening decision is presumably of the highest significance since it is one which may close off access to the criminal process, or may not, as the case may be. For those drawn further into the system of control, the screening decision serves to create a case and to create, or to mark further, a criminal record. The screening decision thus becomes the first of a potentially lengthy series of decisions to be made in the further handling of the case until its career culminates either in a final decision not to proceed further, or in prosecution, with all that this implies for the staining of an individual's life and the formal opening up of the prospects of conviction and criminal punishment.

Degree of generality A second characteristic of police work which it shares with decisions made in other areas of the criminal process is that it involves decisions about cases as well as decisions about policy. Case decision-making centres upon judgements, commonly made by individual officers, which have to be reached about handling specific people or dealing with particular events. Policy decision-making, in contrast, may well be activity involving a number of individuals (acting together, or in sequence, or both) which is directed towards classes of people, events or problems and is intended to influence case decision-making in a general sense.

Case and policy decision-making is associated with the way in which the law is mobilised (Black, 1980). Case decisions are characteristic of much reactively-prompted police decisions (police must decide what to do when a victim or complainant reports a crime) and of some proactively-organised work (police must decide what to do when a speeding motorist is stopped). Proactively-organised enforcement normally applies a policy decision as well, however (officials decide to crack down on drunken drivers at Christmas). And where the concern is to take action of a preventive or prospective sort, policy decisions are involved.

Decision behaviour in case and policy decisions presents a number of contrasts. For example, case decisions on the street (see below) are essentially concrete, practical and non-reflective, that is they have to be made 'here and now', 'on the spot'; indeed a commonly-asserted virtue of the officer on the street is an ability to make decisions in such circumstances – the ability to 'handle a situation' (Wilson, 1968). Such decisions must be made with a degree of immediacy; this means they tend to be made with a high degree of informality. The orientation in case decision-making to individual people or events also gives them a fragmented, particularistic, ad hoc character, and to the extent that any policy is expressed in such decisions, it tends to be in the aggregation of a series of discrete, segregated cases involving independently taken decisions. To a considerable degree such fragmentation is an inevitable consequence of enforcing law by means of a dispersed set of individuals frequently making decisions in low visibility settings and to a considerable degree free of surveillance or control by senior officers (Kaufman, 1960). Furthermore, the particularistic nature of the decisions made here means that individual officers have virtually no holistic conception of a set of cases (Emerson, 1983), in contrast, for example, with other street level bureaucrats (to use Lipsky's (1980) term) like probation officers. The significance of this is that case decisions on the street tend not to be constrained by prior decisions. However, such decisions may be influenced by earlier practice in the more diffused, segregated form of the knowledge generally available to officers about 'normal cases' (Sudnow, 1965) (see below).

Policy decisions, on the other hand, tend to be collectively made. They are abstract in nature, reflective and considered, and occupy a public place in the organisation, since they are intended to have consequences for future case decision-making by numbers of individual agents. Thus they are centralised in character, speaking prospectively to the future in a coherent, generalised way.

Visibility   A third feature of police decision-making is the variable nature of its visibility, that is, its capacity to come to the attention of others. Policy decisions will be taken in private, but may well be very visible - indeed, intended to be visible – in their consequences. Case decisions made in reactively mobilised circumstances will be visible to the extent that they occur in the presence of a suspect or a victim ·or complainant. Proactively mobilised decisions will tend to be visible only to the suspect. The implications for the exercise of discretion vary according to the visibility of a law enforcement decision. Low visibility decisions, involving an enforcement agent and a suspected rule-breaker, are more amenable to bargained outcomes than decisions in which a victim or complainant has an interest, where a paper record or a formal complaint may be involved.

In this latter case a decision about law enforcement may reflect in some circumstances the preferences of the third party (Black, 1980). Furthermore, the more visible the decision process, the more amenable it is to constraint - or at least the application of constraint - by precedent or rule.

Complexity of task   A final feature to note is that, compared with some other kinds of legal decision task, police decision-making is marked by its complexity of choice. The task of policing is characterised by heterogeneity. The conduct subject to policing control varies widely from untoward behaviour of great triviality to major violations of the criminal law of the utmost gravity. The perceived gravity or triviality of an act or event will almost certainly have implications for judgements made about whether to enforce the law or not. This decision, however, is not really a binary choice about action or inaction, for the question of how to act is equally important. Police can choose to do nothing or give advice, warn, threaten, or formally caution. They may sometimes refer people to other agencies or, in domestic disputes, engage in social work or counselling. Or, of course, they may arrest.

In general, it seems that the less serious the behaviour encountered, the wider the array of possible choices about action open to a police officer. In this respect the behaviour of the police almost certainly resembles the behaviour of other sorts of law enforcement official, such as regulatory inspectors (Hawkins, 1984b), or parole officers (McCleary, 1978). On the other hand, other criminal process decisions are characterised by the homogeneity of the issue: a member of a parole board has to decide whether an eligible prisoner is suitable for release or not. Issue and outcome here are essentially binary.

The criterial features of police decision-making, seen in criminal justice context, distinguish these decisions from those taken by other agencies and those taken within other segments of the system. There are, in addition, police-specific constraints which pattern police decision-making. The role of information is primary here, and has been fundamental to all theories of policing developed to date. That is, all have assumed that the basis for police actions is information and have proceeded to produce explanations for outcomes based on this assumption (see Wilson, 1968; Skolnick, 1966; Reiss and Bordua, 1967; Black, 1980. For an exception to this generalisation, compare Manning, 1977, 1980, 1982, forthcoming). The constraints of primary interest in attempting to focus the actual texture and shape of decisions in policing are those of information (primary, secondary and tertiary) and the degree to which there is differentiation and integration of this information within segments of information systems (meaning). The resource-base of policing also modifies information usage. The other factors shaping decisions are, as it were, the result of the social organisation of police decision-making, and are the subject of the following section: usage of information, police strategies and police intelligence systems.

The internal constraints on police decision-making

Information

Information is the difference that makes a difference. Information is of various sorts: primary (that which first comes to police attention); secondary (that which has been processed once or more by any unit within the police); and tertiary (that which has been processed by any two functional units within the police). Information that has been processed more than once by a single unit remains primary information. Information which has made only one loop, such as from patrol to detective division and back, remains secondary information once processed. Such loops could in theory be endless, producing secondary information which has been processed three, four or more times. Information that has been processed by a single unit, sent to a second and on to a third, such as information moving from patrol to detective division to internal affairs and back to patrol, would still be tertiary information once processed by internal affairs-patrol. Source is either the public on the one hand or internal police sources. The assumption lying behind the administrative model of policing (Manning, 1977;

Hough, 1980) is that all demand to the police has the same source, importance and formal status as a message, and produces the same sort of demand. Demand is shaped internally and externally in at least four ways: by the source of the demand, the degree of structure, the availability of resources to respond and the horizon of intent within the organisation (see Manning, 1982). It should be recalled that source effects are fundamental, and that the nature of the 'external world' that is so constructed, that is, how the police view the events as having come to their attention, is an important basis for rationalising police strategies (see Reiss, in Hawkins and Thomas, 1984).

Primary information dominates certain functions within the police department. Units such as patrol and traffic are most dependent upon citizen-sourced information and provide the greatest amount of 'new information' as a result of their stops, enquiries, observations, and any encounter which they initiate on their own (what Reiss and Black term proactive, or police-initiated enforcement). According to various researches, around 86 per cent of police workload arises from citizen calls (Reiss, 1971, p.11). Primary information is also received to a lesser degree by detective, vice and juvenile units but the amount of primary information thus received is unknown since records are not kept on the calls to these units unless they result in an investigation (see, for example, Ericson, 1981, p.84 Table 3.2; Manning, 1980). Primary information is least available to staff units such as internal affairs, administration and research and planning.

Secondary information is present of course in all functional areas of policing, both staff and line, but it is concentrated in juveniles, vice and detective work, since a large proportion of their casework is based upon information received from patrol or traffic. It is previously encoded information (put in police classification or format) which has been decoded for use in internal affairs. Administration is a line function in the sense of organisational authority. The authority it exercises is based on tertiary information which has been twice processed by the unit it is intended to be guiding, commanding and controlling.

Each of the functional units of the police has a series of correlates in objectives and in resources. There is an interaction between information and the social organisation of police work. There is further an interaction to be found between the type of information, the uses (objectives) to which it is put and the means (technology: equipment and resources) by which it is processed, stored and retrieved. Thus, one must imagine how primary information is used to obtain objectives for a functional unit, and how means are employed to gather, process and apply that type of information. Each of the primary, secondary and tertiary information-dominated units has internal features related to the differentiation of the information used, given objectives and technology. There is a covariation in information by function for objectives and technology. Hidden in this covariation is the social meaning of information for police operational and staff units.

A distinction that to some extent elaborates upon the primary-secondary-tertiary classification is the degree of differentiation of the information system. Another term for this is entropy, or the equivalence of the amount of information across the units in police work. Patrol units are most information-intensive and most tied to inputs flowing directly from the environment. These inputs are most likely to be written or recorded in the form of official paperwork such as activity logs and other reports. Recorded data from patrol radio communications are always maintained (these various files and records are not cross-indexed except by the names of the arrestees, although computerised systems could be designed to do this). The traffic unit shares these characteristics. Little new information is gathered once a call is answered or investigated. This task falls to other officers who require both primary and secondary information and are thus less environment-dependent than the patrol and traffic segments, more autonomous in processing information, and more entropic. Given this degree of environment-dependency, juvenile and detective officers are most dependent on primary information passed on to them to create secondary information, and narcotics-vice units are less dependent because a substantial minority of their information comes from their own efforts, or those of their informants. In this way, they resemble internal affairs and research and planning. Administration is most differentiated from the other police line units because of the diversity of information it receives, and its dependence on both primary and secondary information. Although they possess more general, abstract and synthesised information, administrative units depend largely upon the realised and shared information-processing capacities of patrol officers. Administrative and planning and research units possess formidable amounts of technology and their own staff. While the largest proportion of resources, personnel and equipment used to gather information of all sorts is possessed by patrol, the capacity to synthesise information lies theoretically in administration. Administration is very weakly linked to sources of external information.

From an information perspective, primary information is tied most closely to tasks and demands in the environment; secondary information is encoded and amplified by knowledge technology within the system; while tertiary information is created by units that perform integrative functions. As messages move through the organisation from 'bottom' to 'top' they decrease in information content while the meaning of that information is transformed (see MacKay, 1969). MacKay's formulation suggests that producing effects on crime using new information technology is not entirely a question of increasing information levels, or even of improving the gathering, processing or application of information. The problem is rather one of meaning, or how information can be used to effect a change in the organising function.

These distinctions concerning the type, differentiation and level of integration of information are also reflected in police resources. Police technological resources include equipment (hardware) and resources (software). Perhaps the most common example of hardware is computer machinery and related input systems for processing and producing data such as card-reading machines, tape storage and associated memories, and printers or screens that generate or display output. The various trained personnel who maintain, run, adjust and repair the machinery and the programmes they write to put the data into usable format, the forms, flow charts and the.like, are viewed as software or resources. In practice, software and hardware are inextricable.

Information use

The use and implementation of the information symbolised by this technological capacity is limited by certain aspects of police work. Information that is worked on by members, or processed, is not of the same quality, specificity, and amount across units and persons. Aspects of the social organisation of police work ensure that the information available remains located primarily in the heads of officers, and secondarily in their own case files, private notes or log books.' Only under certain specified conditions does it become universally understood, generally shared, reproducible knowledge held collectively by the organisation. The fragmented and personalised character of the knowledge possessed by officers, designed in part to protect them from supervision and discipline, is nowhere systematised into a uniform, comprehensible set of data files that are cross-referenced, retrievable, shared, in universal format, and available to all officers (Bittner, 1970, p.67).

The social organisation of police work amplifies the asymmetrical aspects of primary, secondary and tertiary information flow. It does so for the following reasons. The basic and fundamental knowledge of policing is believed to be the facts at hand gathered on the scene that only the person there can understand fully and in depth. All valid police knowledge is thought to be contextual knowledge, surrounded by unexplicated, tacit assumptions and meanings. The essential knowledge of police work is thought to be substantive, detailed, concrete, temporally bounded, and particularistic in nature. The validity of this type of knowledge is derived from a police belief that police officers should learn and know social life in precisely this detailed and grounded fashion. (In fact, evidence suggests that most officers do not possess this rich knowledge, in part because they do not seek it; in part because they are not trained to do so; in part because they are not systematically rewarded for being active, observant and interested; and in part because they rarely – at least in large cities – have the opportunity to spend a great deal of time in the same area, with the same partner, during the same period of the day.) Often it is worthwhile for the officer to retain information for personal use. Information is rarely shared. The several kinds of files are not cross-referenced, but can only be utilised simultaneously by patrol officers who possess very good memories and an excellent capacity to recall information. No system articulates, for example, detective cases, juvenile records, vice-narcotics units' files (e.g. nicknames, modus operandi, informants), current or past cases, departmental arrest records, current or past charges, police despatch tapes, telephone message files, and intelligence files.

The nature of information in police departments can be best characterised as systematically decentralised and personalised. As has been argued at length elsewhere (Manning, 1977, 1980), the decentralised nature of police work, its craft character, the socialisation pattern for young recruits (see van Maanen and Schien, 1979) and pressure to close incidents and return to service are determinant of what is viewed as decision-relevant information. The clinical nature of the work as defined traditionally and in the police culture (see Manning, 1982), as well as its immediacy and situated character, and the structural characteristics of police knowledge, lead to the discreditation of paperwork, files and systematised information. Personalisation and guarding of knowledge, secrecy, and an exaggerated emphasis upon accomplishing work which terminates immediately, is closed and requires no paperwork also often make primary information-based decisions terminal. Such incidents are record-free and neither produce records nor are their particulars recorded. They are often covered by glosses such as: 'All quiet on arrival'; 'No sign'; 'All in order (on arrival)'; 'Area searched: no trace'; 'No trace on arrival'; or 'No police action'. The systematisation of a layer of information called command and control-relevant or operations-relevant, while leaving open the definition of what is relevant to officers on the ground, means that the operations research and administrative model of police action does not describe the conditions under which information will be entered into the system, but only describes what can occur when in fact it is entered.

Information and police operational strategies

Traditionally, the police have developed their modes of enacting the environment by a gradual shift from maintaining a simple presence and availability to citizens and responding to requests for aid and succour based upon a kind of crude utilitarianistic notion of deterrence via presence and availability, to active involvement in events defined as requiring police intervention. The original justification for policing was as an available and neutral force. Its role was reactive. In time, especially with the development of the detective in the late nineteenth century in London, an additional police role emerged in the Anglo-American policing model. Police were now, with respect to some types of events, to be proactive, to intervene prior to or simultaneously with an event (or actually to create the conditions under which the probability of crime was highly likely, for example acting as undercover agents who bought illicit drugs). The aim of such activity shifts to intervention: the agent works selectively and through informants, and comes to depend on information technology that is used to anticipate crimes or predict or pre-empt their occurrence. Both reactive and proactive strategies focus on criminals or what Pepinsky terms criminality (Pepinsky, 1980, p.45): individuals who have committed, are thought to have committed, or are thought likely to commit in the future, crime. Preventive approaches, on the other hand, seek to reduce the rate of crime (ibid.). Clearly, these are not mutually exclusive approaches, and they interact in complex ways, but the preventive approach seeks to deter or pre-empt crime, uses citizens as cooperative partners, and employs special information technology.

These are termed operational strategies, or modes of deployment (arrayed in time and space) and allocation (the depth of coverage in different positions) of police. There are a set of known correlates of these operational strategies: the time at which intervention is meant to occur, the aim of that intervention, the place or role of the agent in the intervention, the relationship of the agent to the public and the relevant information technology (see Manning and van Maanen, 1977, p.144). They are in turn related to intelligence functions in policing.

Information and intelligence

Intelligence functions are of three types. The first, prospective intelligence, is information which is gathered in advance on the basis of selected targets and causal understandings of the phenomena to be controlled. For example, in vice policing, certain known gamblers may be targeted for surveillance, dossiers compiled and their places of business surveilled. When it is thought appropriate to intervene, previously assembled information is available. Retrospective intelligence, on the other hand, is information that accrues in the normal course of police work, for example the records on arrest, traffic violations, and outstanding warrants, which are gathered and then recalled from storage files to organise an event that has previously taken place. After a robbery or burglary in which suspects are in hand, information may be sought on previous activities for the purpose of investigation or supporting data. Finally, applied intelligence is relevant once suspects are in hand. If a crime has been committed and the police wish to intervene, applied intelligence is used to link previously named suspects with known deeds. This may require analytically devolved data such as forensic materials, and the inferential work of linking suspects to time, place, opportunity, motive and the like. It is the stuff of which great detective films are made, but surprisingly lacking in everyday police work (Sanders, 1977; Greenwood, Chaiken and Petersilia, 1977; Ericson, 1981).

It should be clear that the operational strategies of the police determine the sorts of information/intelligence needs that they develop and maintain and not the other way round. Knowing police praxis, then, allows one to understand the relative degree of development and uses of various types of intelligence, while the uses of that intelligence could not be predicted by reference to the hypothecated value of such types of information. Let us now further review police operational strategies and their relationship to intelligence functions.

Police operational strategies

Preventive strategies are considered tangential to achieving their unspecified aims, and units that carry them out - police community relations and crime prevention units - are thought of as low status, marginal and ancillary to policing (see Norris, 1979). They function without clear goals, direction, purpose or supervision. The agent is defined as 'helper', or 'officer friendly', assisting community members to achieve a better quality of life. Little, if any, prospective intelligence is gathered by community relations and crime prevention officers because there is no theoretical conception of the causes of crime and therefore the type of information required is not defined. Retrospective intelligence stands in isolation from their operations. Applied intelligence is virtually irrelevant, almost by definition. In effect, crime prevention units provide no new primary information, nor perform any analysis that could be viewed as producing secondary information.

Proactive strategies focus on the time prior to which a crime becomes an event, and the aim of the strategy through the agent is to create crime and arrest criminals. In proactive policing, the police actively generate information and attempt to create the conditions of arrest (as in making drugs buys that are later used as the basis for making an arrest for the sale of an illicit substance) or they aim to intercept crime via 'stake-outs', saturation operations, or road blocks. The agent targets and then works either to reduce resistance or to facilitate compliance. Prospective intelligence is gathered to anticipate the commission of a crime, but usually after initial information is received from informants or undercover operatives. Retrospective intelligence is also used: once a crime is known to have been committed and is either written up in case files or arrest records, it becomes part of a new data file which might assist in identifying potential perpetrators of newly discovered crimes. Applied intelligence, although used in proactive policing, has its most frequent use in reactive work.

In the case of crimes detected or viewed by the police as a result of reactive strategies, or brought to their attention by citizens, the role of the agent resembles that of the stereotypical detective. The events at issue come to the attention of the police after their commission; this includes the vast majority of crime, both personal and property offences, as well as much traffic and juvenile crime. Agents rely on citizens to target, especially witnesses, and follow clues to 'solve' the crime reported.

Dominating reactive strategies is the role that technology plays in organising retrospective intelligence. The purpose of information technology in this strategy is to organise and systematise already extant, accumulated data received into a workable format. These sorts of operations are typically constituted by raw statistics-gathering: mapping and charting crimes as to time, location, amount of property involved, and type of crime by district and by unit or person(s) responsible for investigation. Little attempt is made to use the information in a predictive, preventive or evaluative fashion (Rheiner et al., 1979). Typically, retrospective intelligence is gathered through interviewing informants, confessions, or admissions to previously known crimes, or by detectives' interviews of suspects. Once a possible crime has been identified and the police have information as to its content, personnel, location and consequences, both prospective and retrospective intelligence are used.

Other uses of information technology in reactive police strategies are retro-spective in the sense that technology can make available to patrol officers information on other past crimes by suspects currently under investigation, for example outstanding warrants, the most important of this sort of information. Stolen vehicles, licence plates, and drivers' licences and criminal records are among the systematised types of data. For situations where an officer intervenes and is indecisive about the status of the suspect with regard to arrest or detention, such computerised systems may assist decision-making. They will provide the necessary information that will allow the police to hold and perhaps charge a person who might otherwise not be questioned or arrested and charged with a crime or violation for which a warrant has been issued. These arrests represent small, but important, increments for police departments. Traffic warrants, once computerised, can be used effectively in making arrests and in generating income, and have thus gained popularity in some cities.

Sophisticated data processing can contribute little to applied intelligence, the transforming processes necessary to link passive information (files, records, documents, messages) with a crime and thus convert it into active, or suspect-relevant information. It can only store and assemble data, and create patterns upon instruction. The use of latent fingerprint or voice print information to establish suspects is largely a media myth, given the enormous number of data points that would have to be checked to match a given print against a file of prints.

When the place of information gathering, analysis, implementation and use is seen in the context of substantive police activities, objectives, technology and operational strategies, several tentative conclusions can be advanced. In summarising the role of information in police decision-making, one can assert that the information most gathered and used is primary data derived from patrol activities. This rarely penetrates the next substantive levels, nor is it converted into secondary or tertiary information. It is rarely stored, resides in the memories of officers dispersed in time and space, has no uniform format, and can therefore never be retrieved except from the individual who possesses it. Information is differentially organised at different levels such that the most redundancy is at the highest levels, where abstract concepts are used, while the greatest uncertainty obtains at the bottom where more 'command' decisions are in fact made. The integrative actions of command occur after an event of interest has transpired, for example where police have failed to stop an assassination attempt, a string of rapes or robberies, or a corruption scandal that unfolds. Although administrators possess more diverse, general and abstract information, it comes to them in a lagged fashion, and is weakly linked to external sources of facts. The meaning of facts changes as data move up or down the line in the organisation.

When data are available, they are in raw and unintegrated form, and are held in discrete, chunked and coded units in individual officers' memories. When (or because) data are full and rich, they are not entered into the computer in many cases, and when they are entered they are often construed by those who use the system as trivial. Command officers distrust the system as well, and rely instead on their memories, what has happened before in such situations, reports received from inspectors, and personal interviews conducted with those involved. That is, much information is not placed in centralised forms or locations, that which is, is often viewed as trivial, and extant important information is almost entirely of the retrospective intelligence sort, differentially useful to the police, given their strategies.

149

When resources are considered, simple existence of a capacity is meaningless unless it is implemented. When do the police actually use such systems, under what conditions, and what are they used for?

Once one examines the ways in which information flows into police departments and the ways in which it is employed in operational strategies (input/output processes), it is clear that information is:

(a) of little importance in preventive strategies because the relevance of various types of information is not specified, and there is no theory of causation and efficiency that might determine what is to be gathered, stored and applied;

(b) critical in all forms of proactive strategies, but not systematic, centralised and theoretically applied, and least guided by computerised systems (in most police forces, data from detective work, cases and records from other secondary information sources such as juveniles and vice records and files, are never entered in computer records);

(c) most used in reactive strategies where a suspect is known, a crime has been known to have been committed, and there is a previous record on this suspect.

Conversely, where information is most relevant and used is in routine 'housekeeping tasks', such as internal record-keeping, payroll, holiday and sick days taken, message transfer and in storing data for retrieval for review.

The social constraints or filters on calls to the police; the variously organised networks or sources from which the messages flow; demand-conditions generally for the supply of police; contingencies within the organisation having to do with the processing of information and its type, degree of differentiation and integration; the social organisation of police work (especially its clinical nature and record-keeping style); and the strategies of policing, all condition information technology much more than information technology conditions police work. The technology is used to produce and reproduce traditional ways of doing things or practices, and is slowly modifying them (cf Kling and Scacchi, 1982).

The constraints of police decision-making and information-patterning shape the special character of the decisions taken by the police, both in number and type. A somewhat closer examination of police decision-making shows that context or field variables also shape the sort of pressures, values, perspectives and situations which repeatedly are replicated in Anglo-American policing. We have selected three types of police decision-making based on type of information (primary, secondary and tertiary) and array them now against variables which are drawn from the comparative survey made in the first section of this chapter and specified by our other work in this area (see Hawkins, 1984a, 1986; Manning, 1977, 1980, 1982, 1986; Hawkins and Manning, forthcoming).

The structure of police decision-making

Three types of decision-making can be identified. The first of these is 'street' decision-making, which is basically decision-making based on primary data. The second is 'paper' decision-making, which is carried out by investigators, internal affairs units and others who deal with secondary or once-processed data in the form of cases. Finally, there are policy or administrative decisions. Although they are considered as similar for the purposes of this discussion, the degree to which administrative decisions, or those based on twice-processed data, are 'policy' is a variable. There are five variables, or features of decisions, which one can use to describe the context within which police decisions are taken. These are: the discrete nature of decisions; the nature of the espoused reality; features of the job of policing; the audience to which decisions are directed; and the relevance of law as a resource.

Discrete decisions   In primary decision-making, case by case decisions are taken and they are seen as independent of each other both in terms of the physical and social world which produces the events and the response of the officers who dispose of them. The reality of these decisions is that they are in the here and now, experiential, immediate, and based on a non-reflective stance to the events. Intuition is valued and encouraged. There are very limited constraints produced by previous decisions (for example whether an officer has arrested someone previously), but economic constraints may operate (for example if petrol supplies are limited, drunken driving arrests may decline). In decision-making involving cases or secondary data, cases are seen as more immediate sets, perhaps based on notions of 'normal crimes' or typifications of cases (Sudnow, 1965; Waegel, 1981) or series of cases. Cases are seen as quasi-dependent one on another. For example, cases may be clustered or grouped on the basis of offences taken into consideration or there may be bargaining around cases involving several persons. The data include here and now data as well as retrospective reconstructions of crimes and potential or attempted crimes. There may be marginal effects of case-sets therefore, because of the links made between villains, patterns of crime by neighbourhood, or cases worked by given groups of officers in sub-divisions.

There is considerable ignorance about the working and handling of cases horizontally (officers' peers do not share information about cases in any systematic fashion) and vertically (there is little feedback from CID or prosecutors or courts to street decision-makers). There is some sharing of information between detective units and some information shared horizontally. Decision-making involving tertiary data is in theory organised around problems or objectives rather than cases, except in the event of major scandals or crises, which tend to conflate 'policy' and routine-case-orientated decisions. There is a degree of interlocking of actions which is more future-orientated than retrospective in character. The sorts of data utilised are by definition tertiary, but in theory could be any data related to current practice that is required. There is what might be called 'theoretically possible' knowledge of all recorded decisions within the force. The capacity and will to acquire such data is another matter, of course. Although reflection is valued, the nature of experience preceding making one's way to an administrative position is diverse, and may not be cumulative. Discontinuity is the basis for promotion and the basis of practice once promoted has been noted (van Maanen, 1983). Although there are increasing emphases upon management, it is not clear what is to be managed and how officers attain the information, skills and judgement thought to be necessary to managing in the police.

The nature of the espoused reality   Perhaps the fundamental divide in policing is that between what is viewed as the reality of the streets, the 'sharp end', or 'on the ground', and the reality of the administrators, the 'paper-pushers' and the senior officers within the force (see for example Manning, 1977, ch.6, 1980, pp.220-4; Reuss-Ianni and Ianni, 1983). In the primary decision-making world, the paper or records are variously seen as secondary to the immediate and face-to-face reality of interpersonal management of trouble. Reality is street reality. Paperwork is disdained. Paperwork, if done, is a way to cover oneself against the claim that nothing has been done about something, a necessary means of disposing of an event, an offensive resource for controlling an adversary or potential adversary (using the arrest as a tactic for controlling a situation). It can also be used to open a situation, to give indication that further investigation should be done. The aim is generally to close and finish a face-to-face incident with the 'right paper', which ideally concludes the situation. In the case of secondary data, or paperwork decisions, paper is seen as a 'necessary evil', and paper realities and street realities may often come into conflict. This is in part because the notion of what is 'good police work' involves the rule that one should not 'second guess' the actions of an officer, and that one 'had to be there' to appreciate the nuances, pressures and conflicts involved as seen by the officer. These views are widely held up and down the police organisational hierarchy. Paper may conflict with the idea that street decisions can in some sense never be predicted because they are sporadic, uncertain, uneven in scope and potential, and crescive or emergent in nature. Paper may have to be seen through, as well as seen and seen to have been done. The aim is to create, work, close or dispose of cases that have been opened. When tertiary information is used, decisions are to be recorded on paper and are real, even though they stand in contrast to policing on the streets. Paper may be seen as a prospective tool. Decision-makers may not think of themselves as doing real police work when they act in an administrative capacity. Paper must be used to construct and show the relevant social reality. The aim is to avoid scandal, i.e. individual foul-ups or crises (Punch, 1985). The broader aim of administrative action is to display loyalty to the mandate, the law and the relevant political entity.

Features of the job   The job is seen in the street world as a non-reflective task in which intuition is valued and encouraged. The ways in which this non-reflective, action-orientated job are learned are apprentice-like, and are seen as a craft based on a variety of human skills such as humour, interpersonal skill, good manners, the potential to convey the threat of force in a subtle manner without hesitating to use it, and an equanimity.

The audience   The audience is the public on the one hand, and colleagues on the other. The closer colleagues are to self, the more trustworthy and loyal they are expected to be. Thus there is an onion-like series of layers from partner, to former partners, to others on the shift, to others formerly on the shift and so on to the most distant of colleagues, the chief constable. Those working with secondary data value temporary secondments and courses for those already on the job. The orientation is to peers in investigative work, and the courts secondarily. For those taking policy decisions, reflection is valued, as is experience in administration and policing on the ground. The change from street decisions with respect to the quality of decisions made is striking. Administrators develop very different styles of coping with these (relatively) new demands. The orientation of administrators or those working with tertiary data is downward, and outward to other higher police administrators, the media and local politicians, and the Home Office.

The law   Few police know much law, and seem to develop 'recipe knowledge' derived from tutelage by other constables, oral traditions within various sub-divisions, and study for promotional boards. For the primary world of the street, information about the law is gained from other PCs, sergeants and inspectors, especially the charge sergeant when an arrest in made. The law is a resource which if known can augment one's work, but 'too much law' can be an impediment to acting properly in a situation. The world of moral practicality reigns. For those who take paper decisions, the law is a widely useful resource, and assists in drawing up affidavits, forms, statements, testimony in court and in talking with prosecutors. It is, however, seen in a pragmatic and cynical light, rather than as embodying principles of human conduct or proper citizens' behaviour. Policy-making decisions are those in which the law is seen as on the one hand facilitating the achievement of policy ends and being virtually isomorphic with policy; and on the other hand as being in opposition to policy, for example where certain laws are not enforced or are seen as a constraint upon police work, such as the provisions of the Police and Criminal Evidence Act 1984 for custody officers, written records of stops, and access to solicitors. Ideally, law and policy should be in some coherent and recognisable relationship, albeit changing and accommodative.

Observations on the relevance of police decision-making patterns to research in policing

This chapter has taken an analytic position, rather than a descriptive or normative position. The aim has been first to characterise police decision-making within the general framework of naturalism and to describe natural decision-making. This having been made clear, the second step was to contrast the features of police decision-making with decision-making as it takes place in other segments within the criminal justice system. We have focused on the informal, invisible, serial, individual nature of the decisions, and the extent to which they are based on primary data, are creative or constructive, complex and relatively unconstrained by precedent, case-law or policy. The outcomes of police decisions are likely to be loosely coupled, rarely contingent on external controls or decisions elsewhere in the system, and to have considerable consequence for individuals and society. The function of police decisions is multiple, but the gate-keeping or transformational function is one of the most significant. Within the police, variations in decision-making also occur. The effects of types of information on which the decision is based, information usage, strategies of policing, and intelligence functions have been noted. The structure of police decision-making was further differentiated by type of information and five characteristics of decisions. The contrast between police decisions and others in the criminal justice system and within policing, makes visible the nature of police decisions.

The implications of this analytic outline for future research can be best addressed by noting the direction and nature of past research on police decision-making generally. Large amounts of police research have focused on fairly simple and apparently obvious decisions to arrest either adults or juveniles. This research, in an odd fashion, has assumed the original nature of police authority and using a legalistic framework, described decisions as discretionary. It is not clear what 'discretion' in this context means, since the options or choices the officers considered, the alternative scenarios, the events overlooked or ignored, or the fate of these decisions once reviewed, are not studied. Most of the attention of police researchers on decision-making has been directed towards patrol officer decision-making on the ground and with decisions which resulted in an arrest. That is, the research has been concerned with primary information decisions. Some work on detective decisions, focused again almost entirely on the decisions to work a case or priority rankings for cases, is also available. Some work has been undertaken on primary demand (calls to police), but this has been almost entirely normative in character and putative.

There are no studies to speak of which concern tertiary decision-making by higher ranking officers in police, for example decisions about allocation and deployment of personnel, budget requests, strategies in working with the police authority, and negotiations with the Home Office or HM Inspectorate of

Constabulary. Little is known about police budgeting or the allocation of enforcement resources. When the strategies of policing are considered, most research is focused on reactive, patrol-based policing. Some work has been done on proactive policing or policing in respect to drugs and prostitution. A few studies of preventive policing are beginning to be undertaken, some of which come under the rubric of community policing. Most of the notions which have been advanced for the analysis of prevention have been sponsored by Home Office (in Britain) or by the Law Enforcement Assistance Administration (in the United States). The attitude of the police seems less clear. Studies of technology, such as the impact of the police computer and its several facets, have looked at outcomes or consequences of computerisation on crime control and response time. Very little has been done on the ways in which computerisation or other technology alters police decision-making patterns (cf Kling and Scacchi, 1982; Tien and Coulton, 1977).

Accountability and the potential for accountability varies by the visible shaping of police decision-making: the more the demand, type of information, functions and objectives are police controlled, the less accountable are the police. The proactive and preventive strategies have less potential for accountability because police control the allocation of resources, the deployment of personnel, and the programmatic context within which accountability is cast. Technology, which has a potential for providing lasting records of police actions, is confounded by legislation such as the Police and Criminal Evidence Act 1984 which devolves responsibility to the Home Office, the professions and internally-used police data.

In some respects, the chapter has reviewed why police organisations and the decisions which they produce are consistent with the police role within the criminal justice system. Police emphasise individual, discrete, face-to-face primary decisions, and the symbolic and organisational commitment to these decisions is high. The street focus of policing has meant that researchers have pursued this same line, much like tradesmen who want to merchandise a new and popular item. This is simply accepting the common-sense wisdom of the craft as an analytic. This is not an acceptable basis for a programme of research. In particular, we would want to see police decisions treated comparatively and analytically if they are to be studied as just another sort of natural process.

References

Banton, M., (1964) The policeman in the community, Tavistock, London
Bittner, E., (1970) The functions of the police in modern society, National Institute of Mental Health, Chevy Chase, Maryland
Black, D., (1980) The manners and customs of the police, Academic Books, New York
Bordua, D. (ed.) (1967) The police: six sociological essays, Wiley, New York
Carson, W.G.O., (1970a) 'Some sociological aspects of strict liability and the enforcement of factory legislation', Modern Law Review, 33, 396-412
Carson, W.G.O., (1970b) 'White collar crime and the enforcement of factory legislation', British Journal of Criminology, 10, 383-98
Cranston, R., (1979) Regulating business, Macmillan, London
Davis, K.C., (1969) Discretionary justice, LSU Press, Baton Rouge
Davis, K.C., (1975) Police discretion, West Publishing Co., St. Paul
Emerson, R., (1983) 'Holistic effects in social control decision-making', Law and Society Review, 17, 425-55
Ericson, R.V., (1981) Making crime, Butterworths, Toronto

Goldstein, J., (1960) 'Police discretion not to invoke the criminal process: low visibility decisions in the administration of justice', Yale Law Journal, 69, 543-94

Greenwood, P., Chaiken, J. and Petersilia, J., (1977) The criminal investigation process, D.C. Heath, Lexington

Hawkins, K., (1984a) 'Creating cases in a regulatory agency', Urban Life, 12, 371-95

Hawkins, K., (1984b) Environment and enforcement: regulation and the social definition of pollution, Oxford University Press, Oxford

Hawkins, K., (1986) 'On legal decision-making', Washington and Lee Law Review, 43, 4, 1161-1242

Hawkins, K. and Manning, P.K., (forthcoming) Legal decision-making

Hawkins, K. and Thomas, J., (eds) (1984) Enforcing regulation, Kluwer-Nijhoff, Boston

Hough, M., (1980) 'Managing with less technology', British Journal of Criminology, 20, 4, 344-57

Hutter, B., (1984) The law enforcement procedures of environmental health officers, D.Phil. dissertation, University of Oxford

Jamieson, M., (1985) Persuasion or punishment: the enforcement of health and safety at work legislation by the British Factory Inspectorate, M.Litt dissertation, University of Oxford

Kaufman, H., (1960) The forest ranger, Johns Hopkins Press, Baltimore

Kling, R. and Scacchi, W., (1982) 'The web of computing', Advances in Computers, 21, 1-90

Lafave, W., (1966) Arrest, Little, Brown and Co., Boston

Lipsky, M., (1980) Street-level bureaucracy, Russell Sage, New York

McCleary, R., (1978) Dangerous men, Sage, Beverly Hills

MacKay, R., (1969) Information, mechanism and meaning, MIT Press, Cambridge, Mass

Manning, P.K., (1977) Police work, MIT Press, Cambridge, Mass

Manning, P.K., (1980) The narcs' game, MIT Press, Cambridge, Mass

Manning, P.K., (1982) 'Organisational work: structuration of the environment', British Journal of Sociology, 33, 118-39

Manning, P.K., (1986) 'The social reality and social organisation of natural decision-making' (comment on Hawkins), Washington and Lee Law Review, 43, 4, 1291-1311

Manning, P.K. and van Maanen, J., (eds) (1977) Policing: a view from the streets, Random House, New York

Norris, F., (1979) Police community relations, D.C. Heath, Lexington

Pepinsky, H., (1980) Crime control strategies, Oxford University Press, Oxford

Piliavin, I. and Briar, S., (1964) 'Police encounters with juveniles', American Journal of Sociology, 70, 206-14

Policy Studies Institute (1983) Police and people in London, vols.I-IV, by Smith, D.J., Gray, J. and Small, S., London

Punch, M., (1985) Conduct unbecoming, Tavistock, London

Reiss, Jr, A.J. (1971) The police and the public, Yale University Press, New Haven

Reiss, Jr, A.J. (1974) 'Discretionary justice' in Glaser, D. (ed.), Handbook of criminology, Rand McNally, Chicago

Reiss, A.J. and Bordua, D.J., (1967) 'Environment and organization: a perspective on the police', in Bordua, D.J. (ed.), The police: six sociological essays, Wiley, New York

Reuss-Ianni, E. and Ianni, F., (1983) 'Street cops and management cops', in Punch, M., (ed.), Control in the police organisation, MIT Press, Cambridge, Mass

Rheiner et al., (1979) Crime analysis in support of patrol, Law Enforcement
Assistance Administration/National Institute of Justice, US Government
Printing Office, Washington DC
Richardson, G., Ogus, A. and Burrows, P., (1983) Policing pollution, Oxford
University Press, Oxford
Rubinstein, J., (1973) City police, Farrar, Straus and Giroux, New York
Sanders, W., (1977) Detective work, Free Press, New York
Skolnick, J., (1966) Justice without trial, Wiley, New York
Sudnow, D., (1965) 'Normal crimes', Social Problems, 12, Winter, 255–76
Tien, J. and Coulton, K., (1977) 'Police command, control and communications',
in What Works? Law Enforcement Assistance Administration/National Institute
of Justice, US Government Printing Office, Washington DC
van Maanen, J., (1983) 'The boss', in Punch, M. (ed.), Control in the police
organisation, MIT Press, Cambridge, Mass
van Maanen, J. and Schein, E., (1979) 'Towards a theory of organisational
behaviour', in Staw, B. (ed.), Research in organisational behaviour, vol.1, JAI
Press, New York
Waegel, W., (1981) 'Case routinisation in investigative police work', Social
Problems, 28, 263
Westley, W., (1970) Violence and the police, MIT Press, Cambridge, Mass
Wilson, J.Q., (1968) Varieties of police behaviour, Harvard University Press,
Cambridge, Mass

10 Regulation and policing by code

ROBERT BALDWIN

Police forces and officers are involved not merely in enforcement but in regulation. They do not simply put the law into effect, they adopt a number of strategies (one of which involves prosecution) so as to control behaviour in pursuit of a number of ends. Police constables thus regulate behaviour just as factory inspectors regulate health and safety at work. In turn they themselves are regulated and the individual force is subject to pressures in the same way that the regulatory agency is. A useful perspective may result, therefore, by looking at policing not as an enterprise sui generis but as a system of regulation not wholly dissimilar from others. In doing so one can bear in mind Maurice Punch's caution that a common fault with researchers is 'to become mesmerised by the police world and to attribute behaviour uniquely to its culture whereas fruitful similarities, and contrasts, abound with workers in other types of organisational setting' (Punch, 1985, p.187). Trends in policing may be seen in a new light when set against broader developments in regulatory activity.

Accordingly this paper aims to describe certain movements in British regulation; to look at policing under the Police and Criminal Evidence Act 1984 against the background of those events; to consider the role of law and rules in such a system of control and to examine the implications of current developments for socio-legal research.

Developments in British regulation

In the century preceding the 1960s, industrial and social activities were largely controlled in an arms-length manner, that is, there were few specialist regulatory agencies set up to keep watch over specific areas and considerable reliance was placed on control by ministers and the law as applied in the courts. Thus, for example, road transport operators and the railways were regulated by

157

government departments and tribunal-like bodies rather than by agencies with mixed promotional, regulatory and enforcement functions. In the absence of specialist bodies with inclinations to negotiate, advise and educate the citizenry in pursuit of some statutorily defined end, considerable reliance was placed on mandatory laws in regulation. Even in areas defined quite narrowly, this was the case. Thus the Robens Committee on Health and Safety at Work stated in 1972 that people 'are heavily conditioned to think of safety and health at work as in the first and foremost instance a matter of detailed rules imposed by external agencies' (para.28). Such a situation can be distinguished from that in which the enforcers negotiate compliance (by pressure, bluff, advice, education, etc.) or where the parties to be controlled are encouraged to self-regulate.

In the 1960s however, more specific forms of state intervention came into favour. Partly this was due to the need for specialists to control new technologies (e.g. aviation) or newly acute problems (e.g. discrimination); partly because government departments were unwilling to involve themselves in the area (e.g. broadcasting); and partly for ideological reasons. Corporatism came into fashion following the Conservatives' '60s conversion to planning. The Tories' National Economic Development Council (NEDC) was set up on tripartite lines and the incoming Labour government of 1964 followed with the new Department of Economic Affairs and a host of planning agencies such as the Industrial Reorganisation Corporation (1966) and the Race Relations Board (1965).

By the early '70s, the notion of the managed economy had waned and the grip of economic liberalism had become tighter, but the momentum of corporatism was sustained. The new aim was to make tripartism work - if not for the purposes of general planning, then in specific areas. A series of new bodies was created to this end: the Manpower Services Commission (1973), the Health and Safety Commission (1974) and the Advisory Conciliation and Arbitration Service (1975). Consumer and social interests were represented by a number of new groups and agencies such as the National Consumer Council (1975). More narrowly-defined planning functions were revived with the National Enterprise Board (1975) and regulatory bodies such as the Civil Aviation Authority (1972) and Independent Broadcasting Authority (1972) came on the scene. Regulation by specialist bodies, and especially those based on the tripartist philosophy, encouraged a form of control that was negotiated rather than mandated. Thus in the post-Robens era, health and safety at work became deliberately more consensualist. The Health and Safety Commission and Executive were not there to enforce the law by prosecuting offenders. They were set up to advise and assist in the process of self-regulation. There were administratively issued sanctions available (Improvement and .Prohibition Notices) but prosecution was held back as a method of last resort.

By the '80s a further change had occurred. It was less important to make agency regulation and tripartism work than to develop ways of loosening the reins. At the time of writing, the Thatcher government has been in power for seven years and both regulatory policies and strategies have been reconsidered.

Policy changes have come in the shape of privatisation, deregulation and disburdening. The privatisation programme has been three-pronged. The government has sold off public assets to the private sector; 'liberalised' by opening state activities to private competition; and has contracted out public sector services to private industry.

Deregulation involves the wholesale reduction of state control so as to increase reliance on competition. Thus coach services were deregulated in 1980 and controls have been lifted in the fields of financial services, foreign exchange, the retail of spectacles, accounting, stockbroking, opticians and veterinarian services, conveyancing and domestic air services.

Disburdening stems from different roots. Pressure from the small business lobby in the wake of the 1979 Conservative election victory led to a movement to reduce compliance costs. The Department of Trade and Industry argued that disburdening would create jobs, and a task force, the Enterprise Unit, was set up in the Cabinet Office. Now renamed the Enterprise and Deregulation Unit, this group subjects government regulations to cost-benefit testing in the name of economic efficiency. Already the disburdening initiative has led to proposals for the abolition of local bus service licensing, for reducing VAT form-filling requirements and for retraining health and safety inspectors on the interests of small businesses.

Such measures to reduce government control are increasingly combined with a new model of self-regulation. This is not the same as incorporating self-regulatory elements into tripartism - where it is assumed that there is a common solution that can be arrived at by all sides (e.g. Robens' view that employers, employees and the public had convergent interests in health and safety at work). The self-regulation of the '80s is less consensualist and has its roots in a variety of ideas including notions of economic efficiency; the view that only those involved in industry are sufficiently close to the ground to be able to exercise control; a general antipathy to regulation; a distrust of the costs of agency control or an assumption concerning the concurrence of industry's interests in profits and the public interest.

Such movements towards self-regulation are implicit in the deregulatory measures noted above but can also be seen in the creation of new regulatory structures. Thus the control of cable television will, in the wake of the hastily written Hunt Report, be minimal and it is proposed that city financial services will be subjected not to a specialist independent agency's control but to a system of self-regulation within a statutory framework. From another direction, pressure on resources has encouraged the Health and Safety Commission to consider a scheme of 'health and safety assurance' in which employers can be exempted from inspection on satisfying the HSC as to their general safety policies. The Civil Aviation Authority has acted for different reasons again: it is implementing deregulatory measures before the government imposes them.

The trend is increasingly to let the market serve the public interest rather than to create more rigorous laws or to set up more quangos that will devise models of the public interest, establish standards and attempt to force these on reluctant industrialists. Managers will be allowed to manage, under this view, and consumers will increasingly be left to protect their own interests.

Alongside changed attitudes to regulation have come new regulatory strategies. Agency licensing is only one method of government control and, as Steven Breyer has pointed out in the USA (Breyer, 1982, ch.8), there is a series of other 'less restrictive' alternatives such as anti-trust laws, rules on disclosure, taxation and liability rules. These, it is argued, are incentive-based and allow managerial freedom in a way that is impossible under, for example, agency licensing. The message is that it is not enough to revamp old systems of control. It is necessary to consider whether the existing regulatory regime matches the regulatory problem and is the least restrictive system available. Where there is a mismatch, then an alternative strategy is called for. Again with legal rules and procedures for control, the suggestion is that less formal, more flexible norms or processes may be appropriate. These are all notions attractive to the present government (Department of Employment, 1986, para.1.13).

Notable for our purposes is the growing popularity of one control device that complements the deregulation movement. This is the code of practice. The main argument for codes is that they are more flexible, intelligible and accessible than primary legislation; they encourage consistency, guide officials and can be used to advise as well as compel; they are cheap and responsive, relatively free from judicial review and useful in simplifying complex issues. Against some codes it can be said that they minimise parliamentary scrutiny; their legal status is uncertain; they often include rules that are set down in non-justiciable language; they allow ministers illegitimately to 'guide' the judiciary; they are inaccessible; and they are published haphazardly.

The post-Robens era of health and safety regulation can again be cited. The HSC started in 1974 a programme of supplementing and replacing statutory provisions with less formal rules. Now a single hazard may be subject to a series of norms and prescriptions: the general duties of the Act, regulations, approved codes of practice, guidance notes, written standards and leaflets. In countless other areas of control, a major role is played by rules that are often of indeterminate status. Consider the Prison Rules, the Immigration Rules, the Picketing and Closed Shop Codes, the Supplementary Benefits Codes, Home Office Circulars, Highway Code, ACAS Codes and the City Code on Takeovers and Mergers. Whenever modern governments want to skirt round a difficult issue, the temptation is to resort to a code of practice, circular, note of guidance or similar device. The ministerial statement that opposition members need not wrorry as 'this will be dealt with in the code of practice' is increasingly heard (Baldwin and Houghton, 1986).

For the administration, the code of practice has very attractive properties. It not only allows low-level officials to be employed on complex tasks and gives the appearance of consistency, it provides a battery of ready justifications for action but at the same time exposes the agency to minimal threat of legal attack. Agencies challenged with unreasonableness can point to their own rules and cite these as grounds but where they fail to adhere to their own prescriptions they may argue that their publications are merely advisory, that they do not fetter discretions. This is because the administrative rule is often treated by judges as a guide to the exercise of power. In short, codes are useful in 'getting the job done' because they serve bureaucratic needs without rendering the bureaucracy liable to acute legal or parliamentary attack. Judges find it particularly easy to uphold bureaucratic actions by reference to administrative rules. By deciding whether rules are mandatory or advisory (an issue on which the law gives a virtually free hand), the judiciary can decide whether to exercise review or to leave alone - and they can do so on grounds that owe little to the law.

To summarise on regulatory developments, I have concentrated on an institutional and philosophical trend and also on a strategy of growing importance. The movement now is away from agencies that operate in a consensualist manner and in favour of forms of deregulation that mimimalise interference with those who produce marketable goods. Alongside deregulation runs the current of delegalisation and the increasing attractiveness of rules that give the appearance of conformity to the rule of law but which offer limited and sometimes illusory opportunities of redress.

Policing as regulation

Policing involves two different senses of regulation. Police officers control social behaviour by enforcing the law and keeping the peace, but they are also regulated themselves insofar as the law, the courts and the systems of discipline and accountability control the policing process. It is this second sense that I am concerned with, one in which the police are producers (of, say, convictions and the Queen's Peace) who are subject to regulation just as in television the producers of programmes, the independent television companies, are regulated by the law, the courts, the ministers and the IBA.

From this view the Police and Criminal Evidence Act 1984 (PACE Act) effects a change in policing that echoes those developments in other regulatory systems that are described above. The producers, the police, have been deregulated and have been subjected to a set of rules that, especially at difficult points, increasingly rely upon codes of practice rather than primary legislation.

Why state that the police have been deregulated when the PACE Act and codes put into effect a new and very extensive network of rules? The answer lies in the overall legislative strategy of PACE, which is to give broad discretions on such matters as arrest, detention, stop and search, search and seizure, and to 'compensate' by reference to recording procedures and codes of practice.

Let us consider very briefly the nature of police powers on central issues.

1. <u>Stop and search</u>   PACE Act provides for a new general power to stop and search persons or vehicles for stolen goods or other unlawful articles. (Prior legislation was local or specific.)

> Limitations
> a. <u>The Act</u>: 'reasonable suspicion' (s.1(3)); duty to record search (s.3).
> b. <u>Code on stop and search</u>: e.g. Annex B states that such suspicion should have a concrete basis that can be considered and evaluated by a third person: a hunch or 'higher than average chance' are insufficient grounds.
> c. <u>Note for guidance</u>: powers are to be used responsibly and sparingly.
>
> <u>Sanctions for non-compliance with procedure</u>
> a. Civil action against the constable (unlikely).
> b. Evidence inadmissible (<u>R v. Sang</u>, 1980 allows use of illegally obtained evidence, 'technical' breach is unlikely to be 'unfair' according to s.78 of PACE Act).
> c. Complaint ('of little practical use to the individual' - Bevan and Lidstone, 1985, p.62).
> d. Discipline: breach of code, s.67(8).

2. <u>Seizure of evidence</u>   PACE Act provides for general powers of seizure plus extensive new powers to seize anything regardless of whether there was authority to search for it (s.19).

> Limitations
> a. <u>The Act</u>: reasonable grounds to believe it is evidence of an offence and necessary to seize in order to prevent concealment, etc.
> b. <u>Code of practice</u>: e.g. para.5.9 states that premises shall be searched with due consideration for property and privacy.

Sanctions for police non-compliance
a. Civil suit (very unlikely).
b. Exclusion - illegally obtained evidence is admissible but may be excluded as unfair, per s.78.
c. Complaint
d. Disciplinary action for breach of code (what disciplinary action is appropriate where evidence is admitted and a conviction secured?)

3. Arrest PACE Act extends the power to cover non-arrestable offences where a summons cannot be used or appears to the officer to be inappropriate.

Limitations
a. The Act: there must be reasonable grounds to suspect (ss.24,25).
b. Code of practice: no code on arrest but detention code relevant.

Sanctions for non-compliance
a. Civil suit
b. Complaint
c. Evidence admissible
d. No code governing discipline

4. Detention and questioning PACE Act creates new powers to detain for questioning for up to 96 hours and up to 36 hours on police authorisation alone.

Limitations
a. The Act: statutory framework giving general grounds for detention, e.g. to secure evidence or question - s.37(2). Framework for custody officer review, magistrates' review.
b. Code of practice on detention runs to 34 pages

Sanctions for non-compliance
a. Civil action for unlawful detention, assault, etc.
b. Evidence inadmissible - if confession results from oppression, if unreliable (s.76) or unfairness (s.78).
c. Complaint
d. Discipline

As others have pointed out, the effect of the Act is to place the conviction process in the hands of the police in circumstances that are hardly conducive to independent review. The Policy Studies Institute researchers found 'reasonable suspicion' to be no effective restraint (Policy Studies Institute, 1983, vol.IV, pp.233-4), the new provisions on detention and questioning lend themselves admirably to the use of interrogation as a primary method of collecting evidence and they thus shift the true locus of trial away from the courts towards the police station. In this sense the police have been left to get on with the job in the shadow of discipline rather than in the spotlight of the law. This was the philosophy behind the McNee shopping list to the Royal Commission on Criminal Procedure (RCCP) and in debates on the PACE Bill it was clear that the new legislation was offered not as a contribution to the 'fight against crime' but was an attempt to create rules that were 'fair' to police officers. Thus the Royal Commission talked of the need to create rules that police officers could rely on (they 'should not be required to operate with unclear and uncertain rules' (RCCP, 1981, para.2.2) and it espoused the notion that since citizens were finding out about their rights and standing on them, the police had to be given extra powers to reply to those rights. Since individuals would not cooperate, the argument went, compelling powers had to be given. The idea that officers could get by with less than Draconian powers was sacrificed on the altars of (a) not allowing the criminal to escape in the hypothetical worst case; and (b) not placing officers in the 'impossible' position of powerlessness.

The primary legislation gives discretions based on concepts that offer little restraint (e.g. reasonable grounds for suspicion; reasonable grounds for believing) and this increases the burden placed on the codes of practice. The purpose of the Act is to regulate the citizenry but the codes of practice have as a central concern the control of the police. They are the internal rules of the organisation; they do not simply replace the Judges' Rules, they are offered as counter-weights to extended powers and discretions. Nor are the codes merely appendages of statutory powers and duties; the Home Office pulls no punches on their importance. It is stated on the cover of the codes that:

> The codes cover contact between the police and public in the exercise of stop and search powers, and the searching of premises, and in regard to the treatment and questioning of suspects. They therefore represent a major statement of the rights of the individual and powers of the police. (Home Office, 1985)

Codes, rules and policing

Here is not the place to rehearse familiar civil libertarian arguments concerning the inadequacy of codes as checks on extended powers. It suffices to repeat the fundamental point that since powers do not have to be formally exercised in order to achieve de facto results, recording requirements and code provisions can be by-passed on a wholesale basis. For the purposes of this paper, I want to explore the implications of 'policing by code' for the judiciary, the prosecutors and the police themselves.

Courts and codes

The four codes of practice are in the form of a 97-page booklet. Their status is governed by s.67(11) of the PACE Act which states that in all civil and criminal proceedings,

> any such code shall be admissible in evidence; and if any provision of such a code appears to the court or tribunal conducting the proceeding to be relevant to any question arising in the proceedings it shall be taken into account in determining that question.

Police breach of a code involves no criminal action per se (s.67(10)); it leads to no automatic exclusion of evidence but an officer failing to observe the code is liable to disciplinary proceedings (s.67(8)). Where confession evidence is challenged on grounds of oppression or unreliability (s.76(2)), the courts will treat the code as guidance but no more. Section 67(11) closely resembles the provisions on the Highway Code in the Road Traffic Act 1972 and the courts have consistently dealt with that code as an evidential guide only. The courts are even less likely to enforce the PACE Act codes strictly, since the R v. Sang rule states that it is no function of the judiciary to discipline the police by use of exclusionary rules. Bevan and Lidstone in their guide to the PACE Act discuss the relevance of breaches of the code on questioning in cases where the admissibility of a statement is disputed. They argue that 'In fact the Code of Practice offers a ready indication of the sort of standards to which the police must conform and breach of which may amount to oppression' (Bevan and Lidstone, 1985, p.299). This seems a highly optimistic view from the suspect's position. It is doubtful whether the courts will be any more keen to adopt the

163

standards of the codes than they were to 'enforce' the Judges' Rules through the exclusion of evidence. They are more likely to keep alive the old case law on 'voluntariness' which those who framed the PACE Act were so keen to see the end of.

The use of codes in relation to confession evidence demonstrates starkly how such rules achieve the best (or worst) of two worlds. Those who demand evidence for use in court can be assured that breaches of the code will not interfere with conviction; those who demand protection from police misuses of power are directed to the disciplinary machinery. The police officer as much as the suspect is addressed with forked tongue: the evidentiary rules encourage the collection of evidence irrespective of code; the code holds out the threat of severe sanctions for officers who succumb to these legally manufactured temptations.

It is notable in relation to non-confession evidence that Lord Scarman's amendment to the PACE Bill would have deemed evidence obtained in breach of a code to have been improperly obtained. This would have rendered it inadmissible unless the prosecution proved that the impropriety was insignificant or that, given its probative value and the circumstances, the public interest required the evidence to be given. The Scarman clause succeeded in the Lords but was rejected in the Commons when the Lord Chancellor introduced instead s.78. This has no mandatory or onus-reversing effect in the case of breaches of codes. It merely gives the court a discretion to exclude evidence having an 'adverse effect on the fairness of the proceedings'. The last phrase is notable in mentioning fairness not to the accused but with reference to the criminal process. This Sang-like language hints that the courts may again be unwilling to apply the codes strictly by use of the exclusionary discretion. This accords with the view of the Home Office Briefing Guide which stressed that the remedy for breaches of rules lay in disciplinary procedures or complaints rather than in the penalty of exclusion.

Prosecutors may be dealt with briefly. They are likely, independent or not, to consider primarily the chances of securing a conviction. They are unlikely in cases where codes have been breached to refuse to use admissible evidence in court. They will thus be as disinclined as the judiciary to set themselves up as monitors or disciplinarians of the police. They might, with some justification, argue that the disciplinary provisions of s.67(8) relieve them of any such responsibility.

Police officers and codes

Policing by code of practice constitutes a shift from policing under the law towards self-regulated policing in the shadow of law (or discipline). Two principal issues arise: what will be the part played by the code in regulating police behaviour? and is police legitimacy affected?

On the code as regulator of police behaviour, a preliminary point should be disposed of. One may doubt the reliability of self-regulation as a foundation for protected civil liberties without denying the significance of a self-regulatory regime for police work. The codes may again achieve the worst of two worlds by offering scant protection in contentious cases whilst at the same time subjecting police officers to mountainous paperwork in the course of routine work.

The extent to which police officers' behaviour can be regulated by any form of legal rule is dubious. Whether officers distinguish between rules of different status is even more problematic. The lack of research evidence on such matters is remarkable. The Royal Commission made its proposals on recording procedures, custody provisions and codes of practice in the knowledge that the Judges' Rules had been ineffectual but without any evidence to suggest that its own package would achieve better results.

The most extensive recent study, the PSI report (1983), made the distinction between working rules (the ones actually internalised by police officers and guiding their actions); inhibiting rules (which are external and are taken into account because thought likely to be enforced); and presentational rules (which put an acceptable gloss on actions governed by the working rules). The PSI report does not however offer a great deal of help in assessing the conditions under which various forms of legal rule have a genuine regulatory function. It does, however, make the following points:

> rules are not unimportant, they have a very variable influence;

> there are considerable dangers in treating 'more rules' as an answer to bad policing (Policy Studies Institute, 1983, vol.IV, pp.171-2)

> no fundamental change can be effected so long as many police officers believe that the job cannot be done effectively within the rules (op.cit., pp.229-30)

> to make workable rules attention must be paid to the management of the force (op.cit., p.230)

Robert Reiner's useful review in The politics of the police begins with the comment:

> What needs to be more precisely explored is the relationship between formal rules of law and procedure and the sub-cultural rules which are the guiding principles of police conduct. (Reiner, 1985, pp.174-8)

He cautions those of the interactionist tradition (citing Manning, 1977, 1979; Holdaway, 1979, 1983; Chatterton, 1979; Punch, 1979; Fielding, 1984) against the 'extreme rule scepticism' that assumes rules to be largely irrelevant in practice. He argues that the interactionists themselves cite evidence of certain rule-based constraints on police behaviour but is forced back to the conclusion that rank and file sub-cultural autonomy is 'limited to a degree by formal controls, but how much, when and in what way has not been adequately explored as yet'.

Nor does Reiner extract much comfort from the structuralists (citing McBarnet, 1979, 1981; Jefferson, 1980; Brogden, 1982; Jefferson and Grimshaw, 1984a, 1984b) and their argument that the source of deviance is not rank and file sub-cultural autonomy but the encouragement by senior officers, judges and the state elite of deviations from the ideal of legality. His positive suggestion is that:

> If the police can achieve their proper objects within the law then one strain making for deviation disappears. This does not mean that unacceptable practices should be legitimated. But it does suggest that the police must have adequate powers to perform the core tasks which are expected of them. If they do not then the police culture may develop a disdain for legality which will multiply abuses. (op.cit., p.177)

But policing after the PACE Act may be seen as based on codes of practice not primary legislation; on discipline rather than law; as self-regulatory rather than legally-controlled. This suggests a perspective to add to Reiner who, we may note, refers at this stage to the formal rules of law affecting the police rather than the disciplinary constraints of the codes. The point is that a package of wide powers combined with restraint by codes allows officers to perform their core tasks <u>without</u> any disdain for legality. The danger is disdain for disciplinary sanctions. Here the structuralists may have a response. McBarnet has argued (1981) that the wonder of the case law system lies in its ability both to preserve the rhetoric of law <u>and</u> to subvert the principles of legality and the rule of law in practice. The system of self-regulation under codes of practice serves to achieve similar results. The 'ideal of legality' in this sense has <u>already</u> been sacrificed by writing protections into codes of practice, not law. After the PACE Act and the codes the problem of deviation has to a large extent been pre-empted.

As for the legitimacy of the police, the 'deregulation' process only bears on one basis of legitimacy: the idea of the police as observers of the rule of law. To the extent that the PACE Act and codes make it easier for the 'working rules' to be put into effect without overt breaches of the law, police legitimacy stands to be enhanced. Against this must be discounted any increased perceptions of the police as unregulated agents against whom there is little chance of redress through the courts or the complaints, disciplinary and accountability systems. Other factors upon which legitimacy is founded - <u>inter alia</u> the notions of efficiency, minimal force, consent-seeking, non-partisanship, public service and non-discrimination - may depend on factors far distant from the extent and nature of the rules governing police action; and beyond the scope of this paper.

Socio-legal research after the PACE Act

To view current policing as a system of self-regulation sharing characteristics with other such systems suggests certain avenues of research. A clear need, as Reiner, Punch, PSI and others have emphasised, is to explore the relationship of sub-cultural rules to other norms. It is not enough, I am suggesting, to look at the 'legal rules' as a homogeneous group of norms to be set against sub-cultural rules whilst taking into account such variables as differences between the ranks and types of police work, or strategy. The legal rules themselves have to be broken down further according to such factors as status, sanctions, degree of specificity, procedure and enforcement practice. Thus separate attention has to be paid to statutory powers and duties, obligations under codes of practice, disciplinary norms, constraints of the complaints system and rules established by administrators such as force and Home Office circulars.

Many researchers have pointed out the need to look at the organisation of the police, the nature of police work as well as the legal rules. The above discussion and the PACE Act should prompt research for example on whether new emphasis on the codes and on discipline will change the relationships between the ranks. Chatterton (1976) and Holdaway (1983) have described the process of insulation between the ranks and Punch has illustrated graphically how officers may distinguish between illegal activity (which is seen as a breach of duty) and behaviour that conflicts with instructions and disciplinary rules (which involves no breach of duty) (Punch, 1985, p.130). Will the system of control established by the 1984 Act make for more effective supervision or less? Punch suggests that officers are peculiarly resentful of internal controls (Punch, 1985, p.86) and yet others stress the need for effective leadership and lines of authority in controlling deviance (Goldstein, 1977). Self-regulation based on internal rules <u>may</u> be a more realistic proposition than reliance on the courts and statutory rules. It may, on the other hand, lead to a worsening of relationships between ranks, more concealment of methods of investigation and a situation in which there is less policy coordination, less efficient policing and protection of rights, and more paperwork than formerly.

A second complementary approach is to seek inspiration by comparing policing with other self-regulatory systems. For an example we may briefly return to health and safety regulation. Assuming that occupiers (of, say, factories) are expected to some extent to self-regulate in the shadow of regulation, we can analyse the nature of that shadow and consider what the equivalent would look like in the policing context. Thus, the Health and Safety at Work Act 1974 (HSW Act) gave the unions a policing role through the system of safety representatives. This gives those most directly affected by the production process a role both in making relevant rules on health and safety and in instituting enforcement procedures. Transposed to policing, this would imply the creation of an organised reporting system whereby those persons with grievances resulting from contact with the police would be able to gain information and to make representations to a central review body in relation not only to individual past cases but to general issues and anticipated complaints. This body would be capable of monitoring and sanctioning the police as well as making rules for future conduct. The system of health and safety inspection suggests a role for inspectors of policing that goes far beyond anything offered by HM Inspectorate of Constabulary, the Police Complaints Authority and police authorities but does support Lord Scarman's proposal for police authority access to the police station.

The HSW Act recognises that self-regulators need help in the way of advice and assistance and this is provided through inspectoral as well as promotional activity. The implication here is that there is a role for increased education of the police and the public concerning the expectations that may reasonably be made of forces. There might even be a place for an advisory institution. (Is this a role for police authorities?) Health and safety regulation also recognises the need for a sanction against self-regulators that comes between advice or persuasion and prosecution. The HSW Act created a system of improvement and prohibition notices (whereby undesirable activity may be halted by inspectors without immediate recourse to the courts). This prompts the notion of some sort of police authority with powers to monitor procedures (including the disciplinary system) and to order forces to 'cease and desist' from practices (general or specific) that are illegal or in contravention of codes of practice.

A halt must be called to such comparisons for the sake of space. Such suggestions may seem far from inspired, even hare-brained. This kind of exercise may be worthwhile however if it helps to counteract the idea of the police world as unique and if it encourages reconsideration of entrenched perspectives.

To conclude, I have argued that some profit may be derived, both in practical and purely academic terms, from resisting the temptation to see policing purely in terms of the rule of law. It is suggested here that the effect of the PACE Act and the codes of practice has been to move policing in a certain direction - away from the model of an activity regulated by legal powers and duties and closer to self-regulation. In this respect modes of analysis appropriate to other fields of regulation may be more helpful than formerly in explaining such factors as the legitimising role of the code of practice. In the more pragmatic context of policing after the 1984 Act, the response to that legislation should itself take a more wide-ranging and pragmatic thrust. There is little point in researching deviations from law when the ideal of legality has to some extent been abandoned. It is far more profitable to explore the operation and potential of control mechanisms that are appropriate to the enterprise now in operation.

References

Baldwin, R. and Houghton, J., (1986) 'Circular arguments: the status and legitimacy of administrative rules', Public Law, Summer, 239-84

Bevan, V. and Lidstone, K., (1985) A guide to the Police and Criminal Evidence Act 1984, Butterworth, London

Breyer, S., (1982) Regulation and its reform

Brogden, M., (1982) The police: autonomy and consent, Academic Press, London

Chatterton, M., (1976) 'Police in social control', in King, J. (ed.), Control without custody, Cropwood Conference Series No.7, Institute of Criminology, Cambridge

Chatterton, M., (1979) 'The supervision of patrol work under the fixed points system', in Holdaway, S. (ed.), The British police, Edward Arnold, London

Department of Employment (1986) Building businesses . . . not barriers, Cmnd 9894, HMSO, London

Fielding, N., (1984) 'Police socialisation and police competence', British Journal of Sociology, 35, 4

Goldstein, H., (1977) Policing a free society, Ballinger, Cambridge, Mass

Holdaway, S. (ed.), (1979) The British police, Edward Arnold, London

Holdaway, S., (1983) Inside the British police, Blackwell, Oxford

Home Office (1985) Police and Criminal Evidence Act 1984 (s.66). Codes of practice, HMSO, London

Jefferson, T., (1980) Book review, British Journal of Criminology, 20, 2, 178-81

Jefferson, T. and Grimshaw, R., (1984a) 'The problem of law enforcement policy in England and Wales: the case of community policing and racial attacks', International Journal of Sociology of Law, 12, May

Jefferson, T. and Grimshaw, R., (1984b) Controlling the constable: police accountability in England and Wales, Muller, London

McBarnet, D., (1979) 'Arrest: the legal context of policing', in Holdaway, S. (ed.), The British police, Edward Arnold, London

McBarnet, D., (1981) Conviction, Macmillan, London

Manning, P. (1977) Police work, MIT Press, Cambridge, Mass

Manning, P., (1979) 'The social control of police work', in Holdaway, S. (ed.), The British police, Edward Arnold, London

Policy Studies Institute (1983) Police and people in London, Vol.IV, by Smith, D.J. and Gray, J., London

Punch, M., (1979) Policing the inner city, Macmillan, London

Punch, M., (1985) Conduct unbecoming

R v. Sang [1980] AC 402; [1979] 2 All ER 46

Reiner, R., (1985) The politics of the police, Wheatsheaf, Brighton

Royal Commission on Criminal Procedure, (1981) Report, Cmnd 8092, HMSO, London

11 Police accountability: current developments and future prospects

ROD MORGAN

1985 saw the appearance of a spate of articles and books directly or indirectly concerned with aspects of police accountability. The rate of production reflects the prominent place that policing now occupies in social policy and party political debate. It also coincides with the implementation of the Police and Criminal Evidence Act 1984. In the space of a single paper it is not possible to review all aspects of the current discussion – on the one hand the constitutional argument regarding the governance of the police, on the other hand the implications of the new legislation concerning the extent and use of police powers. Nor would it be sensible to make the attempt. These matters have been discussed elsewhere (Reiner, 1985; Spencer, 1985a; Baxter and Koffman, 1985; Scraton, 1985; Public Law, Autumn 1985). I intend to steer a modest course: to chart the government's general position on police accountability, to describe policy initiatives on which the government has embarked, and to consider how these initiatives may affect the climate within which future arguments over the constitutional framework for accountability will take place.

We have to begin with the constitutional position as it is. In numerous statements ministers of the present Conservative administration have stead-fastly maintained their commitment to the doctrine of police operational independence and the tripartite arrangements embodied in the Police Act 1964. This specifies the duty of the police authorities 'to secure the maintenance of an adequate and efficient police force' (s.4(a)) and 'keep themselves informed as to the manner in which complaints made by members of the public against members of the force are dealt with by the chief constable' (s.50). It sets out the duty of the chief constables to 'direct and control' their forces (s.5(1)), enforce the law, and submit each year a written report to their police authorities and to the Home Secretary on the policing of their areas (s.12(1)). And it defines the duty of the Home Secretary when exercising his extensive powers – which include, inter alia, the making of regulations 'as to the government, administration and conditions of service of police forces' (s.33), the standards for police equipment (s.36) and the appointment and performance of Inspectors of Constabulary (s.38) - to act 'in such a manner and to such an extent as appears to him to be best calculated to promote the efficiency of the police' (s.28).

According to the government, this arrangement ensures that policing is a partnership between central and local government and between government and police officers; government providing the necessary resources and administrative framework, and the police their professional judgement as to how law enforcement and order maintenance will best be achieved. To upset this partnership would, according to the government, risk undermining the degree to which the police enforce the law impartially yet in accordance with local needs and conditions. Excessive centralisation - the development of a national police force - would be to rob policing of its local character and bring it too close to the influence of the executive. Greater localisation - granting police authorities powers to dictate the shape of operational policy - would be to risk parochialism and partisan political influence at odds with the letter of the law.

Yet this commitment to the constitutional status quo has not been unqualified. The government has found it necessary to modify the operation of the tripartite structure and operational independence in order to re-establish the legitimacy of both doctrines. The adjustments have not been entirely in response to external criticism and the positions adopted by opposition political parties. Dissatisfaction with aspects of policing is not the monopoly of inhabitants of deprived inner city areas nor of Labour politicians in local government: the broad support publicly expressed for the police in more conservative quarters does not indicate totally uncritical attitudes both as to policy and the structure within which policy is determined. Furthermore, some adjustments pursued by the government have been made in accordance with general policies they have applied throughout the public sector.

Themes in government policy

I suggest the following themes have been prominent in government thinking and provide the background to the policing initiatives on which I wish to focus. I have labelled these themes 'value for money', 'setting priorities', 'self-help', 'consumerism' and 'transparent stewardship'. I am not suggesting that these ideas are peculiar to this administration or are being applied coherently and consistently by it. I am simply maintaining that these slogans are likely to colour the way in which the public defines police accountability and will set the scene within which future debates on accountability take place.

Value for money

This was one of the five keynote aims enunciated in the Conservative Party Manifesto, 1979. Its application to the police may have important consequences for the processes of accountability, and its full impact has almost certainly yet to be felt.

Though the government, in pursuit of its robust 'law and order' policy, undertook initially to exempt the police from the cuts to be achieved elsewhere in public expenditure, there was to be no exemption from the pursuit of effectiveness and efficiency. The Prime Minister's financial management initiative, (HMSO, 1983) set out the doctrine (the application of which was already underway) to be applied to every ministry and service. Objectives were to be specified and measurements for performance articulated. In relation to the police, Home Office Circular 114/1983 on manpower, effectiveness and efficiency in the police service stated the Home Office response. The circular set out 'the considerations which the Home Secretary will take into account in carrying out his statutory responsibility for approving police establishments'. The message was unambiguous. 'Constraints on public expenditure at both central and local government levels make it impossible to continue with the sort of expansion of recent years'. Thus although 'the workload shows no sign of diminishing', the Home Secretary would 'not normally be prepared to authorise additional posts unless': first, his inspectors 'were satisfied that the force's existing resources are used to best advantage'; second, the applications were specific; and third, 'the police authority has signified its intention to fund them'. This last criterion is crucial and is later connected to the 'important role (the police authority has) to play in contributing to the formulation and review of the framework of objectives and priorities within which the force operates'.

That the police cannot in future look to the government for the sort of increase in real expenditure received since 1979 – an increase of one third accounted for principally by pay awards and an extra 12,000 personnel – is clear (see the Home Secretary's speech to the Superintendents' Association on 24 September 1984). This should mean that the search for 'value for money' will begin to bite and scrutiny become closer. The pressure to civilianise police posts and reorganise shift arrangements are symptoms of this process. The Home Office response to the financial management initiative, promoting discussion and research on the development of measures of effectiveness and efficiency (Sinclair and Miller, 1984; Collins, 1985), and use of the Inspectorate as policy promoters and assessors (Home Office, 1984a; Weatheritt, 1986) will mean that the police locally will be required to state and justify their objectives and methods more clearly.

The irony is that the government, in pursuing cuts in public expenditure, has unleashed a process which may provide the police authorities – particularly those Labour-controlled authorities most opposed to cuts in public expenditure – with tools for achieving increased control of policing policy. The mechanisms by which police effectiveness and efficiency are to be measured may enable the police authorities better to penetrate policy and call the police more fully to account. The financial management initiative may breathe new life into the tripartite structure, restoring to police authorities some of the influence which, it is generally agreed, has slipped away from them to the chief constables and Home Office ever since 1964.

Some support for this proposition is to be found in Loveday's (1985) illuminating study of the Merseyside Police Committee. He quotes a senior official of the Association of Metropolitan Authorities (AMA) describing Circular 114/1983 as a 'triumph' for the AMA, linking its content to a Home Office working paper, Police resources and the tripartite structure in which the police authorities are placed 'at the centre of the web'. Chief constables will have to persuade police authorities of an operational need if they are to pay for the additional resources. In turn the Home Secretary will look at 'overall policies which they have agreed together' (quoted in Loveday, p.127).

There is a counter-thesis of course. Loveday also quotes the chief constable of Merseyside, Mr Kenneth Oxford, describing Circular 114/1983 dismissively as largely a 'philosophical document' (ibid., p.126). The metropolitan authorities, which have done most to scrutinise policing, are to be abolished. And the blank cheque given the police by the Home Secretary during the miners' dispute can only be described as a kick in the teeth for the budgetary control which police authority members previously thought they exercised (Loveday, 1985; Spencer, 1985b). Whatever life was breathed into the tripartite structure in 1983/84 was largely squeezed out of it again in 1984/85. Yet, rightly or wrongly, most police authority members with whom I have spoken recently see the events of the miners' dispute as exceptional and transitory as far as budgetary control is concerned. It seems to me that in addition to the government's political need to restore local authority confidence in the role of police committees, they may during that process also find the authorities useful agents for battening down policing expenditure. This point has not been lost on the chief constables.

Setting priorities

The government's commitment to reducing the public sector borrowing requirement is allied closely to its view that the state has assumed responsibility for services better organised by the private or voluntary sectors.

Public services, the government and its supporters tend to argue, are often monopolistic and insufficiently responsive to consumer demands. When services are free at the point of delivery, there is no price mechanism linking suppliers and consumers and no profit element motivating and guiding producers. Furthermore, because finance comes from tax revenues, resource allocation and service delivery is decided either by public officials or elected politicians. The former may be motivated more by administrative and professional convenience than consumer satisfaction, and the latter may be captive to sectional interests. Neither group is likely to be representative of the community at large. Thus, according to this evaluation, consumer-satisfying outputs, or what is to count as effectiveness, will best be maximised if consumer sovereignty is reasserted through a return to the free market. Greater efficiency, it is alleged, would follow privatisation. Accountability (consumer control) of services is maximised when purchasers can choose between competing producers in the market place and providers are obliged, through their quest for profit, to respond to those choices.

These arguments are seldom applied explicitly to policing, though they could be. Defence and security, internal and external, is in most political theories held to be the primary rationale for the existence of the state. The police, like the armed forces, are generally said to provide a public good. Even when they are providing services to individuals, it is the Queen's rather than the individual's peace which is allegedly maintained. Nevertheless, the police are not immune from the suspicion that, like other public services, their priorities may not accord with those of the public at large and, like all state bureaucracies, they tend to over-reach the functions properly provided by the state. Put more mundanely, the police provide a 24-hour emergency service. They are asked to deal with a variety of social service as well as order maintenance and crime control matters (Punch, 1979). So diffuse is this potential mandate or response capacity, it could, if permitted, expand almost infinitely.

When combined with the results of recent research shedding doubt on the effectiveness of much police activity (Clarke and Hough, 1980), the government's approach to public expenditure has led them, despite their commitment to upholding the law whatever the cost, to cast a critical eye over the police budget. Because policing is expensive, and because police decisions have knock-on implications for overall criminal justice and penal system costs, there is a clear administrative and financial need to ensure that the police concentrate on those activities where they are most effective (practically or symbolically) and which are their proper concern (Collins, 1985; Weatheritt, 1985). Thus the government has taken the view that the police should concentrate on 'crime fighting' rather than, for example, minor motoring offences (Conservative Party, 1979). Certain offences - street crimes and burglary - should be targeted (Home Office, 1984b) and others - the supply and abuse of drugs - should be the subject of specific initiatives matched with earmarked resources (Home Office, 1985). This specification of policing priorities by the government ties in with their insistence that forces also should set priorities locally as part of the drive for effectiveness and efficiency. Thus the current vogue for 'policing by objectives' (Butler, 1984a), a vogue matched in other Home Office departments by, for example, the probation service's 'priorities' and the prison department's 'accountable regimes' (Maguire, Vagg and Morgan, 1985).

Self help

The corollary of this attempt to delineate 'core' policing activities (on which the 'professionals' will concentrate) is the promotion of community voluntarism and self-help policing. Again, this process is being applied to other public services such as health and social services.

The first Home Office circular on local consultation arrangements (54/1982) began with the assertion that 'while the police are charged with the prevention of crime and the maintenance of order, those tasks cannot be fulfilled effectively unless the community itself shoulders its responsibilities for tackling the particular problems of an area' (emphasis added). This is a sensitive matter. In none of the numerous statements, circulars and pamphlets put out by the Home Office and police on 'crime prevention' (the rubric under which community participation is generally placed), is it ever stated that certain matters are too trivial for the police to deal with. To do so would be to deny the police image of service to the commuity as well as their duty to enforce the law; even minor matters of public order involve some breach of the law. Thus though the actual consequence of establishing police priorities may be that certain matters are regarded as too trivial for the police to be able or prepared to do much about, community self-help is promoted and justified on a different basis.

The general argument for cooperative ventures in crime prevention is one of corporate responsibility. According to the recent Home Office Circular 8/1984 on crime prevention, 'some of the factors affecting crime lie outside the control or direct influence of the police. Crime prevention cannot be left to them alone. Every individual citizen and all those agencies whose policies and practices can influence the extent of crime should make their contribution. Preventing crime is a task for the whole community.' The circular focused primarily on inter-agency initiatives but touched on wider public participation. For example, community councils, neighbourhood associations and 'Scarman' consultative committees are cited as suitable vehicles for 'persuading the community to do more for itself'. This possibility was taken up by the most recent circular on local consultation arrangements (2/1985), in which the promotion of neighbourhood watch schemes was outlined. According to advice issued by the Home Office Crime Prevention Unit, neighbourhood watch involves 'individuals acting together in an attempt to protect themselves and their property' (Smith, 1984). Initiatives of this sort can, the Home Office also suggests, be generated through greater recruitment and use of special constables (Home Office, 1984b; Laycock, 1985).

It is evident that encouragement for self-help goes beyond the truism that the police only know about and clear up most crimes if the public report the incidents and the persons responsible. Patently, crime prevention is the responsibility of the whole community and successful initiatives do involve a partnership. But the government's emphasis on voluntarism is not being applied to the police alone and it is clear from other services that self-help is not always designed to be an addition or adjunct to what the professionals provide; it may be a substitute. Chief constables are alert to this implication. The crime prevention circular concluded with the warning that 'the suggestions in this circular do not call for a net increase in expenditure; they concern a redirection of effort or of existing resources'. For this reason some chief constables, appreciative that crime prevention initiatives involve manpower commitments, are resisting pressure (much of it from local communities) to form schemes like neighbourhood watch. At least one chief constable has publicly attacked the Home Office circulars suggesting such schemes (Anderton, 1985).

Whatever view one takes of the Police and Criminal Evidence Act 1984, it undoubtedly places extra demands on police resources. That demand can only be met by reducing other activities. The question is whether the reduced activities signify a valued and visibly diminished service to the public at large. If they do, and that process is accompanied locally by the suggestion that the public do more to help themselves, this may stimulate increased scrutiny of what service precisely the police do provide.

Consumerism

Getting public services to state their priorities and find ways of measuring whether their objectives are being met does not ensure the outputs are those the public want. Furthermore, if the public are dissatisfied with core activities provided by professionals, voluntarism and self-help suggest only a marginal solution. The government tends to argue that where services cannot be privatised or voluntarised, they should be consumer-advised. This provides part of the background to s.106 of the Police and Criminal Evidence Act 1984 requiring that 'arrangements shall be made in each police area for obtaining the views of people in that area about matters concerning the policing of the area and for obtaining their cooperation with the police in preventing crime'. The creation of consumer health councils and proposals that parents be given a greater voice in schools management are examples of similar initiatives in other services.

Prior to conducting annual inspections of individual forces, the Inspectorate of Constabulary issues 'inspection notes' to chief constables. In 1985 the notes became more detailed and questions more specific. This was in line with the Inspectorate's emphasis on 'the three Es: effectiveness, efficiency and economy' (Home Office, 1984a, para 1.2). The 1985 notes begin with a request that chief constables comment on their 'statement of objectives' and provide an indication of 'who is consulted, either inside or outside the force, in formulating local policing strategies/tactics'. Subsequent questions suggest the chief constable's answers should refer to consultation outside that which it is expected they will have with police authorities. Under the heading 'relations with the community', they are asked inter alia about formal consultation arrangements resulting from the implementation of s.106 of the Police and Criminal Evidence Act 1984; informal community consultation; liaison arrangements for dealing with juveniles; and liaison with ethnic minorities (including arrangements for monitoring racial attacks). The section concludes with the question 'what evidence is there from meetings, correspondence, etc of the extent to which ethnic minorities, victims and the public generally are satisfied with force policies?'

Part of the rationale for s.106 and its reinforcement by the Inspectorate is, as Lord Scarman put it, that the police

> are now professionals with a highly specialised set of skills and behavioural codes of their own. They run the risk of becoming, by reason of their professionalism, a 'corps d'elite' set apart from the rest of the community . . . if a rift is not to develop between the police and the public as a whole (not just the members of the ethnic minority communities), it is in my view essential that a means be devised of enabling the community to be heard not only in the development of policing policy but in the planning of many, though not all, operations against crime. (Scarman, 1981, paras 5.3 and 5.56)

The importance of police objectives being congruent with community concerns has been emphasised in all the Home Office circulars to which I have already referred. Circular 114/1983 states that 'the Home Secretary is concerned that the police/community consultation machinery . . . should be utilised to the full as a means both of determining local needs and wishes and of explaining policies publicly'. For as Circular 8/1984 argues, 'the public can only be expected to help in preventing crime where initiatives against it reflect their own perceptions and concerns . . . this indicates a need for methods by which the community's fears and concerns can be assessed, and for the formation of closer links between the public and those holding positions of authority'. And Circular 2/1985 explains the purpose of s.106 consultative groups thus: 'effective policing depends on (public) consent being given, and on the police service making decisions which are in tune with the needs of the local community'. The formation of consultative committees, it is argued, will make it 'possible for general policing policies to be adapted to meet identified needs in the light of the expressed wishes of the local community'. By these means, the Home Secretary's 1984 <u>Criminal Justice</u> manifesto maintained, there should be 'increased mutual understanding between the police and the community they serve, providing a platform 'for exploring ways in which the public and the police can cooperate in maintaining a peaceful and law-abiding community' (Home Office, 1984b).

Transparent stewardship

Despite the emphasis on 'policing by consent' and consumer voice, the government is committed to the maintenance of operational independence for the police. The government rejects what I have elsewhere termed the 'directive' model of accountability (Morgan and Maggs, 1985), or what Marshall (1978) terms the 'subordinate and obedient mode'. Instead, as we have seen, the government favours the notion of partnership. However, because there manifestly is no longer policing to which some sections of the otherwise generally law-abiding community consent (Policy Studies Institute, 1983), and because the notion of partnership is vulnerable to the charge that the police may ignore public opinion, the government has allied partnership with what is best described as the 'transparent stewardship' model of accountability. This is a beefed-up version of what Marshall calls the 'explanatory mode'.

The steward model of accountability emphasises the account rendered by one who exercises delegated responsibility. In its most basic form it concerns financial propriety: do the figures add up, has the money been spent on those things for which it was authorised, has cost-effective care been demonstrated over purchasing and organisational methods? However, it can also refer to audits of responsibilities and powers, such as is entailed in the chief constable's duty to submit an annual report. The problem with the provisions for stewardship in the Police Act 1964 is that they are very generalised. There is, for example, no statutory requirement as to what range of information chief constables' annual reports must contain. Thus though annual reports have through a process of precedent and custom come to have a common basic format, there are nevertheless significant variations of emphasis between them. Furthermore, annual reports contain remarkably few hard data on day-to-day police organisation and practice. For example, from almost no annual report is it possible to discover what proportions of manpower are routinely allocated to general uniformed patrol work as opposed to traffic division, CID and other specialisms.

The government seeks to revitalise the legitimacy of operational independence by requiring police stewardship to be fuller and more transparent. The safeguards which the government maintains balance the new police powers incorporated in the Police and Criminal Evidence Act 1984 include reasons for actions having to be given and recorded; officers of designated rank having to make and record certain decisions; and the publication in annual reports of statistics relating to the use of powers (for a detailed discussion see the symposium on the Police and Criminal Evidence Act 1984 in Public Law, Autumn 1985). This is not unlike the obligation now placed on schools to publish examination results. It is said to constitute a public audit which enables consumers better to determine the quality of the local service being provided.

Moreover, the government has exhorted the police to be more open on a voluntary basis through the consultative process. This exhortatory pressure from the centre, mediated by the Home Office, has increased as the public and party political controversy over the extent and use of police powers has gathered pace. For example, the first Home Office circular on consultation (54/1982) adopted the traditional cautionary note about police operational matters: 'the deployment of police officers, the method and timing of police operations, and the stage at which these may be discussed, are matters for the chief constable and his officers'. There was no real encouragement for open discussion. Quite the reverse: the circular warned that Lord Scarman had himself 'recognised that there are some operational aspects of policing . . . [which] it would be wrong to make the subject of local consultation'. However, the second circular on consultation (2/1985) stressed the need for transparency: the police 'should be ready to discuss all aspects of police aims and policy, including operational matters and the outcomes of complaints investigations, as far as they are able to do so . . . and where appropriate . . . the police should be ready to give prior notice of their intention to mount major police operations'. To the traditional doctrine of accountability to the law, the government has added the idea of a public audit as to how the police have used, or intend to use, the law.

Current initiatives

During the next few years the key issue for research will be the use made by the police of their new powers under the Police and Criminal Evidence Act 1984. There are contrasting hypotheses to be tested, some suggesting that despite their ostensibly increased powers, the bureaucratic 'safeguards' may actually inhibit and reduce police resort to actions which, empowered or not, they have traditionally used. These questions have been reviewed elsewhere (see Public Law, Autumn 1985). I can add nothing to that discussion save to say that the nature of the audit the police will henceforth be required to give, and the analyses carried out by research workers, may be scrutinised closely by the new bodies, the growth of which the government has encouraged locally. I refer to the local consultative committees which now cover most of the country and to schemes for lay visitors to police stations (Home Office Circular 12/1986).

Police/community consultative committees

The background to and development of consultative groups has been fully described elsewhere (Morgan and Maggs, 1984 and 1985; Morgan, 1986). The following points need emphasising here. First, except in the Metropolitan Police District (MPD), where the Home Secretary as police authority has used his powers under the Act to make the formation of consultative committees a statutory requirement, there is nothing in the Act which requires that committees be formed. Indeed, during passage of the Bill, the Home Secretary repeatedly resisted pressure that he build a blueprint into the Act specifying what s.106 'arrangements' should be. As is customary on these occasions, the watchwords were flexibility and local autonomy. Policing conditions varied; it was for the police authorities, in consultation with their chief constables, to determine together what consultative arrangements would suit their localities best. They might decide, the Home Secretary argued, there was no need for formal arrangements at all. It might suffice for local constables to go along, as the need arose and as they always had done, to parish council meetings. In consequence, s.106 is couched in the vaguest of terms. There is no specification as to what the consultation 'arrangements' shall comprise; how 'the views of the people' shall be obtained; what 'matters concerning the policing of the area' should or can be discussed; or how the 'cooperation' of the people should be enlisted.

This aspect of the legislation is significant because, having resisted laying down a statutory blueprint, the government has virtually imposed a blueprint interpretation of s.106 nationally (Morgan, 1986). Indeed, most police authority members (whose responsibility s.106 arrangements are) and senior police officers are under the mistaken impression that the creation of formal consultative committees is a statutory requirement. Their mistake is understandable. Both the Home Office circulars on consultation arrangements (54/1982 and 2/1985) emphasised the flexibility of local arrangements. Nevertheless both circulars assume throughout that committees will be formed. Thus despite the references to informal consultation, or attendance by constables at parish councils, the circulars refer repeatedly to consultative 'groups', their membership, their links with beat officers, their need for chairmen, and the frequency, venue and openness of their meetings. Most importantly, there is an assurance that the administrative costs of 'groups' will qualify for central government police grant.

The assumptions in the Home Office circulars have been reinforced by other processes. I have referred already to the instructions from the Home Secretary that consultative committees be formed in the MPD (in particular, the then Mr Whitelaw lent his personal well-publicised weight to the formation of the consultative committee in Lambeth). There have also been general enquiries of chief constables and police authorities from the Home Office police department asking for information about action taken as a result of the circulars. But the most important influence has probably been that of the Inspectorate of Constabulary. Several police authorities and chief constables decided initially that they had no need of special consultative committees in their areas; that their traditional methods were adequate. Almost without exception these chief constables have been leant on by the Inspectorate, have succumbed, and have in turn persuaded their police authorities of the need to form some type of committee. There is now scarcely a force area that does not have consultative committees (Morgan and Maggs, 1985).

The application of the blueprint goes deeper. The arguments for local flexibility for consultation arrangements apply just as much _within_ police authority areas as _between_ them. Most police authorities exercise responsibility for areas encompassing very different policing characteristics; many include large urban concentrations with inner city problems alongside extensive rural hinterlands. If there is a case for constructing modes of consultation tailored to localities, one would expect to find substantial variations within police authority territories. But this is scarcely ever the case. Not only have most of the 41 provincial police authorities adopted a model for their formal consultative groups which is broadly on the lines the Home Office recommended, but they have in almost every case imposed that model uniformly throughout their force area, usually by sub-division.

The irresistible interpretation for this development is that though s.106 is a devolved police authority responsibility (with wide discretion as to interpretation), in fact the process of implementation betrays the centralised influence of the Home Office. The considerable effort expended by the Home Office to ensure that consultative committees are appointed is indicative of the importance the government attaches to the creation of mechanisms through the working of which it can be claimed there is policing by consent, thereby bolstering the case for the operational independence for the police. It will almost certainly then be argued that Labour Party proposals to revise the Police Act 1964 in order to bring operational policy under local democratic control are unnecessary and motivated by politically partisan objectives. Furthermore, the rapidity with which police authorities set up consultative committees will no doubt be interpreted as an indication of the authorities' vigour, and thus of the desirability of maintaining unchanged the tripartite structure for police governance. In fact, the background evidence suggests that the reverse interpretation is equally plausible.

Lay visitors to police stations

There is no statutory provision for lay visitors to police stations. There is a Home Office circular (12/1986) commending their creation. It is likely that the circular will be followed by pressure from the Home Office similar to that exerted for the formation of consultative groups.

The first lay visitors' scheme began operating in Lambeth in 1983. The constitution was hammered out by a sub-committee of the Lambeth Police/Community Consultative Group from whose members the first panel of lay visitors was drawn. The Home Office, acting on behalf of the Secretary of State as police authority for the MPD, was closely involved. In July 1983 the Home Secretary announced that pilot lay visitor schemes were also to be introduced in six provincial police authority areas. He indicated that he would be monitoring the experiment. Unlike the Lambeth scheme, five of the six provincial experiments decided initially that visitors should be elected members of the police authority. Only one authority, Cheshire, decided to appoint special community panels for the purpose. In Cheshire the members were appointed from respondents to an advertisement and the volunteers underwent a training programme devised for the purpose. The Cheshire scheme became operational in September 1984, since when two of the other provincial pilot schemes have decided to appoint community volunteers to their panels (see, for example, Walklate, 1986).

In July 1984, following a meeting with representatives of the Association of Metropolitan Authorities, the Association of Chief Police Officers and the participating local authorities, the Home Secretary announced that he was pleased with the experiments and was proposing to issue a circular 'commending lay visiting wherever there is felt to be a need for it' (Hansard, 31 July 1984). The Home Office circular on lay visitors, like those on consultation, stresses local autonomy. It is 'for individual police authorities to decide whether the establishment of (lay visitors) would be useful'. However, the Home Office apparently has little doubt they would be useful: the letter accompanying the circular claims that the potential of lay visitors 'for promoting public confidence in the work of the police flowing from a better understanding of what goes on within police stations has already been demonstrated'. This is despite the fact that no evaluation has taken place.

According to the circular, lay visitors are appointed to enable 'members of the local community to observe, comment and report upon the conditions under which persons are detained at police stations and the operation in practice of the statutory and other rules governing their welfare, with a view to securing greater public understanding of, and confidence in, these matters'. Each police authority is reminded that it 'will wish to consult the chief constable before settling on the membership of its visiting panel', and members of consultative groups are among the suggested groups from which panel members might be drawn. The link between lay visitors and the police authority which appoints them is emphasised, as is their function to report on what I have called the transparent stewardship of the police. Visitors should have access to the areas in 'stations in which persons are detained pending interviews, release or production in court, including cells, charge areas, detention rooms and medical rooms'. They should also, with prisoners' permission, be able to see the 'custody record relating to a person's detention, treatment and welfare' and it is anticipated they 'will wish to satisfy themselves about the extent to which (the documentation) properly records the action taken in his case'. Finally, it is suggested that visitors record their visits (an example of a standard form which might be used is attached to the circular) in triplicate (copies for the station commander, chief constable and police authority) and report regularly to the police authority.

If, as I anticipate, panels of lay visitors will soon be operating in most of our major cities – those areas where hostility to the police is greatest and where police authority criticism of operational policy is most marked – and if the work of lay visitors is fed into the consultative groups, then they also are likely to exercise a significant influence on the police accountability debate locally. It is to the possible nature of that influence that I wish in conclusion to turn.

Local consultation and inspection: the hypothesised implications

I began by saying that I would not attempt a review of the arguments concerning the constitutional governance of the police, that I would restrict myself to a review of the likely implications of initiatives already being pursued by the government. Such a neat demarcation is not viable. It is not possible because of course the operation of consultative groups and lay visitors' schemes is itself dependent on the meanings which participants and onlookers attach to the exercise. These meanings are in turn charged by the constitutional arguments which, in part, have given rise to the policy initiatives.

This point is best illustrated by the well-publicised case of the MPD. Because the MPD lacks a locally elected police authority, and the unique constitutional arrangements for London are widely considered to be inadequate, the Home Secretary's decision to make consultative committees a statutory requirement in

London is considered by many to be a confidence trick (Greater London Council, 1983; Christian, 1983; Spencer, 1985a). Consultative committees have no powers and cannot formally call the police to account in the sense of instructing them to change policies of which members disapprove. Thus, according to the critics, not only has the existence of consultative groups not changed anything constitutionally, but, more damagingly, it has made constitutional change less likely by presenting a false impression of accountability. For this reason many Labour Party-dominated London boroughs resolved to boycott MPD-organised consultative committees and set up borough police committees instead. In response, the Commissioner of the Metropolitan Police issued instructions that borough police committees were not to be recognised or dealt with by the police locally. Officers were reminded that no borough council had a 'right to veto or determine the format' of a consultative committee, and 'any failure by the local authority to respond to the approach by the police or refusal to participate in the process will not invalidate the group' (Commissioner of Police of the Metropolis, 1985).

The MPD case is particularly controversial. However, the argument over consultation in the MPD is far from unique. Data we have collected in the provinces suggests that, partly because of the wider arguments concerning constitutional accountability, many local politicians and community groups perceive local consultation to be a 'talking shop' confidence trick not worthy of participation. For some local politicians that argument extends to police authorities also. To participate is to perpetuate a charade. Furthermore, the 'con trick' critique is by some observers allied to a more sinister interpretation of consultative groups. This view is particularly prevalent among personnel with voluntary and statutory agencies working in the inner cities with young people likely to be in conflict with the police. Despite the fact that s.106 is a police authority responsibility, consultative groups are perceived by these observers to be creatures of the police, and vehicles for the greater dispersal of social control (Cohen, 1985; for commentary see Bottoms, 1983). Consultative groups are said easily to be co-opted to a police view of reality, are mechanisms for gathering police intelligence, promoting neighbourhood 'narks' and facilitating greater police penetration of the community (Gordon, 1984; Wolmer, 1984; Scraton, 1985).

I have two brief comments to make about these claims. First, the manner in which many consultative groups are conducted lends itself to these cynical interpretations. Many groups are dominated by the police, though in defence of the police it should be said that this domination is typically at the urging of lay members. Some groups are attended by almost as many officers as civilians; some are held in police stations; many are serviced by police personnel; and possibly a majority have their agenda filled by items suggested by the police or police contributions (visits to police stations, presentations by specialist officers, police statistics, etc). My second point is rather different. Some critical commentators make rather glib references to 'social control', police 'intelligence' and community 'penetration'. They pay insufficient attention to the possibility that these processes may be at the behest of and carried out on behalf of sections of the community as well as, or instead of, being against some other section of the community. The beneficiaries may not be powerful. What if neighbourhood narks concern themselves with racial attacks or child neglect? These questions can only be settled through empirical study.

Returning to my general theme, the more the police refuse to provide operational information, the more they resist rendering an account about resources and priorities, the more they refuse to discuss complaints by hiding behind spurious 'operational' or 'sub-judice' defences, the more prevalent will be the boycotts and the cynicism to which I have referred. By so acting, the police will merely fuel the demand for something they oppose, namely amendment of the Police Act 1964 along the lines now being proposed by the Labour Party.

Of course not all commentators who support radical constitutional reform (and subscribe to the view that s.106 was cynically motivated by the need to provide a palliative to prop up the status quo) propose existing consultative groups be boycotted (Spencer, 1985a). Nor are many groups now boycotted by Labour councillors, even in the MPD (Morgan and Maggs, 1985). The most thoughtful commentators in this field have conceded that whatever constitutional reforms are introduced, there will nevertheless be a need for local consultation, though it may take a rather different form from that prevailing in most areas at present. Lea and Young, for example, argue for the community consulting 'the police as part of the process of formulating its needs, not that the police consult the community in formulating its strategy (1984, p.260; for a contrasting police management perspective, see Butler, 1984b). Some writers even take the view that consultative groups may be more effective in making the police responsive to neighbourhood needs than would result simply from police authorities ostensibly exercising control (Savage, 1984; Reiner, 1985). And finally, there is that group of commentators, which includes Lord Scarman, who argue that police authorities, as presently constituted, have an unrealised potential to influence and call the police to account. They argue that the existence of consultative groups might persuade police authorities to 'act more vigorously' (Scarman, 1981, para 5.65; see also Regan, 1983).

From these various perspectives one can distil a number of hypotheses, which in our own research we are seeking to investigate. Does the existence of consultative groups increase the degree to which the police publish accounts of that which they do or propose to do? Do they, either because members become more knowledgeable or are provided with additional channels of communication, influence the attitudes of police authority members, their agenda and their procedures? Will consultative groups influence the manner in which the police determine their priorities and allocation of resources? Will they enhance the degree to which the police work with the community and other agencies on crime prevention initiatives, etc? Will members adopt views similar to the police about what the problems of crime and order are locally, or will they challenge the police picture?

None of these questions will easily be answered, not least because the formation of consultative groups is only one of several policy initiatives (to some of which I have already made reference) which are currently affecting policing. After the Home Office circular on lay visitors has taken effect, similar questions will have to be asked about that initiative, with particular reference to the development of the custody powers in the Police and Criminal Evidence Act 1984.

Finally, putting on one side all the problems about the questionable representativeness and accountability of consultative groups, it should be said that part of the rationale for their formation – the idea that the police should be more responsive to community needs and wishes – begs many difficult policy questions. Is it, for example, desirable for the police, and indeed other public services, to be more responsive locally? The case is not self–evident. Though the overall service provided by the police arguably constitutes a public good, police activity also entails divisible and more or less exclusive benefits to individuals, groups or agencies. A patrol mounted in one location means the absence of a police presence elsewhere. Time spent advising householders about domestic security may mean less attention being paid to victims elsewhere. Increased responsiveness to one group of needs and wishes means less responsiveness to others, and so on (see discussion in Jefferson and Grimshaw, 1984). It should not be forgotten that the original justification for providing certain services through public agencies is to insulate them for one reason or another from consumer sovereignty exercised in the market place nationally or locally.

Secondly, there may be a case for saying that in policing matters consumers are not necessarily the best judges of their own welfare. They may have very limited experience of their potential needs and imperfect knowledge of crime conditions. There is, for example, what I am coming to think of as the 'dog shit syndrome'. The average citizen has not experienced burglary and is probably unaware of the burglaries that have occurred in his or her street or village, though some local crime surveys, such as those conducted in Merseyside and Islington, indicate that concern about burglary and other serious crime is considerable in some areas. On the other hand, everyone has trodden in the dog shit or seen the bus shelter vandalism and wants something done about it. Were the police to do more about these nuisances they might be able to do less about the burglary, to which, when it does occur, most citizens expect a rapid and visibly painstaking investigatory response (Maguire, 1982). Yet, to take the sequence on, the painstaking investigatory response which seems central to the satisfaction of burglary victims may have little bearing on their goods being recovered or the offender apprehended.

I am not in any way suggesting that there is room for complacency about consumer wishes or that the police should be arrogantly indifferent to them. On the contrary, as I have indicated earlier, one of the functions of local consultation is to explain to consumers what the pattern of crime is locally and what the police can reasonably be expected to do about it. Where the police think it right that they should resist consultative group wishes, it is for them to make the public aware of where the other demands for their services are coming from and how they are recorded (message pads, letters, emergency calls, etc). Whatever form consultative groups take, the messages the police receive via them will only ever constitute one small part in a larger jigsaw of communication between police and public. The shape and content of that jigsaw need to be articulated.

Conclusion

Whatever view one takes about the wider constitutional debate regarding the governance and accountability of the police, the information flowing from the government's financial management initiative and the record of consultative groups and lay visitors is likely to be a crucial factor influencing the legitimacy of the status quo and the demand for change. It is too early to predict outcomes; the research in these areas has yet to be done. What is clear, however, is that in this debate the ground rules are being renegotiated continuously. From existing evidence it is apparent that there is enormous variation in chief constables' policies and consultative group practice from one part of the country to another. I have in mind, simply as one example, those areas where the police are refusing (contrary to Home Office advice) even to provide breakdowns of local crime statistics or written statements of manpower resources. I compare that stance with other areas where the police are showering local politicians and consultative groups with police data: see, for example, the information supplied to the Lambeth Community/Police Consultative Group after the disorders in Brixton on 28 and 29 September 1985 (Metropolitan Police, 1985).

It is also apparent that practices are still developing, that local authorities and police are watching closely precedents in other parts of the country. As the party political controversy gathers strength, as the problems of the inner cities deepen, community leaders, local politicians and police officers are beginning to be aware of the implications of the initiatives in which they are engaged. For the researcher that means walking a tightrope. In our own work on consultative groups we are finding that our respondents frequently turn our questions round: what now shall we do? It seems that many participants are aware, like Lord Scarman, that 'everything is still to play for' (Scarman, 1985).

Note

This paper arises out of a research project on police community consultation funded by the Economic and Social Research Council (ESRC) (reference number: E06250029) and the Police Foundation. It could not have been written without the assistance of my colleagues in that project, Dr Christopher Maggs and Mr Paul Swift, both of the University of Bath. Any errors of fact or judgement, however, are entirely my own.

References

Anderton, J., (1985) 'What price law and order?', Police Review, 14 June
Baxter, J. and Koffman, L., (1985) Police: the constitution and the community, Professional Books, Abingdon
Bottoms, A.E., (1983) 'Neglected features of contemporary penal systems' in Garland, D. and Young, P. (eds), The power to punish, Heinemann, London
Butler, A.J.P., (1984a) Police management, Gower, Farnborough
Butler, A.J.P., (1984b) Policing by objectives, paper presented to the British Association, Norwich, September
Christian, L., (1983) Policing by coercion, GLC/Pluto Press, London
Clarke, R. and Hough, M., (1980) The effectiveness of policing, Gower, Farnborough
Cohen, S., (1985) Visions of social control, Polity, Cambridge
Collins, K., (1985) 'Efficiency revisited', Policing, 1, 2, 70-6
Commissioner of Police of the Metropolis (1985) Instruction – Consultative Procedures, s.106, PACE, A7 Branch, 20 February
Conservative Party, (1979) The Conservative Manifesto, Conservative Central Office, London
Gordon, P., (1984) 'Community policing: towards the local police state', Critical Social Policy, 10, Summer
Greater London Council, (1983) A new police authority for London, Police Committee Discussion Paper No.1
HMSO (1983) Financial management in government departments, Cmnd 9058, London
Home Office (1984a) Report of Her Majesty's Chief Inspector of Constabulary 1983, HC528, HMSO, London
Home Office (1984b) Criminal justice: a working paper, HMSO, London
Home Office (1985) Tackling drug abuse: a summary of the government's strategy, HMSO, London
Home Office Circulars:
54/1982 Local consultation arrangements between the community and the police
114/1983 Manpower, effectiveness and efficiency in the police service
8/1984 Crime prevention

2/1985 Arrangements for local consultation between the community and the police outside London

12/1986 Lay visitors to police stations

Jefferson, T. and Grimshaw, R., (1984) Controlling the constable: police accountability in England and Wales, Muller, London

Laycock, G., (1985) Property marking: a deterrent to domestic burglary, Crime Prevention Unit Paper 3, Home Office, London

Lea, J. and Young, J., (1984) What is to be done about law and order? Penguin Books, London

Loveday, B. (1985) The role and effectiveness of the Merseyside Police Committee, Merseyside County Council, Liverpool

Maguire, M., (1982) Burglary in a dwelling, Heinemann, London

Maguire, M., Vagg, J. and Morgan, R. (1985) Prisons and accountability, Tavistock, London

Marshall, G., (1978) 'Police accountability revisited', in Butler, D. and Halsey, A.H. (eds) Policy and politics, Macmillan, London

Metropolitan Police (1985) Report on the Brixton disorders 28/29 September 1985. Prepared for the Lambeth Community/Police Consultative Group. Agenda item CP107/1985

Morgan, R. and Maggs, C., (1984) Following Scarman? Bath Social Policy Papers, University of Bath

Morgan, R. and Maggs, C., (1985) Setting the PACE: police community consultative arrangements in England and Wales, Bath Social Policy Papers, University of Bath

Morgan, R., (1986) 'Police consultative groups: the implications for the government of the police', Political Quarterly, Jan-March

Policy Studies Institute (1983) Police and people in London, vols.I-IV, London

Punch, M., (1979) 'The secret social service', in Holdaway, S. (ed.) The British police, Edward Arnold, London

Regan, D., (1983) Are the police under control? Research Paper 1, Social Affairs Unit, London

Reiner, R., (1985) The politics of the police, Wheatsheaf, Brighton

Savage, S.P., (1984) 'Political control or community liaison? Two strategies in the reform of police accountability', Political Quarterly, Jan-March, 48-59

Scarman, Lord (1981) Report of an inquiry into the Brixton disorders, 10-12 April 1981, HMSO, London

Scarman, Lord, (1985) Address to NACRO annual conference, London, 14 November, unpublished

Scraton, P., (1985) The state of the police, Pluto, London

Sinclair, I. and Miller, C., (1984) Measures of police effectiveness and efficiency, Research and Planning Unit Paper 25, Home Office, London

Smith, L.J.F., (1984) Neighbourhood watch: a note on implementation, Crime Prevention Unit, Home Office

Spencer, S., (1985a) Called to account: the case for police accountability in England and Wales, NCCL, London

Spencer, S. (1985b) Police authorities during the miners' strike, Working Paper No.1, Cobden Trust, London

Walklate, S., (1986) The Merseyside lay visiting scheme, Merseyside County Council, Liverpool

Weatheritt, M., (1985) 'Police research', Policing, 1, 2, 77-86

Weatheritt, M., (1986) Innovations in policing, Croom Helm, Beckenham

Wolmer, C., (1984) 'Neighbourly nosing', New Statesman, 21 September